D0260986

ALL TEACHERS BRIGHT AND BEAUTIFUL

ALL TEACHERS BRIGHT AND BEAUTIFUL

ANDY SEED

headline

First published in 2013
by HEADLINE PUBLISHING GROUP

1

Cataloguing in Publication Data is available from the British Library

Hardback ISBN 978 0 7553 6220 2

Typeset in Adobe Garamond by Palimpsest Book Production Limited, Falkirk, Stirlingshire

Printed and bound in the UK by Clays Ltd, St Ives plc

Headline's policy is to use papers that are natural, renewable and recyclable products and made from wood grown in sustainable forests. The logging and manufacturing processes are expected to conform to the environmental regulations of the country of origin.

HEADLINE PUBLISHING GROUP
An Hachette UK Company
338 Euston Road
London NW1 3BH

www.headline.co.uk
www.hachette.co.uk

To Ellen, a wonderful teacher
and friend, with thanks for all
you have done.

Acknowledgements

Many people deserve appreciation for their help, advice and encouragement with this book. I am particularly grateful to Jo Roberts-Miller, my editor, and to Emma Tait at Headline; your patience and understanding have been greatly valued.

I'd also like to thank the following family members, friends and ex-pupils: Mike Barfield, Beryl Cosens, Jan Dean, Ian Dodgson, Penny Dolan, John Gascoyne, Matt Goodfellow, Vicky Hajba, Irene Helliwell, Andy and Jane Holmes, Liz Howden, Sue Lake, Cindy Lankshear, Matt Lawson, Pete and Sally Maynard, Maxine Rodgers, Geoffrey Seed, Laura Shewan, Lesley Simpson, Sally Stone, Andy and Pauline Straw, Sheila Silvester, Heather Towse, Craig Turton, Russell Walker and Jess Welburn.

Finally, I must mention the exceptional staff and children of Amotherby and Reeth Primary Schools: thanks!

Contents

Prologue

Martine

A surprisingly powerful September sun rose into the sky on a clear Monday morning, rapidly warming the ancient temporary classroom at the back of the little Dales school. I felt its heat on my back and I noticed some of the children turn to avoid its glare as they sat writing their News. I moved across the room quietly and opened some of the windows, not wanting to disturb the heavenly calm as twenty-five eight- and nine-year-olds scribbled away in their jotters. I was enjoying the interesting mix of characters that made up my new Class 3 and the first few days of term had been almost serene.

The door opened and Joyce Berry, the enthusiastic, cosmetically enhanced headteacher, noticed my surprise as she introduced a rather stern-looking parent governor to the class.

'Sorry to interrupt you, Mr Seed; it is lovely to see your class working so hard but, children, this is Mrs Sykes, one of our new school governors. Some of you will know her from the village, I'm sure. She's going round the school and observing each class for half an hour, so she'll just sit in the corner while you carry on with what you're doing.'

I had forgotten. It was in my diary, I recalled, but it had somehow slipped my mind. Not that there was any concern, with the children working so well on a quiet task. I found Mrs Sykes a chair, smiled warmly and gave Joyce a no-problem-at-all nod as she left the room.

'They're just writing their news from the weekend, Mrs Sykes. I'll give it five more minutes then ask some of them to share what they've been up to.'

Any reply was interrupted by the scrape of a chair as a broad, unkempt girl stood up.

'Mr Seed, I need toilet.' It was Martine.

'Martine, you mean, "Please may I go to the toilet?"'

'Please, I'm bustin'." Her jiggle emphasised the point.

I nodded as Mrs Sykes drew a small notebook out of her black handbag. There was something very likeable about the tousle-haired Martine Clarkson, despite her rather chaotic approach to life.

I was leaning over Fraser Garth's shoulder studying his rugged, farmer's boy handwriting in which he matter-of-factly described 'cutting maggots off a sheep's bum' when the wasp flew in.

It wasn't a piddly little workaday wasp but one of those really big menacing ones. I heard the commotion before I saw it: a squeal followed by a succession of bumps with children yowling as they ducked and flapped.

'Keep still!' I bellowed. Some of them tried but most involuntarily swayed or swiped at the angry-looking insect as it freely toured the room.

'Stay in your seats,' I advised. 'It's much less likely to sting you if you keep perfectly still.' Then it came over to me. It really was a big so-and-so. I confidently stood motionless until it inspected my face, at which point I ducked manically and took a lash at it with the dinner register, missing by a distance. There were laughs from the older boys followed by more screeching as the wasp set off for the other side of the room.

Seeing my example, the irrepressible Lawrence Quantick unsuccessfully assaulted it with his jotter, which only succeeded in driving the airborne pest towards the nervous Vicky Rushworth, who yelped with tight eyes and hunched shoulders before flinging herself on to me for protection.

'Stop trying to hit it,' I ordered guiltily. 'If we leave it alone it might go out. Stephen, open the door please.'

'I'm terrified of wasps,' wailed the shaking Vicky.

'Me too!' chorused several children as I glanced over to Mrs Sykes who was busily recording the whole episode in her notebook.

After another thirty seconds of flapping, wailing and fuss from the children, the yellow fiend landed on a window. I saw my chance and, grabbing and rolling up a clutch of papers, I stealthily advanced on the crawling wasp. The whole class watched as I drew back my arm.

'No, don't kill it, that's cruel!' It was Lisa Bowe, an evidently sensitive girl and an early junior animal rights activist – something very rare in rural Yorkshire in the 1980s. I was tempted to ignore her but could feel Mrs Sykes' eyes on my back.

'Mash it, Mr Seed!' called big Howard Sedgwick, and most of the boys chorused agreement. But I withdrew my arm and asked Lisa to fetch me a water pot from the painting cupboard. The tiger-striped insect, seeming to anticipate my plans, scuttled to the top of the window just out of reach. Someone offered me a chair to stand on. I felt its grey plastic seat sag dangerously as I stepped up. The wasp was now within reach and I was just about to clamp the pot over it when the classroom door clattered against the wall and Martine appeared, causing me to lose my balance.

'What's goin' on, like?' she cried, seeing the entire class out of their seats and craning for a view of the 'killer hornet' as some of them were calling it.

'It's just a wasp,' I said. 'Come in and sit down and get on with your work.' Fat chance.

'But, Mr Seed, toilet's broken and I ain't bin yet.' She held up a white plastic bolt for everyone to see. 'This fell out of the back o' the bog.'

'Please don't use that word, Martine.' But she wasn't listening. Several of the children were making 'Euurrgghh' sounds and suggesting that she had picked up something decidedly slimy.

'That's disgusting!' said Vicky Rushworth, sticking out her tongue.

Martine's face tightened. 'You can talk, Vicky. I saw you throwing salad in the loo on Friday.'

Before I could intervene, Helen Guy piped up. 'Aye, that's true, I wondered what that lettuce were doin' there. Wouldn't flush either.'

'Be quiet girls!' I called, almost falling off the chair, but Vicky had the look of the unjustly accused and couldn't hold back.

'That's not fair – Beverley made me do it. She was really hungry at lunchtime and didn't want to wait for a hot dinner so she got a salad and just ate the meat and bread but she doesn't like lettuce so she gave it to me under the table cos I was going to the toilet and she told me to flush it down the loo and—'

'All right!' I was tempted to go into the classic, 'Well, if Beverley told you to jump off a cliff, would you do it?' routine but this was not the time. 'Right, Vicky, stop there – I'll deal with this later. Sit down. And, Martine, put that bolt on the shelf and go to the toilet quickly.'

I glanced back at the wasp. It had taken off again.

My next tactic, amid the continuing ducking and flapping of the children, was to try to shoo the wasp towards the open door using the *Times Concise Atlas*. It seemed to be working at first but then the wasp landed on Anna Reed's neck. The poor girl was so terrified that she froze, her hands shaking and her eyes the size of golf balls.

Advice rained in on the unfortunate victim from all quarters, including me, but the wasp looked disturbingly interested in investigating the inside of her collar. I hurried forward to intercept it but was beaten by Lawrence Quantick, who decided that the best solution was to whack Anna's neck with his jotter. She screamed at full volume but the insect had already sensed the attack and taken off. I added Lawrence to my mental list of miscreants then stopped to minister to Anna who was now in tears and threatening to get her dad to come and deal with her assailant.

I put an arm round her and vainly hoped that Mrs Sykes would see the funny side. Anna's sobs subsided and the class calmed down a little, too, as the wasp once more landed on a window.

'It didn't sting me, did it?' she said.

'I don't think so.' Although her neck was so red it was hard to tell.

'Mr Seed, you didn't notice that I had my hand up, either.'

'I'm really sorry, Anna. What was that for?'

'Ricky wrote piss off in his News.'

The whole table's eyes lit up. 'Er, he what?'

'He wrote piss off – look.' She reached over and slid an exercise book away from the pale, slight boy next to her.

'I never,' he said, with anxious eyes.

I studied his jotter, knowing that the writing would be difficult to decipher since Ricky had significant learning difficulties. As expected, the page was a smudgy scrawl of pencil. The letters were large, ill-formed and in many cases back-to-front but I could just about make out a tangled block of script:

i wnt to Tims bufday pratee i got a piss off cayk

'It's all right,' I said, smiling towards the inert Ricky but addressing Anna. 'He's just put that he went to Tim's birthday party and was given a piece of cake.'

'But it does say—'

'Yes, it was just a spelling mistake, that's all.' I looked round for a wasp update and noticed that it was still on the windows.

Briskly if forlornly ordering everyone to sit down and finish their work, I marched straight over to the window and pulled it open. Using a plastic ruler I managed to flick the infuriating insect towards the gap, where it detected fresh air and winged out swiftly to a cheer from the class. I didn't waste a moment.

'Right, Howard, please close all of the windows and the door.' It was time for a deep breath. Mrs Sykes continued to scribble. I went on, giving my voice as much authority as I could muster, 'Listen carefully, everyone. We've wasted enough time this morning. I want you all to sit in your places without making a sound. I want you to finish your writing quickly then check it carefully. Understood?'

There was a broad mumble of 'Yesses', followed by about forty seconds of beautiful silence.

Then Lawrence put up a hand. 'I'm too hot now, Mr Seed.'

'Tough.' They had to know who was boss; a bit of sun wouldn't hurt.

With five minutes left before playtime, a kind of sanity returned as selected children read out their News and I picked out sections for praise before the class discussed some of the more interesting items sensibly.

Mrs Sykes finally put down her notebook and listened intently as I managed the remnants of the lesson and encouraged individuals to speak clearly and strive to make improvements to their writing. I hardly dared look, but detected what might even have been a half-smile from her at some of the more charming comments made by the class. Somehow, despite the hornet invasion, a rescue had been accomplished.

It was at this moment of hard-earned calm that the door burst open and Martine walked in. She had a toilet seat around her neck.

'Mr Seed, it's really broken now!'

Chapter One

Lawrence

I stopped the bike at the top of the hill and looked down over the village where we lived: Applesett. The warm weather had continued for two weeks and I'd decided to make the most of it one Sunday afternoon in early September, taking out the shiny new touring bike to which I'd treated myself with birthday money.

Applesett was a remarkable place: a classic Dales stone village, situated at the confluence of three valleys and hidden away from the main road through Swinnerdale, giving it a tranquillity that was the envy of so many communities. From here I could survey its long sweep of sturdy cottages bordering a tapering, sloped green with the homely white pub in the centre.

All I could hear was the call of lambs drifting off the fells and the chatter of swallows perched on the power line above my head before the distant rattle of a truck drew my eyes down towards the bottom of the scene where the village's magical waterfall was tucked away in a cleft among the rocks.

To my right, over the mossy dry stone walls, the great soaring bulk of Spout Fell rose up to nearly 2,000 feet. I turned away from the jumbled farmyard ahead and into a tight, lumpy lane next to a series of small fields thick with lush grass, where I was greeted by the warm smell of cow muck. In the distance, I could see right across the main valley of Swinnerdale to the stout fortress of Castle Heywood, where we'd first arrived in the Dales.

I turned the bike on to the rising road and headed up Buttergill, the little-known, tight valley behind the village, with its steep arching hills and scatter of lonely farms. The light played off the fells in the distance as I wheeled past the colours of early autumn: hazel, brambles, long twists of ivy swamping the walls and pink spots of herb Robert. In every field a scatter of rabbits scurried away at my approach.

As usual, I passed no traffic on the dead-end road and so made haste along the rising and falling track, until I reached one of my favourite spots, a tiny bridge over the dale's peat-brown stream. I stopped and listened to the gentle tumbling rush of the beck, twisting between mossy boulders and alder roots. Two pheasants bobbed away for cover on the far bank amid the knapweed and cranesbill. Once more there were no sounds except for the buzz of bees and the yack of rooks in some distant trees.

Heading back I cut across a grassy track down the hill into the village and swept my head back as a tortoiseshell butterfly sailed across my path. Remarkably it turned and fluttered by my side, matching my speed as I rumbled down the path for some distance. With great joy I raced the orange-speckled creature back to the houses, once more delighting in this remarkable place where we lived.

As soon as I arrived at the minuscule front garden of Craven Bottoms, our lopsided house next to the chapel, I was greeted by my two boys, pensive Tom, just over three, and raucous Reuben, now sixteen months old and unstoppable. Barbara, my wife, was pulling weeds out of a flower bed.

'Good ride?' she said.

'Wonderful; what have the boys been like?'

'Same as usual: Tom was trying to look at books while Reuben wanted to throw plastic animals at him. I got them out in the sandpit eventually. I'm afraid it's more or less empty now.'

'Except for those teddies and that jigsaw.'

'Yes, and the worms they found.'

'Anyway, cup of tea?'

'Ooh, yes please, but I've got some exciting news first.'

My heart missed a beat: our interpretation of 'exciting' wasn't always the same.

'What?'

'Do you remember Doug and Rosie from York?'

'Erm, vaguely, yes. I think you knew them better than I did.'

'Well they rang twenty minutes ago to say that they're looking for a house in Swinnerdale. Doug's got a job at Ingleburn Secondary and they're renting a small place down the dale.'

'That'll be fun to see them again. But, if they are the ones I remember, aren't they quite, er, *alternative* for the Dales? Doesn't Rosie weave her own bread and all that?'

'Well, yes, but I've invited them over for a meal anyway.'

I went to make the tea, trying to picture the couple I'd last seen about four years ago.

The following morning I got to Cragthwaite Primary School at quarter past eight and was, apart from the headteacher Joyce, the first to arrive. The school was situated at the back of Cragthwaite village, which was one of broad Swinnerdale's larger communities, about six miles from Applesett, and another handsome place. The building itself was a squat, plain affair, built around 1970 when four tiny outlying Victorian schools were closed. It housed four classrooms, my own being a tatty 'mobile' outside the main structure.

As usual, the caretaker-cleaner Pat Rudds was pushing a mop around inside, looking fed up.

'Morning, Pat. Is it your ankles again?'

'It's always me flamin' ankles. They're swollen like cottage loaves. Ma doctor dun't give a chuff, neither.'

I was about to answer when a voice cut in from behind. 'Get some onions on them, that's what my mother always did.'

It was Hilda Percival, the diminutive rascal of an infant teacher. She noted Pat's surprise then leaned over to me to whisper. 'Never did 'er any good, tho'.'

Hilda was a Cragthwaite resident, now in her sixties, and had taught in the village for over thirty years. As usual, she went away chuckling at her own gag.

I headed for the staffroom and waited for the brief but unpopular pre-nine o'clock meeting that Joyce had recently established. A moment later the bulky figure of Val Croker, the deputy head, crashed through the door. She was carrying two large bags in one hand and a stuffed owl in the other, which she threw across the room at me.

'There you go, be careful with that.'

I caught it by the base, reacting quickly out of sheer surprise. 'Er, wow, thanks Val.'

'You are doing a woodland project, aren't you? If you take your rabble to the woods you've no chance of seeing anything alive so you may as well have something dead to study. I've got a weasel too – I'll bring that tomorrow.'

Before I could answer, Sue Bramley the marvellously efficient classroom assistant came in, followed by a jangle of beads which heralded Emma Torrington, the chaotic Class 1 teacher aged somewhere in her early thirties.

'Hello, everyone!' she beamed. 'Oh Sue, give me lots of coffee, please. Nice owl, Andy.'

I decided to hide the bird before Hilda saw it and made lots of awful twit jokes. She entered a moment later, complaining as usual that she had better things to do than blether in the staffroom. Val sat down and looked at her watch.

Sue noticed. 'I heard the phone go just now. Joyce might be late.'

We all wondered if it was worth nipping into our classrooms.

'Well, here we are, another school year, another bunch of empty-headed kids to sort out,' said Val, blowing on her pint mug of coffee.

'Oi, I was teaching your lot last year, they must have learned something,' I protested.

'I meant the new starters in Emma's, you soft pillock,' said Val shaking her head.

Hilda invited herself into the conversation as always. 'Oh, over the holidays they'll have forgotten everything you taught them, don't worry about that.'

'Aye,' said Val, 'they come in wearing their new shoes, they call you mum, they babble to all their mates about their week in Scarborough or Spain, but as soon as you get down to some work they look blank.'

'Most of them never read during the summer and half are scratching their bottoms with some scrofulous sheep disease,' said Hilda.

'Oh, come on you two,' I said. 'It's not that bad.'

Emma laughed. 'Pay no attention to them, Andy. You should know by now they do this every September – they just need to have a good moan and get it out of their system.'

'I wish the little beggars would get the worms out of their system,' said Hilda. 'I keep telling them that biting their nails will lead to itchy nethers. That Martin Fawcett can't leave his backside alone . . .'

Sue groaned. 'Oh, can we change the subject please, Hilda.'

'How about scabies, then?'

'No, don't tell us about Melanie Peacock from 1969 again,' groaned Val. 'I've heard that seventeen times before.'

'Actually, I think I've got a rash meself,' said Hilda, getting up and examining her leg. 'Oh, hang on – I've been sitting on a protractor. It could be a forty-five degree burn.' We all groaned and hoped that Joyce would rescue us.

Lawrence Quantick surveyed the owl with great interest. 'It's a tawny, isn't it, Mr Seed?'

'I think so,' I said, wishing I'd checked with Val.

Lawrence was extremely keen on nature, like many of the children in my class. He was an interesting boy, an off-comer, as the locals called outsiders, who had moved to the dale two years before when his father had bought the caravan park in nearby Shawby. He was regarded by the locals as being a little posh, but I would have described him first and foremost as overenthusiastic. That, and unable to keep his mouth closed for more than four seconds. But he was a likeable character all the same.

'We have a stuffed fox at home, Mr Seed. Shall I ask if I can bring it in?'

'That would be great, Lawrence. Just make sure that you do ask.'

An idea popped into my head at that moment. With the owl, Val's weasel and a fox, we could make a wonderful woodland table in the classroom. I had already planned a walk in some nearby woods for the following day and decided that we could collect twigs, acorns, conkers and the like to create a large, impressive display, using the wall behind, too. I began to get really excited about the idea and had some difficulty switching my attention to the forthcoming session on adverbs.

The following day the class was lined up in pairs outside the school, ready to walk down the drive and up the lane to the nearby woods. A parent, Mrs Lawson, was accompanying us and I was delighted to see that the weather was once again fine.

'Right children, reminders,' I called, waiting for them to turn to me. 'Remember that we are doing two things on this walk. One, looking for signs of woodland animals: tracks, droppings, signs of feeding and, er, birds and animals themselves, of course.' I hesitated, knowing full well that we would scare off every living creature within two miles. 'Your job is to spot these things and sketch them in your pads and try and identify them. Don't lose your pencil.'

A hand went up. It was Martine. 'I've already lost mine.' I gave her a spare then asked what our second objective was.

Lawrence blurted out. 'To collect bit and pieces!'

'Yes; leaves, seeds, fruits, twigs, that kind of thing, to make a display.'

'Fruits?' said Martine. 'You mean like bananas and stuff?' Everyone laughed.

Lawrence interrupted again, 'No, he means like hawthorn berries – they're fruit aren't they, Mr Seed?'

'Correct, yes, but please put your hand up, Lawrence.'

He put his hand up.

'Yes, Lawrence?'

'My mum's bringing the fox at lunchtime in the car. She didn't trust me to carry it in this morning.'

'Excellent. Right, stay in your pairs everyone and no shouting or running. It's time to go.'

We got about five yards down the path before Ricky needed the toilet.

The woods were actually a long, narrow copse beyond Sunters' farm next to the school and had a handy footpath running down the middle. The children crept through it in wonder, as if they'd never been in woodland before. At least two walked into trees as they shuffled forward with their heads down hoping, no doubt, to uncover the footprints of bears, wolves and wildcats.

Seeing that some children were starting to wander off, I gathered them back up again.

'Listen please, Class 3, I have a very important reminder. Remember there are probably poisonous mushrooms and berries in this wood so don't touch any fungi and ask Mrs Lawson or me before you pick any berries.' The word poisonous seemed to do the trick and several of them moved about much more cautiously, as if a toadstool might lurch out at them at any moment.

Ricky and his partner-in-crime Gary Blacow didn't seem perturbed, however, and were soon running up to me with a succession of items.

'Mr Seed, we've found a acorn,' said Ricky.

'Lovely. That's *an* acorn, Ricky.'

'And I've got an conker,' whooped Gary.

Bless them, they weren't the greatest minds in the school. Two minutes later they were back. Gary held out his hand.

'What are these, Mr Seed?'

'They're beech nuts.'

Ricky furrowed his brow. 'But there aren't any beaches round here.'

With any other child I might have thought this was a joke, but not with poor Ricky. As he ran off to find more wonders, I saw a fat wasp on the trunk of a nearby ash and wondered if this was my nemesis from a week before. I smiled and said in a comedy voice, 'So, we meet again, Doctor Vespa.'

'Yer what, Mr Seed?'

I hadn't seen Trudy Hammond waiting behind me.

'Oh, er, nothing. What do you want, dearie?'

She giggled and said what I feared she'd say. 'I need the loo.'

Did these children do nothing but drink? I called over Mrs Lawson and asked her to help the sensible Trudy locate a convenient shrub. I just hoped that no one was in it gathering specimens.

I went to see how the rest of the class were doing. Most were noisily collecting twigs and leaves but a few were quietly drawing. I overheard two boys, Tim Musgrave and Jason Fisher, who didn't see my approach from the other side of a large tree.

'Hey,' said Tim, 'did yer see that bird fly up there? I think it wer a woodpecker.'

'Don't look at it,' replied the sullen Jason. 'You'll only have to write about it later.'

Despite this cynicism, most of the children were having a wonderful time, even if their sketches were at best minimalist, and the carrier bags with which they had been issued were soon bulging and tearing. When I called them together to head back to school we had owl pellets, rabbit bones, leaf skeletons, pheasant feathers, a dead bee, some squirrel-raided hazelnuts, several kilos of sycamore seeds, an immense pile of pine cones and approximately 2,780 conkers. We also had a Mars Bar wrapper that Lisa insisted we couldn't leave because it was litter and could kill a passing hedgehog. I refused, however, to take the deer turd that Lawrence wanted to bring. At any rate, we would certainly have enough for a display.

Back at school, Mrs Quantick arrived with the stuffed fox at lunchtime, bringing it into the classroom while the children were in the hall for dinners. It was a magnificent specimen, mounted on a long base, with one paw raised threateningly and its mouth wide open as if in mid-attack, displaying two impressive rows of jagged teeth.

'She's lovely, isn't she?' said Mrs Quantick who was dressed from head to toe in Barbour.

'Fantastic,' I said. 'I'll make sure that we look after, erm, her well. And we're OK to keep her here for a couple of weeks? I'd like to make a big woodland display.'

'Of course, no prob, super idea. How's Larry getting along?'

'Larry? Oh, Lawrence! Er, yes, fine. He's enthusiastic, very enthusiastic.'

'Super! That's just want you want, Mr Speed, I'm sure. Nothing beats a blast of enthusiasm.'

I nodded hesitantly but before I could ask her the fox's story she was gone. In the meantime, I hid the animal in the small classroom store cupboard, then rushed around the room to set up the next teaching session.

At the start of the afternoon, Lawrence bounded into the room. 'Did my mum bring the fox?'

'Yes, thanks, it's great.'

'It's actually a vixen, the taxidermist told us. Shall I tell the class all about it?'

'That would be excellent, Lawrence,' I said, tempted to call him Larry for fun. 'But it will have to wait until tomorrow because we have science and art to fit in next.'

'Awww, I won't take long, really, Mr Seed, I'll keep it brief.'

I looked at him and we both knew perfectly well that he never kept anything brief.

The next lesson began with me asking the class to write a list of woodland creatures that they had seen or had found evidence of, using books for identification. Jason came up to me after I'd finished speaking. He was a child that didn't endear himself to people easily.

'Mr Seed, I can't find my pen.'

'Well, just use one of the spare ones on my desk, Jason.'

'But it's a special pen; it was a birthday present from my dad.'

He described the cartridge pen and I asked the class if anyone had seen it but they hadn't. 'When did you last have it?'

'This morning, before we went out on the walk.'

'Have you checked your drawer and bag?'

'Yeah, I've looked twice.'

'You didn't take it on the woodland walk did you?'

He looked doubtful. 'I don't think so. I don't remember taking it.'

'Anyway, it'll turn up I'm sure, Jason. You need to get your work done now.' He went away muttering that he had to find it, and I was soon confronted by a line of other children needing help.

At half past three, the room was empty again and I breathed a sigh of relief. There was some superb artwork drying on the tables:

paintings of treecreepers and voles and badgers, each made with real care and attention to detail. The most magnificent was Lawrence's stag, which he'd insisted on doing almost life-size. I couldn't wait to get them cut out and put up on the wall.

I brought three large branches in from outside, then stapled some azure paper to the largest wall space for a background. I arranged two cupboards in front and covered them with green paper before laying out the best of the children's woodland finds, along with some moss I'd brought from home. Next I cut out the painted animals and began to attach them to the wall.

An hour and a half later I added the large branches then brought out the stuffed animals as the centrepiece of what was a truly magnificent display, even if I said it myself. The fox, of course, was at the centre. I added a large label then stepped back to admire my work. After a few seconds the door swung open and the unwieldy figure of Pat Rudds filled the doorway. I decided to keep quiet and let her enjoy the honour of being the first person to see the display.

She bustled in dragging a mop and bucket, with her head down as usual. I said nothing. Pat shuffled forward, heaving the bucket to the side then stopped to rub her lower legs. It was late and she evidently thought the room was empty. She looked up and let out a walloping scream, tumbling backwards and crashing into a pile of Maths books.

'Bloody Norah! Bloody helling bloody Norah.'

My heart was now racing. 'Are you all right, Pat?'

She screeched again. 'Eurrrk, you made me jump. It was bad enough with that flamin' fox there.'

'Sorry, Pat.' I went over to her and noticed that the fox was right opposite her, its fanged mouth facing the door.

'What a bloody place to put that thing. I 'ate foxes 'n'all . . .'

I tried very hard but couldn't help a slight chuckle. 'At least you know it's there now, Pat.'

'Well, you may laugh but ma nerves are shot now and it won't do me ankles any good. You'll 'ave to move it a bit or someone else'll 'ave a shock like me.'

I was about to go over and shift it when the door opened again and a well-built, suited man came into the room. I didn't recognise him.

'Hello, can I help you?' I said.

'Jason tells me he's lost his pen,' he said abruptly.

'Ah, you must be Mr Fisher, then, his dad.'

'It was a very expensive present that pen – a Parker. Have you looked for it?' He seemed in a real hurry and came into the room without being invited and started glancing about. Pat raised her eyes and went over to her mop.

'I haven't had time to look, Mr Fisher. I've been rather busy.'

'Well, it needs to be found. He's only had it for a few weeks.' He crouched down and started to peer under the cupboards before pulling out drawers and rifling through them. I didn't know what to say.

'Erm, I have asked the class if they've seen it, Mr Fisher, and Jason has looked for it today. I wonder whether he took it on the woodland walk this morning and dropped it.'

He stood up and dusted his knees, giving me an unexpectedly severe look. 'He told me that he didn't take it on the walk, Mr Seed. I hardly think he's lying.'

'Could it be at home, then?'

'It's his school pen – he keeps it here. Another child's probably taken it.'

'I really think that's unlikely. We don't have a problem with that sort of thing in Cragthwaite.' I was finding it increasingly difficult to disguise my dislike for this impudent man.

He looked at me again, glanced round the room, then at his watch. 'Well, I am not happy, Mr Seed. That pen needs to be found.' He walked out swiftly.

Pat Rudds, leaning on her mop, watched him stride down the path. 'What a delightful man. Don't envy yer dealin' with the likes of 'im.'

I nearly said what I wanted to say but thought it best to hold my tongue, knowing Pat and the village's thirst for gossip. Instead I grabbed a huge pile of marking, forced it into my bag and headed home.

The following morning the classroom buzzed with approval and curiosity as children came in and saw the grand woodland display. They pressed round the animals and admired the fox in particular while Lawrence stood guard alongside and recounted its story.

'It was injured trying to dig into our hen enclosure,' he said. 'My dad found it tangled up in chicken wire and unconscious.'

'Ma dad shoots 'em,' said Gary.

Lawrence ignored him. 'It had lost a lot of blood and the vet put it down, so we took it to the taxidermist in Ingleburn.'

'The what?' said Martine.

Lisa filled her in. 'The man who stuffs animals.'

'What's that got to do wi' taxis?'

The questions flowed forth. 'Are the eyes real?'

'What's he do with its guts?'

'Can I put me 'and in its mouth?'

''Ow much are they? I might get me dog stuffed when it pegs out.'

I reluctantly called the children back to their seats and took the register before asking once more if anyone had seen a Parker pen. The whole class spent ten minutes scouring the room without success before we were called to assembly. As the class lined up, Jason continued to mutter that someone must have taken it.

It was about three weeks later that I took down the woodland display, its leaves now curled and grey, the conkers dusty and shrivelled. I returned the owl and weasel to Val with thanks and told Lawrence to ask his mum to pick up the fox. In the meantime, I put it in the store cupboard for safe keeping.

Lawrence's memory, however, was not as reliable as his enthusiasm and when there had been no sign of Mrs Quantick for several days, I quite forgot about the large stuffed animal that was wedged in the old cupboard at the back of the room. The reminder that it was still there came rather too abruptly for comfort late one afternoon as I absent-mindedly opened the cupboard door looking for some tissue paper. My eyes were unexpectedly confronted by a gaping red mouth of fangs, snarling eyes and a raised paw. It gave me such a shock that I spontaneously yelped, while the cup of tea in my left hand decanted mostly on to my trousers. My eyes flicked round to see if Pat was watching.

She wasn't but when my heart finally calmed down I had to laugh.

Chapter Two

Estelle

The week that had started so well with the woodland walk began to turn sour. On Friday, I arrived at home to find Barbara with a glum face. The boys were crawling all over her, seeking fun, but I could see right away that there was something wrong.

'What's the matter, are you all right?' I said, moving to sit down beside her, as my two sons transferred their attention to me, hoping that I'd be more responsive.

'I'm all right but our mortgage isn't.'

'What do you mean?' I said with a grimace, as Reuben accidentally put his full weight down on my groin.

'They've put the interest rate up again.'

'You're joking! It was only a few weeks ago they did that last time.'

'It's not looking good. Things were tight before but now we're really struggling. I'm cutting back on everything I can but if I can't sell lots of Christmas decorations this year, well, I don't like to think about it.'

We sat there in silence contemplating this shock, as our oblivious little sons demanded to play. My salary was still on a low grade and concepts like overtime didn't exist in teaching, while Barbara's wooden craft business was a very small-scale operation involving a lot of time and effort for not much reward.

She could see my mind working over the problem. 'Well, we've got a simple choice, really,' she said. 'We either live on economy lentils and have no holiday or I get a proper job. You can't earn any more at the moment so it's down to me.'

'Unless I try and get promotion.'

'Well, yes, but those sorts of opportunities just don't come up in the Dales. Think how long Val's been a deputy at your place.'

'That's true. What sort of job would you consider? And there's the whole childcare thing.' I looked at Tom who, as usual, was just sitting quietly against me while Reuben bounced about.

'Something part time, I don't know what yet, but I'll start to look. I'm sure Iris will have the boys and it's not all that long until Tom'll be starting school.'

I thought about our kindly neighbour and friend Iris Falconer across the green and felt reassured that she'd be the perfect babysitter if the need arose. That was something at least.

Estelle Wood was smart, outspoken, energetic and nosey. A slim, athletic nine-year-old with long brown hair, she had quickly established herself as the 'head girl' in Class 3, partly by virtue of being the eldest, but mainly through sheer force of personality. She had ears like radars and a mouth which was rarely shut.

'When's the student teacher starting?' she asked me early in October as I walked to the classroom.

'Estelle, how did you know about that? I haven't told anyone.'

'I overheard you talking to Mrs Berry about it last week.'

Well, at least she was honest. The conversation with Joyce had actually started at the beginning of term when the headteacher called me into her room. She'd redecorated the walls in a lush red and added a comfy armchair into which I appreciatively sank. As always, I found the aroma of her expensive scent almost overpowering.

'Now Andy, love.' She shuffled through piles of papers with her long fingers then gave me a characteristic warm smile. 'Ah, here it is.'

I wondered what I was in for now as her eyes flicked over a page. 'I'm not in trouble am I?'

'Don't be silly, I wouldn't allow it.' She looked up. 'You've been teaching, what, four years now, haven't you?'

'It only feels like two but, yep, it is four,' I said.

'And you're doing a terrific job. In fact, I don't know what we'd do without you with all the sports and Design and Technology and creative things you do.' I waited for the blow. 'Well,' she went on, 'St Mark's College asked me last year if we would have students and I said no but they've asked again and I can't really turn them down, especially as I'm friends with one of the course leaders.'

'But isn't Cragthwaite a long way for them to come?'

'Yes, but they're getting so desperate for schools that they're laying on a minibus for students right up the Dale.'

'Are these postgraduate trainees or younger students?'

'They're undergrads in their second year, so mainly aged nineteen. They're sending two: one infant specialist and one who wants to do juniors.'

'And you'd like me to have the latter?'

'I think you'll be an excellent mentor, Andy. You don't mind, do you?' She fluttered her long eyelashes but there was no need: I was quite keen on the idea, thinking that it might just give me a few hours' free time in the coming weeks to do marking and planning.

'OK,' I said. 'When do they start?'

'Good! There's a prelim one-day visit in early October then they do a four-week teaching practice from the eighth. Your student's name is Kim Bennett.'

Estelle wanted to know more. 'Is it a he or a she, Mr Seed?'

'Her name's Miss Bennett.'

'Ooh, I wonder what she's going to be like . . .'

Kim Bennett arrived the next morning at eighty-thirty for her preliminary visit. With striking features, long legs and a swirl of dark hair she looked more like a fashion model than a primary school teacher.

'Hi,' she said, flashing perfect white teeth and extending a hand. 'It's Kim; I'm really excited to be here.'

'Andy Seed. I'm glad that you're here. I mean, it's good to have you here, er, Kim.'

'Is it OK to call you Andy?'

'Er, yeah, sure – as long as it's Mr Seed in front of the children.'

She giggled. 'I can't wait to meet the kids. I'm so looking forward to teaching them – college is OK but I just want to get stuck in, in the classroom.'

'Good, well, there'll be plenty of opportunity for that next week when you start properly.'

Within a few minutes children started arriving and all of them stared wide-eyed at Kim. With the exception of Estelle, I hadn't told the class that we had a student with us but a gaggle of the older girls clearly knew, no doubt courtesy of their leader.

After the register I addressed the class. 'Right everyone, I'd like to introduce Miss Bennett to you. She's another teacher who is going to be helping you over the next few weeks.' I made a special effort to avoid the word student.

Kim gave a little wave and grin, waggling her head from side to side. Most of the children seemed unsure what to make of her. I quickly regained their attention.

'Now, look this way. Miss Bennett is just observing today, not teaching, so it'll be a normal Thursday.'

Martine put up her hand. 'What's observing mean?'

I looked around. 'Who can answer that?'

Estelle volunteered. 'It means watching something sort of carefully.'

'Good explanation,' I said.

Martine scratched her head. 'So Miss Bennett will be watchin' us? Sort o' like a spy?'

Kim laughed and answered herself, 'No, nothing like that. I just want to get to know you all and see how you do things.'

Estelle certainly wasted no time getting to know the new student and, during Maths, I overheard a conversation they were having.

'How old are you, Miss Bennett?'

'I'm nineteen, twenty in January.'

'Oh wow, my birthday's in September.'

'Did you get any nice presents?'

'Yeah, a Sony Walkman, some clothes and loads of books.'

'Great, I've got a Walkman – good aren't they?'

'You're really pretty,' said Estelle. 'Do you have a boyfriend?'

At this point I moved over to Estelle's table and asked to see her work. Kim smiled and moved away to talk to one of the boys. Estelle had hardly even started the questions I had set.

'Estelle, I know it's exciting having a new person in the room but you shouldn't be just chatting to Miss Bennett like that and certainly not asking her personal questions. Come on, you need to catch up with this work.'

'Sorreee,' she said, aware that it was unquestionably cheeky.

'What's your student like then?' asked Val the following day in the staffroom during morning break. 'She's a bit of a looker, I'll say that.'

Emma spoke before I could answer. 'A bit of a looker? She's beautiful!'

'What does the man think, though?' added Hilda, putting me on the spot.

'I can't say I've noticed . . .' I said, hoping that the joke would let me off the hook but it only seemed to make matters worse.

'He's blushing like a pound of cherries!' squealed Hilda, causing me to redden more.

'Of course I've noticed she's attractive, but to answer Val's question, she's really overfamiliar with the children – I had to have a word with her about it twice. It doesn't help having Estelle in the class who thinks she's the same age . . .'

'Oh yes, young Miss Wood,' said Val. 'I taught her older brother a few years back.'

Sue nodded. 'They're not short of confidence those kids.'

'Gobby is the word I'd use,' said Hilda.

'Dead right,' said Val. 'But they've got brains, too.'

'So, anyway, Andy,' said Hilda, steering the conversation back to a place I didn't want it to go. 'You need to get on top of this student and be firm with her by the sound of it.'

'Hilda!' called Sue, while Emma screeched with laughter. 'You can't say that!'

But I was already heading out of the door.

* * *

Five days later, Kim was back in the classroom sitting beside me after school and going through her plans for her first lesson the following day. I'd suggested Art since it was something that all the children enjoyed and didn't require as much preparation for differing abilities as the more academic subjects.

'I'm going to do wax resist,' she said enthusiastically, although it wasn't really obvious from her written lesson outline. 'We did it at college and I loved it. I think the pictures will make a lovely display – really colourful.'

'OK, what theme have you chosen?'

She clearly hadn't thought of this. 'Erm, well, I was going to let them just choose but maybe autumn? We could do leaves with lots of oranges and reds. Yeah, actually, green ink washed over reds and yellows would be really striking.'

'It sounds good,' I said, not wanting to dampen her excitement. 'Have you checked that we have the inks for that? And other resources?'

'Oh, er, I'd just assumed that you'd have those things. I saw wax crayons.' She flashed her dazzling smile once more and I sensed that she was used to getting away with things on its account. That and her low-cut top which, despite a superhuman effort, my eyes were continually drawn to. I didn't dare suggest that it wasn't appropriate clothing for a teacher and hoped that Joyce would make the point.

'Well, we do have Brusho inks, actually, but they're in powder form so you'll need to mix them beforehand. What paper will you use?'

'Er, white . . . ?'

'Yes, it needs to be white for wax resist but what size and thickness?'

'Oh, can you get different thicknesses?'

* * *

The lesson began with a lot of noise and this was maintained throughout. Kim just didn't appear to have the knack of speaking to children in such a way that they would listen to her. She didn't wait for quiet when addressing the class and so had to raise her voice above the chatter. This had the effect of just making the children talk more loudly. I was tempted to intervene but didn't want to undermine her so early on in her session.

I felt sorry for Kim as she battled against the subsiding attention in the room but I knew that she had to go through this by herself in order to learn. Casting my mind back to my own days as a callow student teacher facing just such a class of cheeky kids in a village near York, I wondered if I was really any better. Theory and lectures were of limited value when it came to teaching; the only place to test your mettle was at the deep end. At the moment, Kim was flapping about trying to keep her head above water and it was tempting to throw her a line but I knew that I shouldn't.

'I want you to do some lovely pictures, OK?' she said through the din. 'Look at the autumn leaves out of the windows, draw them in wax crayon then wash over the page with green ink from the pot over there.'

Estelle's hand was up right away. 'What paper do we use?'

More questions from others followed.

'How big do we draw them?'

'Do we fill 'em in or do line drawings, like?'

'Can I do the 'ole tree?'

'Can us use any colour, Miss?'

'I don't get what yer mean by "wash t'page". You mean clean it or summat?'

There then followed ten more minutes clarification by Kim with the rising noise of chatter once more making attention sparse.

'OK, off you go!' said Kim.

Martine came trundling up. 'Yer what, miss? I didn't hear any o' that.'

She was followed by Ricky who, as ever, looked confused. 'I don't know what to do.'

The lesson was chaotic. Children were shouting, scraping chairs, moving about and using vast amounts of paper, scrawling huge messy sketches with as many colours of wax crayon as they could find. The green ink soon ran out and two boys asked if they could make some more. Kim nodded and rushed around, trying vainly to keep everyone on task.

I was finding it very hard just to sit and watch but this was the way the college had asked us to be. I had to let her make mistakes. She certainly knew how to do that, and while watching the mayhem I willed her to stop everyone, sit them down in silence and remind them of the exact task and the remaining time which was rapidly ebbing away. She looked flustered and some of her eye makeup had streaked with sweat.

'Noise down, please, Class Three!' she called. They took no notice.

Martine was finding out what would happen if you mixed every colour of ink. The answer was a horrible mess. Jason was snapping and flicking bits of crayon with a ruler, while Lawrence decided to experiment and see if wax resisted paint as well as ink: he emptied the art cupboard and tried every kind of substance.

Estelle, meanwhile, couldn't help herself and was asking Kim where she bought her clothes, in between telling her what the boys of Class 3 were really like and even what she thought of the other teachers.

At one point, Estelle wandered by me so I called her over for a word.

'Estelle, haven't I told you that you really can't talk to teachers like that?'

'Yes, Mr Seed, but she's a student, not really a teacher – she's still at college.'

'That makes no difference. I want you to stop having these conversations with her about clothes and presents and boys and so on. All right?'

She nodded guiltily. 'Sorry.'

'And please clear up some of the mess on your table.'

'I will and I'll make sure the others help.'

'Good.' I expected her to walk away but she lingered.

'Mr Seed . . .'

'Yes, Estelle?'

'Do you think Miss Bennett's pretty?'

When the bell for home time rang I surveyed what was left of my room. Every surface was covered with splashed, frenzied pictures that looked more like infants' artwork. There was ink on all the desks, the walls, the floor and some of the books. The sink area looked like Vikings had rampaged through it and no one had put any chairs up. My nerves were frayed and Pat would be furious. Kim, meanwhile, her own attire festooned with rainbow splatters, came over to me smiling.

'What did you think?'

I spent an hour going through the lesson with her, trying to be sensitive about the main issues. She gradually became quiet and, as she went to catch her minibus, I was left feeling somehow that I was in the wrong, seeing her face tired and flushed. I wondered if I'd been too harsh as I went round the room, trying to repair some of the devastation, but much of the sympathy I had for her drained away when I saw that she'd used an entire year's supply of ink and most of the expensive cartridge paper.

Joyce walked in, smiling. 'How did she get on? Oh.'

I outlined the calamity that was Kim's first ever lesson.

'Oh dear, I'm sorry, Andy. And I'm afraid that I'm not going to lighten your mood either.'

'What do you mean?' I said.

'Remember Jason and his missing pen?'

I nodded.

'Mr Fisher has made an official complaint to the governors.'

I picked the phone and heard the soft Dales tones of Adam Metcalfe.

'Now then, Andy.'

I was at home chewing over Kim's calamitous start and the dismal pen episode, and was pleased to have something take my mind off school.

'How's the farm?' I asked.

'Same as usual: we get by.'

Adam farmed high up beyond Swinnerdale in a bleak, wet valley called Rawdale, known locally as Reddle. With his steadfast wife Ruth and four young children, he somehow managed to eke out a living raising hill sheep on the worst land in the area. Since meeting him after he'd preached at the chapel in Applesett two years before, the family had become good friends and Adam's gentle wisdom and practical, forgiving approach to life was just what I needed at this time.

'I'm going over to Arkleton tomorrow night,' he said, 'dropping off some logs for my sister. There's a sheep sale on at the auction mart – we could stop by for an hour if you fancied it.'

I jumped at the chance: not only had I said to him some time ago that I'd love to see where all the buying and selling of livestock happened locally but it would be a good chance to talk with him in the car on the way over.

'Let it blow over is my advice,' said Adam, as his old Vauxhall strained up the hill out of Reddle towards the greener valley beyond. I'd told him about Mr Fisher's complaint but, as usual, he put me at ease.

'There'll always be complainers,' he said, 'in every walk of life; some just need to get it out of their system and some'll never be pleased whatever you do.'

'I just wish he hadn't taken it to the governors.'

'Oh, they've got more important things to think about than a lost pen, I reckon.'

'True . . .'

'And the head supports you – she knows you're a good teacher. Just carry on doing what's right.'

As ever, he put things in perspective, and when he told me of the struggles he had on his farm with awful weather, dead animals, rising feed prices, crumbling buildings and new European directives, I didn't even bring up the subject of my wayward student teacher.

It was dark by the time we pulled into the muddy stone town of Arkleton and Adam steered his car towards the big sign saying *Auction Mart.* We wheeled past row upon row of Land Rovers, each one hitched to an aluminium trailer, then big livestock wagons and battered pick-up trucks.

'Busy tonight,' he said.

We put on wellies and walked across to the open-sided sheds where hundreds of sheep were huddled in small square holding pens with burly men clanking open gates and pushing them through.

'These are all waiting to go through to be sold,' he said. I couldn't believe the number and variety of breeds. Adam pointed them out. 'Them're Suffolks, then we've got Herdwick cross, Dalesbred, Swardle, Texels, Blue-faced Leicesters, Mashams and Teeswater over at the back. A lot of mules, too, of course.'

'Cross-bred?'

'Aye, you're learning.'

We clambered over some metal barriers and towards small huddles of flat-capped farmers. The night air was cold but there was a busy excitement about the place. A painted board on the side of one of the buildings proclaimed *Belly clipping service available*. Elsewhere were chalked notices:

Night milkers wanted
For sale: cattle crush
Win £5 in beef semen vouchers

Everywhere there were scraps of paper listing future sales for maiden heifers, suckled calves, store bullocks and stirks, or shearlings, gimmer hoggs, tups and horned draft ewes.

'Come on, we'll go into the ring and see my friend Rick in action,' said Adam.

'Who's Rick?'

'Richard Suggett – he's the auctioneer.'

We pushed through a door and entered the nerve-centre of the auction: a dimly lit old building with a large circular pen in the centre, floored with sawdust. Eight or nine serious-faced men stood at one side of the ring eyeing four nervous sheep, while opposite, the white-coated auctioneer kept up an amplified babble. Around the circle were ancient wooden benches in rising tiers upon which were perched grizzled old farmers, red-faced lads and a handful of children. There were only four women in the room, two of whom sat by the auctioneer scribbling furiously on piles of paper. The whole place reverberated with the low chatter of men weighing up livestock.

We climbed over the benches to the back row which afforded a good view of the whole frenetic scene. I had no idea what was going on. What amazed me most was that gangs of sheep were hustled in and out of the ring so rapidly, most being sold within 40 seconds.

'These are this year's lambs from all over the country,' explained Adam. 'That's why there are so many breeds – we've got lowland stuff from Bilthorpe way, hill sheep from the Lakes, upland from Wales or Scotland.'

'I thought they'd be mainly local.'

'A lot of them are but farmers'll travel because it's a good auction and they'll get fair prices here.'

A single stumpy lamb was ushered through the gate and into the ring. A short, ruddy man pressed his hand into its rump and waggled some fingers. The auctioneer had already begun his jabber of prices and bids, only a few of which I could make out.

Fifteen, fifteen, I'm looking at fifteen, who'll give me twelve, twelve there, twelve and a half, thirteen, thirteen, come on, thirteen for a good lamb . . .

I tried to work out who was who and eventually, with some guidance from Adam the scene began to make sense. Yardmen brought the lambs through from the pens once they were weighed and as soon as the previous sheep were sold and out of the ring the next group was pushed in with a clatter of gates, sometimes with the selling farmer, crook in hand, nudging the anxious animals around the ring so that everyone had a good view. The sour-faced men lining the round pen opposite the auctioneers were the buyers, working with quick flicks of their fingers to register interest and bids.

'Some of them are buying for ten or more firms so they'll be dashing out for the phone or getting paper messages all the time,' said Adam.

Sometimes pairs of lambs were ushered into the ring, sometimes tens and occasionally tightly packed huddles of thirty. In each case the auctioneer, standing at his platform, announced the average weight and named his fair price before dropping a little to invite bids. He then launched into a frantic gabble if competition was keen and, within half a minute, banged down his knobbly stick and the lambs gratefully hurried off away from the stares of the rugged farmers as the exit gate was opened.

Twelve scraggy, long-haired sheep with red markings were next and one of them leapt up at the gate as it was barged through into the pool of light in the middle of the room. A few prods from the buyers brought a brief flurry of offers before the tall, curly haired Rick rapped the gavel and announced a sale.

'Fourteen twenty to Clarke.'

An unshaven, round-faced buyer shook his head. 'I di'n't bid on them.'

The auctioneer raised his eyebrows. 'Well why did yer look at me like that then?'

'I did nowt.'

There was a rare moment of hush in the arena before a tall fellow in a worsted jacket lifted a finger and mumbled, 'I'll 'ave 'em.' This brought a moment of panic with the paperwork before the next lambs were pressed in and the flow continued. The unshaven man withdrew a few yards shaking his head.

'I think Rick's tired,' said Adam. 'He started at half four and he's not had a break.'

I looked at my watch. It was eighty-thirty. 'So he stands up and talks the whole time without a break?'

'Sometimes he does six hours with just a cup of tea.'

Another sale was completed while we were talking and a bobble-hatted Dalesman in a battered wax jacket and mucky wellingtons stepped forward and pressed something into the hand of the buyer.

'What's going on there?' I asked.

'He's given him luck money. It's a superstition thing – kind of expected, too.'

The smell of fish and chips drifted across the ring and an ancient pair of shepherds opposite us pushed lumps of batter into their mouths with fat black fingers.

'Cup of tea for the buyers please!' called Rick the auctioneer. 'Put extra sugar in Mr Clarke's.' The assembly laughed.

'He's a bit of a joker is Rick,' said Adam. 'Anyway, this job'll be on for a couple more hours yet – shall we go?'

Rick's flying patter faded away as I wandered past the Land Rovers having forgotten all about my troubles at school.

On the following Monday morning, I sat and watched Kim Bennett lead a simple and mercifully quiet English lesson involving using thesauruses. I was pleased to see that she had taken on board most of my advice and was considerably sterner with the class, insisting on their attention when she spoke. I positioned my chair near Estelle as insurance.

At only one point did the session slide dangerously away from control; Kim had put an exercise on the blackboard involving changing words in sentences. The fifth sentence was:

The old man went for a walk in the woods.

The instruction was for the children to replace the underlined word with another word, using a thesaurus for ideas. It was going well until Kim stopped the class and went through the sentences, asking for examples of improvements.

'What about number five?' asked Kim, sounding confident.

Lawrence's hand shot up, as did Estelle's. I noticed that Lawrence had the large *Oxford Thesaurus*, rather than the slim children's version that the others were sharing.

'Yes, Lawrence?' said Kim, pointing.

'The old man went for a mince in the woods.'

I nearly spurted out the tea in my mouth but the class just chuckled until Martine blurted, 'Yer what? 'E bought some mince in the woods?'

At this point there was uproar and I couldn't help intervening as poor Kim fought to salvage control.

As the bell went and the children filed out, I went over to her, just as she gave a large sigh.

'Kim, that was a good lesson, well done!'

She stared at me for a moment, almost in disbelief. 'Really?'

'A huge improvement,' I said smiling, and her own face split into a huge grin. 'It's really hard to get things right when you start out – I wasn't so brilliant myself – but the main thing is that you are enthusiastic, you like children and you are willing to take advice on board. Well done!'

'Oh, I'm so relieved; I really appreciate it.' She stepped forward and panic arose as I thought for a moment that she was going to hug me: no doubt some child would see it.

But she was reaching for her notes. 'Thanks so much,' she said.

'It's my playground duty, I'd better go out,' I said, turning for the door and she added that she would come out, too, as it was a requirement of the course.

Out on the windy tarmac we watched children running and spinning and kicking balls with that boundless energy that the young possess. Estelle saw us and approached.

'I might become a teacher,' she said, looking at Kim. 'Or maybe a lawyer or a TV reporter. It's hard to choose, really. I like your coat, Miss Bennett.'

I held up a hand. 'No, Estelle, I have the perfect job for you.'

'What's that?' she said.

'An auctioneer.'

'What's that?' she said again.

'You help sell sheep and cattle to farmers . . .'

'Ooh, that's good – I like animals.'

'. . . And you get to talk all day.'

'I'll do it!'

Chapter Three

Jason

Under a scudding late October sky the children of Class 3 boarded Mr Ripley's wobbly old coach with great excitement. We were heading to Hauxton Airbase, having been invited there by the father of Anna Reed, one of the younger girls. He was a Squadron Leader flying Tornado interceptor aircraft and had told me some weeks previously that he could ensure a memorable visit for the children.

'I'll take them into the hangar, show them the aeroplane, then they can each have a go at sitting in the cockpit.'

'Seriously?' I said in disbelief. 'Isn't there, er, a security issue or something?'

'It's no problem, really. I'll have a word with the boys at the gate and we won't tell the Commander,' he laughed.

'Well, if that's OK, I'll check with Mrs Berry the head but I'm sure she'll be fine. The boys will love it, particularly.'

'They certainly will, Mr Seed. The Tornado's an impressive piece of kit.'

I'd arranged the trip to coincide with Kim Bennett's teaching practice, thinking that it would be excellent experience for her to be involved in organising a visit. She had continued to improve over the previous three weeks and was gradually getting to grips with the mammoth task that was becoming an effective primary school teacher.

I let her deal with a dispute involving Lawrence as we climbed on to the bus. He hurried up the aisle from the rear seats carrying a pained expression.

'Miss Bennett, I was on the back seat and Jason's just pushed me off.'

'Jason, is that true?' she said moving towards the scene of the crime.

'What?'

'Did you push Lawrence off the back seat?'

'I was here first – he was pushing me.' Several children nearby contradicted this version and it was obvious that he was not telling the truth.

'Right, Jason, I want you to move please. Come and sit at the front behind the driver.'

He pulled a sour face and for a moment I thought that he might defy her request. The coach went quiet. Kim looked him in the eye, pointed and gave her voice authority. 'Now!'

Reluctantly, he stood up and moved forward, muttering as he went. Finally, everybody sat down and, after counting them all, I gave the driver the thumbs up to go.

I sat down next to Kim. 'You handled that very well; good stuff.'

'Do you think so? I wonder if I was being a bit harsh with him.'

'You've got to be tough with Jason, he's an awkward customer.'

'I've certainly learned that . . . He was a real pain in PE yesterday and almost spoiled that game of benchball. I know he's really good at sports but he wants to do everything all the time – he never gave some of the others a touch of the ball.'

I looked around to make sure that no one was listening. 'Hmmm, you can help a child with work and with behaviour often, too, but when someone has an arrogant personality it's very difficult.'

Kim reduced her voice to a whisper. 'What sort of home does he come from?'

'Parents have lots of money – they run some kind of business. He's an only child and spoiled by all accounts. His dad doesn't help his case, either.'

'Is that the one who complained about the pen?'

'Yeah . . . we had to take apart the whole classroom and Joyce asked everyone in school about it. She was really good and got the governors to support me over the situation, telling him I hadn't done anything wrong, but he still wasn't satisfied. He's still telling Jason to look for the pen.'

'Oh flip, and there was me giving his boy a stern telling off just now . . .'

'No, you we're right. We can't treat him any differently just because he has narky parents.'

At this point I looked up and noticed that Mrs Lawson, our trusty parent helper, was watching the two of us leaning close and whispering. Her eyes shot away but I could register that they were rather wider than usual. Not wanting her to get the wrong idea, I stood up immediately and started looking business-like, walking up the aisle and checking that everyone was sitting sensibly.

'Are we nearly there yet?' asked Estelle.

'Very funny,' I said, wondering whether to chat to Mrs Lawson or if that would simply make things worse.

At the airbase we had to cross a road from the car park to reach the inner gate. I let Kim organise the children at the kerb.

'Remember to look both ways as you cross, and to listen for

traffic.' Unfortunately she didn't ensure that everyone had heard, and started ushering them on to the road before I could intervene. I noticed Jason step out without looking at all.

'Jason Fisher! Watch for traffic!' I boomed. He made a cursory glance then ran across. 'And don't run! You've been told before about that.'

Everyone looked over towards him and once more his face betrayed a seething resentment that he'd been singled out. I went over and spoke more softly to him.

'It's for your own safety, Jason. Please try and listen, then do as you're told.'

He didn't answer but just looked at me with an irksome defiance before I glanced at Kim as if to say, 'Watch him.'

The upright, moustachioed Squadron Leader Reed was waiting at the gate in his flight gear and ushered us through with great enthusiasm. We could see giant hangars everywhere and the runway with several large and small aircraft on the tarmac beyond. The children babbled with excitement and there was a lovely 'Wowwww!' when he led us through a wide door and into a vast metal-framed building. There was a sleek, grey Tornado jet just a few metres away.

'Welcome to RAF Hauxton everyone,' said our host. 'If you all spread out facing this way I'll introduce you to the aircraft.'

I dug out my notepad, ready to jot down some facts, and I could see Kim wishing that she'd thought to bring one. I smiled and tore out some pages for her.

'Right, well, this machine's full name is a Panavia Tornado ADV,' said Squadron Leader Reed, 'as my daughter there knows.' We laughed as Anna hunched her shoulders and mouthed that she didn't. 'It is what we call an interceptor, meaning that its main role is to find and deal with enemy aircraft that are heading our way.'

I wondered whether this was all too much to take in for the clutch of young, ruddy-faced Dales kids standing there but my class listened rapt throughout. Our guide astonished us with a series of facts about the plane, telling us that on one short flight it used as much fuel as a car would in its entire lifetime and that each of the missiles strapped to its wings cost more than a typical house.

We learned about swing-wings, the vast power of turbofan jet engines, and the huge amount of training that pilots and navigators had to undergo. Finally, he stopped and invited questions. Every child raised a hand.

'Does it 'ave guns?'

'Is it faster than the Russians?'

'Have you ever crashed?'

'Are yer sometimes scared when flying this?'

'Have you ever been in a war?'

And from Ricky the inevitable, 'Can I go to the toilet?'

Lawrence asked if it had an ejector seat and what happened when you used it.

'Ah,' answered the smiling pilot, 'good question. It does have an ejector seat and I hope I never have to use it. I've been on the training machine that simulates being shot out of the cockpit by an explosive charge and, believe me, it's very scary . . . Oh, that reminds me, Mr Seed. We do go on a survival course in case we ever have to bail out and they give us this emergency kit – I thought you'd like one.' He passed me what looked like an old-fashioned metal tobacco tin about the size of a pocket dictionary.

'Thanks,' I said, while several marvelling children leaned across for a closer look. They were fascinated by the idea of survival and asked several more questions before our guide looked at his watch and said, 'Right, one last question.'

Again, all the hands went up. I indicated to Kim to choose.

'Gary,' she said.

'Can we fly in it?' he asked in all seriousness.

The Squadron Leader chuckled. 'No, but you are allowed to sit in the cockpit, two at a time.' A rousing cheer rent the air of the hangar and some of the boys dashed forward in an attempt to be first in line. Jason was one of them and I saw him dig his shoulder into Ricky's back in his desperation to make the front, eliciting a wail from the scrawny boy.

Kim reacted first. 'Jason, come here!'

'I can only let you on board if you're sensible,' said the pilot, noting the kerfuffle. 'The rule is you sit down for a short while and touch *none* of the controls. We don't want to wipe out Hauxton with a nuclear bomb. Well, not before I've had a cup of tea, anyway.'

The children half-laughed and I reluctantly sent Jason to the back of the line, wishing it hadn't been him once again.

The first young would-be pilots climbed the twin steps into the jet, their eyes shining with wonder. Kim took some photos and we all laughed again as the children's heads disappeared into the cockpit and gave us an idea of just how big the plane was.

Several airmen appeared to enjoy the moment, too, and it was difficult to ask each child to leave the cockpit. Finally, it was Jason's turn and I went up with him before he dropped into the pilot's seat and reached for the throttle. I was about to suggest that he didn't move it when there was a loud wolf whistle from across the hangar. I looked out and saw Kim climbing up the other steps and leaning over to look under the canopy.

It was clear that she was used to such treatment and ignored it, instead turning to the scene in front of her and calling out, 'Jason! You were told not to do that.' I looked across just in time to see him flicking various switches on the control panel in front. He seemed genuinely disappointed that no missiles were instantly launched.

That evening I sat on Tom's bed at home and with a sigh asked him to choose a story, tempted to add, 'something short'. Reuben, as ever, was jiggling about on my lap but he did look adorable in his little stripy pyjamas, his fringe of thick fair hair almost reaching his eyes.

Tom took his time, as was his way, and his finger alighted on the very book I had feared, the *Thomas the Tank Engine* compendium. It wasn't that the stories weren't charming or the railway characters fun; they were just so long. I wanted to be downstairs next to our log fire, with a good cup of Yorkshire tea.

For what felt like the twelfth time that month, I began the tale of Harold the Helicopter, reading at maximum bedtime story speed. Reuben, who was too young to appreciate the Rev Audrey's quaint language, soon grew bored and went into a moany wriggle, while Tom listened intently, his eyes glued to the pictures as he twiddled his hair. I, meanwhile, started to fall asleep. Wasn't it supposed to be the other way round? I stifled another yawn and tried the old trick of turning two pages at once.

'You've missed some!' said Tom. 'Where's the bit where Harold flies really fast?'

'Whoops,' I said sheepishly and resigned myself to ploughing on.

Fifteen minutes later they were tucked in, although neither looked sleepy, while I trudged downstairs to tell Barbara about the airbase visit and find out how her day had been.

'You're kidding!' she said, mouth agape. 'He really flicked some switches in the plane? What if something goes wrong when they next fly it?'

'And it would have to be Jason, too. He was causing trouble all day. I was glad to have Kim there to help – she dealt with him really well.'

'What's she like this student, then? You've not really said much about her since that first lesson disaster.'

'Kim? Well, she's doing much better now, although she's still got lots to learn . . .'

'No, I meant what sort of person is she?'

'Er, she's, er, nice really, just a typical young student, like we were a few years back I suppose.'

'I heard that she's stunningly attractive. You haven't mentioned that.'

Was I blushing again? I really hoped not. 'She's, yeah, a pretty girl but not my type.'

Barbara laughed. 'You are allowed to say if she's fit or not. Honestly, men!'

'Anyway, who told you she was fit?'

'Who do you think? Mrs Dent at the shop has a cousin who lives next door to one of your parents.' I might have known it would be the village gossip. 'They'd seen Kim arriving one morning at school – apparently a couple of dads at the gate couldn't help staring.'

'Well, she does have an amazing figure . . .'

'Oh, so you've obviously been staring, too.'

'Oi, stop it, Barbara Seed – you're just winding me up.' I lobbed a cushion at her. 'Anyway, what about you? Found any jobs in the paper?'

'There's really not a lot. I might be able to get something in the grocers in Ingleburn but it's long hours and the pay's pitiful. Otherwise the ads are for the usual things: agricultural sales reps and holiday cottage cleaners. I have enough trouble keeping this place half-tidy and my knowledge of nitrogen-based fertilisers is remarkably close to nil.'

'Hmmm, well, we were told it's no good looking in the papers.' I tried not to sound too depressed. 'Remember what that woman at Castle Heywood told us: all the locals grab the part-time jobs via their secret extended family network. We don't stand a chance.'

'It's not their fault that they're all related to each other. We'd do the same if we'd been brought up here – it's just the Dales way of things.'

'I know, I know . . . but what are we going to do? I can't bear the thought of having to sell this house. Remember how hard it is to buy places in Swinnerdale.'

'I can't bear the idea of leaving Applesett, either. I love this village.'

'So what *are* we going to do?'

'Well, there is one idea. It's a bit mental but . . .'

'What?'

'I had coffee with Iris this morning and she said what about delivering the post. Her neighbour's son does it and he says they do sometimes have part-time work going.'

'Well, Tom would be in heaven if you had a red van: Postman Patricia! But, could you really do that? Getting up at four in the morning or whatever it is?'

'Well, for a start it's in Ingleburn, not around the dale, so it would be delivering on foot or by bike, and secondly I've always loved the idea of being a postie, ever since I was little.'

'Really? You never told me that.'

'And I'm at my best early in the morning – you wouldn't know that either because you're always asleep – so that's not a problem. I would finish around eleven o'clock, too.'

'Wow. How did Iris know all that?'

'She didn't. I rang the sorting office this morning and they put me on to personnel. They're sending me an application form.' She smiled and I could see genuine excitement in her eyes.

'Amazing . . . I can't wait to see you in uniform.' This time she threw the cushion.

The following day I was home at five o'clock. Now that Kim was doing nearly half the teaching, I could often finish early. My marking had been done in school hours and I was contemplating the joy of an evening at home without a hefty pile of exercise books to trawl through. A battered 2CV was parked just outside the house as I arrived and I wondered if we had visitors or if there were French hikers about.

Inside I was greeted by a short, humorous fellow in handmade clothes and a sunny-faced woman of about thirty-five with a vast frizz of wavy hair: Doug and Rosie, our acquaintances from York.

'Andy! How ya doing?' they both called. I could just about recall meeting them previously but it certainly didn't feel like a case of old friends to me. Rosie gave me a big hug anyway and Doug waggled his glasses and held out a hand.

'Good to see you here,' I said as Tom and Reuben ploughed into my legs and demanded cuddles.

'Yeah, great to be here. What a village!' said Doug.

Barbara came in with a tray of drinks. 'They've just been looking at a house – the one behind Sam Burnsall's at the top of the green.'

'Oh, right,' I said. 'It's quite big, isn't it?'

'It's divine,' said Rosie, her eyes alight. 'Needs a lot of work, but that's why I'm married to a woodwork teacher.'

'CDT, please: you demean my status,' said Doug.

'So, er, are you putting in an offer?' I asked.

'It's an auction job,' said Rosie. 'We're definitely going to bid and we've now sold our house in York so we have *cash*.'

'Wow, it'll be great having you around if you get it,' said Barbara. I nodded a little half-heartedly.

'Anyway,' said Doug. 'Come on you two, we want to know the truth about this village: is the beer any good in the pub? Do the children all have funny noses? Where the axe murderer lives – dish the full dirt.'

We laughed and Barbara said, 'Right, well, if you like the smell of cow poo, don't mind cold monsoons and being regarded as foreign, it's wonderful.'

At school the next morning I'd arranged to meet Joyce in her office to discuss Kim's progress. We were getting to the end of her four weeks' teaching practice and we had to decide whether to give her a pass or not.

'I know you think she's improved since the first disastrous art lesson,' said Joyce. 'How's she doing at the moment?'

'Well, things could only get better after that and they have. She's listened to just about everything I told her and her class control is now not bad.'

'I'm sure you've done a great job mentoring her, Andy – I have full confidence in you. So, the question is, will she make a teacher?'

'I was doubtful at first but I really think she could do it. She enjoys being with children and she has worked hard. She's dealt well with awkward individuals like Jason and Estelle, once she realised it doesn't work to be their friends.'

'Well, even if she doesn't make it she can always become a model. I've never seen such a bonny girl.'

'Don't you start all that as well, Joyce!'

'Sorry . . . right, so a pass, then?'

'Yes, just.' I stood up to go.

'Wait, Andy; there is something else I need to talk to you about.' Her smile straightened out and I sat down again with an uneasy feeling in my stomach.

'I'm afraid our friend Mr Fisher rang again yesterday, just after you went home.'

'Oh, not the pen again, surely?'

'No, I think he's resigned to that being lost. He says Jason is unhappy in your class because he's being unfairly picked on by you and Kim. He says he gets told off and shouted at when he's done nothing wrong.'

'Does he really believe that?'

'It does sound like it, yes. But try not to worry; I've told him that I have every confidence in you as a professional, and I explained that Miss Bennett is a student on her first school experience.'

I groaned. 'What's the school policy with impossible parents?'

'Leave him to me. I know what Jason's like, Andy. I've told Mr Fisher that I will personally investigate how his son is treated in Class Three – I'll pop in next week some time – and ensure that he is treated fairly. Which he already is, I know.'

I thanked her, took a deep breath and prepared to try and sound upbeat for Kim. After her haphazard start, it was going to be good to tell her she had passed, despite the spectre of Mr Fisher.

Chapter Four

Ricky

Teaching is a strange job because the work is never finished. Unlike a carpenter who completes a well-made door, or a taxi-driver who safely delivers a passenger, it's never possible to be completely satisfied with the teaching of a child: there is always more they can learn and more you can do.

Quite often I was tempted to work late into the evenings to make my preparation better but tiredness and the knowledge that I was neglecting Barbara by doing so would draw me away from plans and the gathering of learning resources. I used to tell myself that I was doing my best and that was all I could do, but sadly there was a time when the best wasn't enough for one child in my class.

It was the second week of November and Swinnerdale was shrouded in damp; a cold wet mist secreting the higher hills under low, mean-looking clouds. Darkness hemmed in the day, at beginning and end, and at school some of the children gave the impression that they were preparing to hibernate.

One of these was Ricky Dawber. The Class 2 teacher, Hilda, had warned me about Ricky but she hadn't warned me enough. I recalled the conversation as I sat at my desk listening to the poor, pale child struggling to make any sense of his native language in written form.

'He's a nice lad, is Ricky,' Hilda had said. 'As quiet as a mouse but not as clever.'

'And is he always ghostly pale like that?' I'd asked. 'I never really noticed when he was younger.'

'Aye, he's not your average liver-cheeked Dales lad, is he? But be grateful for small mercies: he's slow but he's never trouble. Well, apart from wanting the toilet every five minutes. He should carry a peg, that youth.'

I brought my mind back to the present and listened once more to Ricky painfully trying to deconstruct simple words as he read to me. I'd snuck in some books from the infants especially for him but he simply couldn't remember his sounds and only a handful of sight words. I just didn't know what to do; he wasn't making any progress at all.

Over the weeks I'd tried to find a subject that interested him: usually with boys it was one of cars, football, tractors, dinosaurs or something similar, but Ricky appeared to have no hobbies or interests at all. Unless staring counted. I'd have to talk to Joyce about trying to get help for him.

I sent Ricky back to his table to sit down. He walked about three paces then returned with his hand up.

'Yes, Ricky, you can go to the toilet,' I said.

He turned and left the room, then reappeared ten seconds later to put down his reading book.

I surveyed the class, glad to have full control of it back now that Kim had finished. It was also a relief to see an end to the looks and giggles that the children gave whenever they passed the two of us having a meeting in the classroom about her lesson plans.

In the staffroom at break, I asked Val if she had any suggestions for getting Ricky moving.

'A firework under his chair? No, seriously, I have actually noticed him out on the yard – I've never seen a child so inert. He just stands there most of the time. I think he wants checking out by a doctor.'

Sue came in just as I was about to reply. 'Joyce says to remind you all that it's Remembrance Day tomorrow and Mr Dobson is coming to plant a tree by the drive at eleven o'clock.'

'Who is Mr Dobson?' asked Emma. 'I must have missed that meeting.'

'He's Cragthwaite's resident war veteran, of course,' cried Hilda. 'Korean not World. And, if you ask me, he's very well turned out, that gent. If I wasn't a confirmed spinster and highly respectable I'd like to see more of his medals, I can tell you.'

After break, Joyce came into my room, just as I was explaining to the class what Remembrance Day was all about.

She whispered in my ear, 'It's just so I can say I've watched Jason in class when I speak to Mr Fisher – just carry on and ignore me.' The children watched with intense curiosity, wondering why the headteacher was sitting on my chair.

'Right, come on everybody, look back this way,' I said briskly clapping my hands. 'As I was saying, tomorrow is Remembrance Day.' I wrote it on the blackboard in scratchy chalk. 'What word does remembrance come from?'

Estelle put up her hand. 'Remember?'

Before I could say, 'Good,' Lawrence blurted out, 'It could be membrane, too.'

'No, Lawrence, it's definitely remember,' I said as Joyce stifled a snort. 'What are we remembering?'

Several hands went up but it was always the brighter ones and I wanted to show Joyce that I did try and encourage everyone to think.

'Martine, any idea?'

'Er, is it Bonfire Night? Remember, remember the fifth of November!'

'Good try but tomorrow is the eleventh, not the fifth.'

Several of the children were stretching, trying to get their hands as high as possible. Lawrence had resorted to waggling and two or three others were making straining sounds almost as if in pain. Ricky, as ever, just sat and stared blankly, his mouth slightly open. I considered asking him but knew that his answer would be what it always was: 'I don't know.'

Eventually Cathy Lawson confirmed that the day was about remembering those who had died fighting for their country. I listed the two world wars and asked if the children knew of any other wars.

Ian Tattershall suggested the recent Falklands Conflict, then Lawrence's hand went up. 'The Battle of Hastings.'

'Well, yes, that was part of a war but it was over nine hundred years ago and we don't really remember people who died that long ago.'

'I can remember,' said Lawrence. 'It was King Harold – he was shot in the eye by William the Conker.'

'Conqueror, you div,' said Jason behind him.

'Jason, please don't use words like that.' I glanced at Joyce. 'Anyway, Remembrance Day starts with World War One, so I'm talking about wars that are later than that – more modern ones.'

At this point some joker whispered 'Star Wars', and I knew it was time to move on.

Joyce stood up to speak. 'Excuse me, Mr Seed, but you've just reminded me that we haven't sent the poppies round today. Has anyone brought any money?'

A few hands went up so Joyce asked two children to go and collect them while I jotted down a few more words on the board including *cenotaph*, *veteran* and *Korean War*, then quickly explained what would be happening at our special service the following day. I mentioned that Mr Dobson would be coming from the village to plant a tree to help remind us of all those who had died.

As the children copied out the words and the poppy sellers toured the room with a collecting jar, Joyce came over to me again, speaking in a hush. 'Andy, would you read the "Ode of Remembrance" tomorrow please – we'll just do the final "They shall not grow old" verse. Mr Dobson's going to say a few words, then I thought it would be good if the children asked him a few questions. It's not every day that we have a war veteran in school. Is that OK?'

'Yes, sure,' I said. 'While you're here, have you noticed Ricky? I'm very concerned about him. He's really struggling in class, just not progressing, and he just looks so, well, blank. I'm at a loss what to do.'

She nodded. 'You know, I was just watching him and I do think something's up. He wasn't like this last year. I'll call his mum and we'll have a meeting about him.'

I turned round, sensing a restlessness in the class, and saw Jason snatch a handful of poppies from Trudy Hammond who was holding the tray.

Joyce saw him too and stepped in. 'Jason Fisher, how dare you just grab all those poppies. Put them back!'

'But I paid 50p so I want a few.'

'You get *one*, like everybody else.'

'That's not fair – Martine only put 10p in the jar but I put in loads of money.'

'Sit down and be quiet. You've disturbed Mr Seed's lesson enough already. Come and see me in my office at twelve o'clock, we'll sort it out then.'

Good old Joyce.

The following morning at five to eleven the whole school stood on the patch of lawn at the front of the school, shivering. At least it wasn't raining. The hills around the village were now looking drab, and everyone could sense winter's grip on the Dale beginning to tighten.

Mr Dobson stood erect in his smart camelhair coat and navy tie, his grey hair slicked back, while Joyce explained that we would have a minute's silence at eleven o'clock. It was clear from the expression on Emma's face that this was going to be like half a lifetime for the smaller infants. At least it wouldn't be a problem for Ricky.

The moment came, marked by a sad peal of church bells, and one hundred children, along with a clutch of pensive adults, stood surprisingly still without a sound. It was very moving. At the end of the minute I read the Ode:

They shall grow not old, as we that are left grow old:
Age shall not weary them, nor the years condemn.
At the going down of the sun and in the morning,
We will remember them.

Val stepped forward and lifted up the small rowan sapling, placing it in the prepared hole. With a solemn dignity, Mr Dobson reached forward with the spade he was given and lifted a pile of earth, dropping it gently over the roots. Even Hilda watched quietly, the reverential air rendering her for once quipless. Arthur Fawcett,

Chairman of the school governors then finished off the planting, while Mr Dobson stepped forward to speak to the children.

He talked in measured tones, his authoritative voice ringing out through the cold air as he explained what an honour it was to have served his country. He referred briefly to lost comrades, which I could see confused many children, then spoke about the importance of learning about the dreadfulness of war so that we all strive to avoid it in the future. The children clapped politely then we sang a hymn and went inside.

At half eleven, Joyce brought Mr Dobson into my classroom and said that he'd be happy to answer any questions for ten minutes. It was at this moment that I deeply wished I had prepared and vetted my class's response. At least plenty of hands went up.

I pointed to Lawrence. 'What was it like in the war?' he asked.

Mr Dobson took a moment. 'Well, in Korea, where I was involved in the conflict, it wasn't pleasant. We were mainly fighting the Chinese with tanks and artillery, and as an officer I had to make lots of difficult decisions involving men's lives. Like everyone, I did my best and tried to maintain the honour of the British Army. I don't like to go into detail about the battles, really, er . . .'

'Let's have another question,' I said.

Jason's hand went up. 'Did you kill any Germans?'

'No, you're perhaps thinking of World War Two. I was in the Korean War about six years after that.'

I tried to look apologetic and turned to Dan Alderson, who was holding up one arm with the other. 'Yes, Dan?'

'Did yer shoot anyone?'

I stepped in, seeing our visitor becoming rather flustered. 'I don't think it's really fair to ask Mr Dobson that. No more questions about killing, please.' About half the hands went down.

I should have guessed the next question, from Martine. 'Did you injure anyone?'

Once more, I appealed for different kinds of questions but drew only a pause. Then, amazingly, Ricky's went up.

'Did you want to go to the toilet, Ricky?' I said.

He spoke in a shadow of a voice, barely audible. 'No, I got a question.'

I smiled broadly; it was the first time he had ever responded like this. 'Go on then, Ricky.'

'Did you go in a Tornado?'

'A tornado? You mean like a whirlwind?'

'A plane.'

Once more I stepped in, seeing Mr Dobson's bafflement, and explained about our visit to the RAF base. He was still confused but I was delighted that Ricky had for once participated. It offered, however, such a tiny grain of hope.

At the end of the following week, Joyce dropped into my room again, after school.

'Two things,' she said. 'One, Ricky's mother has just called. You know she took him to the doctor? Well, they've confirmed he has diabetes.'

'That explains a lot,' I said, partly relieved but also concerned that Ricky would have to manage the condition. 'It's probably why he was always going to the loo and why his concentration was so poor.' I wondered if he'd be able to cope. We discussed having a meeting about the treatment then Joyce glanced at her watch.

'I've got to dash, but I thought you'd like to know the other thing. I spoke to Mr Fisher, having observed Jason last week . . .'

'Yes?'

'I don't think there's going to be any more problem with complaints.' There was a half-smile among the lipstick.

'What? How? What did you say to him?'

'I told him that you were an excellent teacher, I had seen Jason's unsatisfactory behaviour myself, and watched it being dealt with fairly . . .'

'Right . . .'

'And if he didn't like it he could, of course, take his child somewhere else.'

'What did he say to that?'

'Not a lot.'

I wanted to smile but I was thinking about Ricky; if only his problems could be solved as quickly.

When I arrived home, Barbara also looked to be in rather a good mood.

'What's the news?' I said.

She lifted her shoulders and her eyes twinkled. 'There was a phone call this morning from the Royal Mail.'

'And?'

'I'm now a postie!'

We gave a little cheer and, comically, both Tom and Reuben joined in, even though they were watching TV and had no idea what we were talking about.

It was nearly a month later that Ricky Dawber left Cragthwaite Primary. For some time his fate was to travel far down the dale each day to a special school. An educational psychologist had diagnosed serious learning difficulties exacerbated by his medical condition when untreated.

Eventually, Ricky did make sufficient improvement to join the mainstream secondary school in Ingleburn when he was old enough, even if he spent his days in the remedial department, as it was then called. In time I saw him there, a gawky youth of thirteen, struggling over a written exercise as I was given a tour of the school as part of a primary-secondary liaison scheme. He looked up, surprised to see me, then gave something like a brief smile. It was a few years later that I bumped into his mother in Cragthwaite and learned something that still brings a tear to my eye.

''Ow do, Mr Seed,' she said with a resigned expression that never seemed to change.

'Hi, Mrs Dawber. How's Ricky getting on these days?'

'Oh, yer know, still strugglin' away, poor lad.'

'How old is he now?'

'Gerrin' on fifteen now; oh aye, he's a big long dollop these days.'

'Well say hello from me.'

'Do you recall that day yer saw 'im at Inglebu'n, a couple of years since?'

'At the secondary school? Yes, of course.'

'You know, when 'e saw you, 'e thought you was comin' ter tek 'im back t'primary, here.' She gave her head a shake. 'I dunno, that lad . . .'

Chapter Five

Dan

'Byyy, it's nitherin' out theear, Mr Seed.'

I turned round knowing who it would be: only one child in Class 3 had an accent that impenetrable, and his name was Dan Alderson. A wiry, weather-beaten boy, Dan lived on a small, isolated farm near the bleak settlement of Millscar high up on the north side of Swinnerdale. I'd seen his home once, when out on a walk with friends, and remembered the squat little farmhouse with just a clutch of bent outbuildings standing alone in a vast area of rolling heather and rushes called Faggergill. It didn't even have a proper road, just a rough track that climbed and dipped miles to the village below.

'Cold is it, Dan?' I said as the other children hopped and bustled into the classroom on a gusty November day.

'Aye, a proper backend blower as me dad 'ud say.'

I smiled, surprised that he hadn't used something even more earthy; I loved listening to Dan's dialect with its blunt North Riding expressions but he was often inclined to use uncouth language without realising it might offend someone. On several occasions I'd had to warn him about swearing and using unsuitable words but he always seemed genuinely surprised; clearly this way of speaking was the norm in his household.

I sat the class down and reminded them that they needed to bring wellies to school the following day for the sponsored walk around the playing field.

'It's your last chance to get sponsors tonight, too, so do ask your families and friends and neighbours.'

A hand went up. It was Estelle. 'Mr Seed, why are we doing a sponsored walk in November? It's freezing.'

I felt like saying, 'Good question', but instead answered, 'Mrs Berry is very keen that all the children do more exercise. Lots of you come to school by bus or car so she thinks it'll help us all to keep fit.'

Dan raised his eyebrows. 'Hell, ah walk miles on t'farm all t'time. Ah'll be about jiggered t'morrer.'

More hands went up. 'How many times are we walking around the field?' asked Lawrence.

'We're aiming for fifty but you do as many as you can.'

'Who are we raisin' money fer again?' asked Martine.

'Dr Barnardos. They help poor children around the UK. Remember, we had that talk back in September?'

'Us cud do wi' some o' that cash – ma 'ouse is a dump,' whispered Dan to Gary Blacow.

'Anyway,' I said, 'we are supposed to be doing English now, not discussing the walk. Right, please open your jotters and put today's date.'

The lesson was a spelling activity centred on 'silent g' words and I began by putting a few examples on the board and asking the class to think of some more and write them in their books. As always, some found it easier than others and I quickly toured the strugglers providing them with clues. Dan was one of them.

'Ahm reet flummoxed wi' this, Mr Seed,' he said blowing out his ruddy cheeks.

'OK, well, can you think of a small, hatted figure who lives in the garden?'

'Aye, me granddad.'

'Gnome, Dan. G, n, o, m, e.'

'Oh, aye, one o' them daft little model fellas. Thes not so many o' them kinda things at Faggergill End.'

'No, I suppose not.' I smiled. Eventually I got him to produce 'gnat', then moved on.

After some practice in using the listed words, for the final part of the session I told the class that I was going to think of some tricky 'silent g' words and give them clues to see who could guess the words first. To add an element of motivation, I split the class into three teams.

After 'gnash', identified by Estelle's group, I moved on to 'gnarled'. 'Right, this is a word that describes something sort of lumpy and twisted,' I said, looking up.

I saw a sea of blank faces with a few individuals mouthing guesses or looking around for inspiration. No hands were raised so I gave an extra clue. 'Think of a tree that's old and worn out.'

I could see the tension building as three or four recognised the concept but still, no one ventured a guess until, suddenly, Dan jumped to his feet and pointed at me.

'Av gorrit: knackered!'

The class splurted into whoops of mirth until I calmed them down and spoke. 'No, Dan, that's a silent k.'

At home that evening, I retold the story for Barbara who loved hearing about Dan's adages and gaffes.

'Do you think he's ready for the concept of *faux pas*?' I said.

'How was it that Hilda described him? "Blunt as a ferret's bottom"?'

'It was something like that; anyway, tell me about your day – how's the job going?'

'Well, there's some news first. Rosie rang this afternoon and they've got the house!'

I was amazed. 'In the auction? I thought loads of people were after it. How much did they bid?'

'Fifty-five thousand.'

'Whaaat!'

We both laughed and Barbara shook her head. It sounded like a fortune to us. We discussed when they might move and how we might help them before Barbara started to tell me about her new life as a four-day-a-week postie.

'I'm a bit slow at sorting at the moment, but everyone says I'll speed up in time – they're all really friendly. Well, more or less.'

'What's the round like?'

'Well, it seems to encompass every elderly person in Ingleburn. It's all those bungalows behind the church and the estate next to it. They were very chatty and keen to say hello but it does mean everything takes longer.'

'Well, what time are you supposed to finish?'

'About ten-forty-five.'

'And what time did you finish?'

'Twelve-twenty.'

We laughed again, then Barbara assured me that our boys had a great time with Iris across the green where they were given freshly squeezed juice and Marks and Sparks treats. 'Much better than they would've got here.'

'I tell you what,' I said, looking at my watch. 'Let's ask Holly if she can babysit for an hour or two and we can pop down the pub to celebrate the new job. The boys'll be asleep by now.'

Half an hour later, the doorbell rang and we were greeted by the sunny face of eighteen-year-old Holly Weatherall, the daughter of John, the builder and captain of the darts team who lived down the bottom of the village. She was glad for a few extra pounds and we were delighted to have a rare chance to be out together.

We hurried across the green, through a scouring wind and into the cosy glow of The Crown, Applesett's steadfast pub with its perpetual log fire and warm welcome from the landlord, Dennis Helliwell.

'Good to see you two out together,' he called as we shook ourselves warm. 'Pint for you I presume, Andy, and for Barbara?'

'Ooh, it's a celebration, so I think I'll go wild and have a large G&T.'

At the bar, ancient Sam Burnsall, now in his nineties, was perched on his corner stool, as always, and the monster farmer Big Alec Lund from Town Head stood silently, blocking out most of the light.

Barbara and I sat near the fire and I told her about the following day's sponsored walk.

'In November!' she said. 'The field'll turn to mush. Joyce must be barmy.'

'That's what we all pointed out, but she's trying to work it in with some kind of healthy schools scheme from County. Anyway, at least it's good exercise for me if I join in – I don't go out walking much at this time of year so I do feel unfit. I need to do some more sport.'

'Oh come on, you've got your darts here . . .' Barbara said with a snigger.

I ignored her mockery. 'I'm not good enough for the football team and there's only snooker locally – not exactly energetic.'

Dennis came over to collect our glasses. He'd evidently been listening. 'What about table tennis? There used to be a table in the village hall.'

Barbara smiled. 'A bit of ping pong is hardly going to have you fighting fit.'

'I used to play back in the day,' said Dennis. 'It's quite active when you get good at it – clever players can make you run around all over.'

'I love table tennis,' I said, recalling how I used to play every day in the sixth form. 'That's a great idea, Dennis; I might go up to the hall at the weekend and have a look.'

Eighty-five children, all clad in coats and wellington boots, filed out across the tarmac of Cragthwaite Primary's playground, through the biting November wind and on to the soggy field. They were followed by three well-wrapped but disbelieving adults. I was one of them.

'Aye, Emma's not daft keeping hers inside, is she?' croaked Val. 'I don't blame her for putting her foot down, though. Half of her class would get pneumonia and the other half would blow away.'

'Well, I am going to do one lap, so I can say I've joined in,' said Hilda. 'Ladies of my age shouldn't be route marching with a gale up our bloomers.'

'I'm going to do as many as I can,' I said. 'The kids reckon they can beat me.'

'Rather you than me,' said Val with a grimace. I could see she was gasping for a fag. 'Lambert and Butler have only sponsored me for five laps.'

Val then growled at the children to stand on the edge of the field and reminded them they had to go around the football pitch without cutting corners. 'Be honest about how many laps you do and when you finish go and write it on your sheet, then sit in the hall and do quiet reading. Mrs Berry will be in there supervising. Are you ready?'

'Yesssss,' they chorused through the wind, edging forward.

'Oh, and remember, it's NOT a race. Go.'

Immediately, eighty-five children charged forward running at full pelt. Two slipped over and received a face full of cold sludge.

'WALK!' roared Val.

They walked, if comically quickly. The three of us followed, woolly hats wedged on and hands tightly in pockets.

After a couple of laps, the children slowed down with the older ones well in front and already bored with the circuit. I looked at my wellies, which were now thick with ooze: the thin grass was beginning to disappear as the course cut up. A child overtook me squelching along.

'Are thee paggered yet, Mr Seed?' I might have known it would be Dan.

'I'm taking it easy, Dan – so should you.'

'Nay, ahm used ter fells up past Millscer but you tekkit steady thissen.'

I laughed as he turned to wave.

'Sithee, Mr Seed!' and he strode forward.

Thirty minutes later the younger children had all dropped out, along with Val and Hilda. Many of mine were cold, and notes of rebellion were sounding among the less fit.

'I'm freezin'.'

'This is borrrring!'

'Can't we go in? Class Two have gone in.'

'I'm tellin' me mam that we're being slaved.'

'It's too muddy – ma kegs are clarted, Mr Seed.'

The last child had a point. By now the course was a quagmire. Only the striding Dan made light of it. 'Tis just a spot o' plother,' he said before squelching past to keep up with the biggest boys of Class 4 who were determined to do the most laps.

After another hour I was inside, worn out myself from trudging through the circular swamp that now enclosed the football pitch. I clutched a steaming cup of tea as I stood by the hall windows and watched the last windswept mob of hardened farmer boys slog on. There were six from Class 4 and just one from Class 3: Dan Alderson.

'He may have a potty mouth but you've got to hand it to the lad,' said Hilda who had sidled up next to me. 'They'll have to stop soon, though – it's nearly home time.'

Ten minutes later they were all inside. They'd made a pact to stop, having reached a satisfying number.

'One 'undred laps, flippin' 'eck!' cried Dan, beaming broadly as he came into the hall. Everyone turned to him and Joyce shook her head and looked up. He peeled off his shabby old coat then lifted his hat to release a cloud of steamy heat as everyone watched.

'Byyy, ahm lathered wi' sweat,' he said, then I could clearly see the moment when he stretched and realised just how tired he was. I braced myself. 'Well, ahm fair bu—'

'Dan! I do hope you'll remember what we said about language.' It was Joyce, stepping in with perfect timing.

'I wa' gunna say I wer fair bushed, Mrs B.'

The head and I looked at each other and chuckled.

'That's good,' said Martine, joining the moment. 'I thought fer a minute yer were gunna say buggered.'

* * *

On Sunday afternoon I found myself in Applesett Village Hall shifting stacks of old chairs from the back of the building. The dust, cobwebs and biting cold made it less than pleasant but then I found what I was looking for: old, battered and with a chunk of surface missing from one corner – a full-sized table tennis table.

With difficulty I slid the two halves out from behind the chairs and located an old broom to brush it down. It must have been there for years and certainly looked like it had seen some action. There was no sign of a net but I unfolded the legs and, with a struggle, set the table upright. It really was in a state and almost useless until the corner was repaired. I needed to get it home into the garage right away to try and patch it up but felt I'd better check with someone first. Then it occurred to me that I was on the Village Hall Committee. I gave myself permission and headed outside to find someone to help me lift it.

I knocked on Andy Cheeseworth's door, which was just across the green from the hall. The young, scruffy builder sleepily opened it. 'Now then, Seedy, what are you up ter? I haven't forgotten a darts match 'ave I? No, it's Sunday.'

'Can you give me a hand carrying a table tennis table to my garage from the hall?'

'What, are you nicking it?' he jested. 'Getting me to assist in your filthy crimes.'

'It's bust and I'm going to try and fix it.'

'Oh, right, starting up a youth club?'

'No, I just want to make it usable and maybe have a game or two – do you play?'

'Of course I play! I play everything and I'm brilliant. See you off anytime, lad.'

'Right, OK, a challenge – let's get it fixed then.'

He disappeared to find some shoes and in no time the ancient table was in my workshop, as I laughingly called the garage with its wonky home-made bench and box of cheap tools. Barbara heard the noise and came in holding a grouchy-looking Reuben.

'What on earth are you doing? Why have you brought that in here?'

Reuben's eyes lit up when he saw the tools. 'Biff biff!' he said.

'No, Daddy's biff biff is a bit dangerous for you, darling. You can maybe help him with your plastic hammer.'

'The table's broken here,' I said, pointing to the mangled corner. 'I'm going to try and fix it.'

Barbara shook her head. 'It's broken more than there. Anyway, that has got to be an antique – you'll lower its value if you repair it.'

'Yes, it could fall from 10p way down to three.'

Reuben strained forward to climb on the big green table but Barbara reined him in. 'It's too cold in here for you, Reubs. We'll leave Daddy to do his biffing in peace while we snuggle down by the fire with Tom.'

I wasn't really listening, however. I was already digging around in my toolbox, anxious to get to work on the table before the weekend ran out.

Three hours later I emerged from the garage, dusty, grimy and numb from the November cold. Barbara was watching TV in the front room.

'I've fixed it!' I declared.

'Look at the state of you! Why didn't you come out for your tea when I called? Your sandwiches'll be curled up by now.'

'But I've fixed the table.'

'Well done, dear.'

'Where're the boys?'

'I've put them to bed, even though it was your turn . . .' She saw my surprise. 'It's nearly eight o'clock, you know.'

'Really? I thought it was about half six . . . Anyway, I'm starving. After I've had my butties shall we go and have a game of ping pong?'

'What? On a freezing night like this? I'm not going to carry that table back up to the hall now.'

'No, I meant in the garage.'

'Eh? There's not enough room in there. And I thought you said there was no net.'

'There isn't but I'll rig something temporary up.'

'What about bats and a ball?'

'I found my old TT stuff in that cubby hole under the stairs. They're a bit manky but they'll do.'

'Why don't you ask Major Asquith next door for a game? I bet he's good.'

'Come on . . .'

'But you'll only mope when I beat you.'

'You have no chance!' I ran up the stairs to wash my hands before rushing downstairs to wolf the dry sandwiches.

Barbara insisted on putting on several more layers before venturing back into the garage. In the meantime I found a broom handle and balanced it on two cans of beans for a temporary 'net'. The bats were rubbish: my cheap sponge rubber model from school days and a really flimsy pimpled thing. I'd need to get a decent one before facing Cheesey, that was for sure.

Barbara appeared, looking doubtful. 'It's arctic in here! And what if Reuben starts crying?'

'Bring the baby alarm – it should work.'

'But I'm only playing for five minutes. It's too squashed anyway.'

'Oh, stop moaning and pick up a bat.'

Two minutes later we were both laughing and warming ourselves up as we plinked the little white ball back and forth over the wooden divider. It really was great fun and I remembered how much I enjoyed the game. Barbara was quite a good player, too.

'Shall we have a match?' I said. 'First to twenty-one, OK?'

'Oh, go on then – you boys and your competitiveness . . .'

She soon showed, however, that she wasn't interested in losing. After she served fast, I ballooned the return too high and she gleefully whacked it into the corner.

'One-love!' she cawed.

'Right, Mrs,' I said, attempting to smash her second serve, only to see it ricochet off the broom handle.

'Two-love, do you want me to go easy?' she smarmed.

I decided to employ one of the weapons that used to bring me success in the common room: spin. Slashing an angled bat across the ball I made it hop over the net, almost fizzing with rotation. Barbara pushed it back but the ball flipped sideways and shot on to the floor.

'That's not fair! You've got a spinny bat.'

'Want to swap?'

'No, I like this one. But I want you not to spin it.'

'That's part of the game, I'm afraid. Two-one.'

She grumbled, watching the ball jiggle about on the rough concrete floor of the garage. As she bent down to pick it up there was a strange noise.

'What was that?'

She stood up, red-faced. 'Nothing.'

'Did you trump?'

'No I did not trump!'

'Well, what was that sound?'

But she was already walking to the door, in a strange crab-like sideways action. 'I just need the loo.'

I shook my head, mystified even more when I heard her guffawing as she went up the stairs. What was going on? I put my head round the end of the hallway but she had gone up to the bedroom. And they say men act strangely, I thought.

Barbara appeared again, just a minute later, looking more composed. She also looked slightly different.

'Two-all, my serve,' she said, trying hard not to collapse into a giggle.

'What is going on?' I said, looking at her. Then I realised: she was wearing different trousers. She saw my realisation and exploded into one her trademark snorting hoots.

I pointed, scarcely able to breathe. 'Your trousers split!'

It took her five minutes to calm down but when she did she said, 'I will only play table tennis with you on the condition that you never tell anyone what happened, especially that darts team of yours.'

'That's not fair! If it happened to me the whole village would know already.'

'That's different. Do you want to play or not?'

We finished the game and afterwards I kept my word, content to amuse myself with the thought of what Dan Alderson would have said about such an episode.

Chapter Six

Vicky

She stood up slowly, a pudgy, plain-faced girl with long, fair hair. Her name was Vicky Rushworth and I'd called her over to my desk to check up on her reading.

'What book are you on at the moment, Vicky?'

'It's about an Owl.'

'And what's it called?'

'*The Owl who Went in the Dark*, or summat.'

'*The Owl who was Afraid of the Dark*?'

'Yeah, that's it.'

'Are you enjoying it?'

She shrugged. 'S'alright.'

I listened to her read: she toiled through the words slowly and deliberately, lacking expression or a feeling for the text. I asked a few questions to gauge her comprehension and found that she understood the basic story but missed the nuances and touches of humour. It didn't surprise me: Vicky was the classic plodder.

'Do you read to someone each night at home, Vicky?'

'Sometimes.'

'It's important, you know. Ask your mum and try and do it every night.'

She nodded unenthusiastically.

'What about other books?' I asked. 'What other kinds of books do you like?'

'Dunno, really.'

'Are you interested in horses or animals or anything like that?'

'I've got a pet rabbit.'

'Well, maybe you can read books about rabbits and other pets. Do you have many books at home?'

I guessed the answer would be no and I was right; Vicky's parents weren't readers. There were very few books in the home and, unsurprisingly, she hadn't caught the reading bug: that love of books that gives children such a precious advantage in their learning.

I sent Vicky back to her place wishing that I could have praised her more. Her work was so dull, like her attitude, however, that I often struggled to find positive things to say to encourage her.

I'd discovered in my first few years of teaching that it was vital for every child to be given praise and small regular boosts to build up their self-confidence but with Vicky I found it strangely difficult. Even with a troublesome character like Jason, I'd been able to find something – in his case his sporting prowess – as the basis for commendation. With Lawrence I delighted in his enthusiasm and with the dippy Martine I could admire her cheerfulness. Even with poor Ricky, I'd given frequent little pats on the back for his stoic outlook and willingness to try and overcome so many problems. But I just didn't know what to say to Vicky.

A few days later I was sitting in a staff meeting while Joyce rattled off a list of Christmas activities for which we had to prepare. I couldn't believe that it was mid-December already.

'The tree for the hall is here now and Pat'll put it up tonight. Val, will you arrange for some top juniors to decorate it? I'm also going to put out the post box for children's cards. Actually, it's looking a bit tatty – Andy, would you be a dear and make a new one? I know you'll be able to do it in a jiffy.'

I mumbled, 'OK,' scribbling a reminder note and wondering how I'd find the time.

Joyce continued while we all flicked manically through our diaries. 'Christmas dinner is on Friday this week, the carol service in the church is next Tuesday, the nativity play on Thursday at 2pm and 7pm, with a dress rehearsal on Wednesday, and the disco on the afternoon of Friday twentieth. All got that?'

'I hope we don't all get this bug that's going round or we're going to be like Mrs Harker's turkey: badly stuffed,' said Hilda, smiling at her own line, as ever.

'Well, I have four away today so it's definitely doing the rounds,' said Val.

'Six of my little ones are off,' added Emma.

I joined in to say I had three absent while Hilda reported four.

'Is it just a cold, do you think?' asked Joyce.

Val put down her coffee. 'Well, it's not flu but it's some kind of lovely seasonal virus. Sore throats and runny noses then a cough, according to my lot.'

'Oh, just what we need . . .' said Joyce. 'Well, life goes on. Did I say we'd have a carol practice on Monday? Let's say 10am. Oh, and is anybody offering to put Christmas displays up in the entrance area and hall? We'll need a Bethlehem scene backdrop for the play, too.'

Half an hour later the meeting ended with Joyce dashing off to her office before everyone stood up creakily and used the opportunity to exercise the traditional moan.

'This happens every year, we must be bloody daft,' said Val.

Hilda shook her head. 'No wonder so many kids are off – it's stress, not a cold. That or glitteritis.'

'And we've still got cards to make, costumes to sort out for the nativity and lines to learn,' said Emma. 'There's no time for any actual work.'

'I like Christmas, you bunch of Scrooges,' I said, just to wind them up.

'Good,' said Val. 'You can decorate the hall and entrance.'

On Sunday morning, at just before seven, Barbara shook me awake. I turned over groggily and hoped it wasn't really happening.

'Wake up, scruffyhead. I've made you tea.'

I tried to open a crusty eye. 'Whatimeisit?'

'Early for you, obviously, but I'm off now so you need to listen.'

I heaved myself into a sitting position, recalling that she was out for the day at a craft fair selling her home-made wooden decorations.

'The boys are already downstairs,' she said. 'They're playing nicely at the moment but it won't last long so you'll need to be down there soon. They'll want breakfast in a few minutes anyway.'

'What time are you going to be back?'

'Late, and remember, after the fair I'm going to see Emily – she only lives a couple of miles away.'

'Oh yeah.' I didn't remember.

'There's plenty of food for lunch and tea – don't give them two lots of trash. And I know the weather's horrid but try and get them outside for the day. *Postman Pat*'s on at eleven; you could hoover the dining room and upstairs then. Got all that?'

'Yep, you have a really good day, sell lots,' I said, trying to sound awake before leaning over to give her a croaky kiss.

'OK, gotta dash, bye!'

I waved and then, fatally, plonked my head back on the pillow for a snooze.

It was quarter past eight when I felt a strange rocking sensation and heard a familiar voice.

'Daddee, wake up. You need to get up.'

It was Tom. He was sitting on top of me and bouncing up and down.

Once more I rubbed the crustiness out of my face and tried to sit up. There was my big-eyed eldest son, now nearly three and a half, with thumb in mouth.

'What's up, Tommy?'

'You need to see what Reuben's done.'

I reached for my tea which was stone cold. 'Oh dear, what's he done?'

Tom pulled at my arm. 'Come and look.'

I put on a dressing gown and wearily followed him downstairs, the trepidation building as we descended. Tom pushed open the dining room door and I was presented with a scene of pure guilt.

Reuben, a broad, bruising toddler of just over eighteen months, was sitting next to our big wooden table on one of the chairs. On the table were the remains of Barbara's breakfast: an empty bowl with spoon and an empty cup. She'd had hot oat cereal; I could tell because she always had dark, sticky muscovado sugar sprinkled on top. The sugar pot was in Reuben's hand, or rather my son's hand was in the pot, rammed down to the bottom because the pot was almost empty.

It wasn't hard to see why the pot was empty. A significant portion of the sugar was on his face, pebbledashed in a huge ragged ring around his mouth. The rest was equally distributed between his woolly jumper, trousers and the carpet, in each case welded on by the trail of drool he had generated in response to finding this rich, black treasure left open. He made no effort to hide the evidence or run away; he rather just sat there in a sucrose-induced stupor. Even with the waste, he must have consumed a quarter of the jar. I went to fetch a basin.

Ten minutes later I had wrestled him out of the sticky clothes and was well into the expected tantrum phase as I attempted to wipe his face. Reuben had always objected to having wet cloths applied to his skin, which was unfortunate as his body usually required this at least eleven times a day. He was extra cantankerous at this moment, too; perhaps resentful that I was removing the sweet face-coating that he was saving for later licks or, more likely, because the stuff was fused to him like Araldite.

Eventually he was restored to cleanliness and once he'd screamed at me some more to show his disgust he demanded to be picked up.

'Cuggee!'

I gave him the required carry and went to make some tea, only to find poor Tom lying on the floor with a book, and a long-suffering expression.

'Can I have some brekky?'

I quickly fed the poor tyke and myself something, then tried to put Reuben down so I could get washed and dressed. He made very strong objection via a series of groaning wails and I wondered if he was preparing to be sick. For the next fifteen minutes I wandered around with a heavy toddler in one arm and a washing up basin in the other.

Just as my bicep was giving out he saw Tom playing with Lego in the front room and reached towards it.

'Miiiine.'

I put him down and he made a grab for the brightly coloured bricks. Tom, well-used to this state of affairs, moved to the other side of the room and began instead to pick wooden blocks out of the basket by the TV. Reuben, meanwhile, took hold of the Lego car that Tom had made and started brrrming it along the carpet and out of the room up the hallway.

'Shall we make a big tower, Daddy?' said Tom, aware of the opportunity.

'OK, I'll get the bricks out, you build it up. Use the heavy ones first.'

He bounced with excitement and began constructing a base from the hard beech blocks.

'Let's make a tall one, shall we, Daddy?'

'Right, good idea.'

Tom arranged the bricks with deliberation, reflecting his analytical temperament, and soon the tower was over a metre high.

'We'll make a *really* big one, shall we, Daddy, shall we?'

I nodded just as the throbbing engine impersonation grew louder again and Reuben turned back into the room, pushing the model car.

Tom stood up and added two more bricks to the construction.

'Let's make a really, really tall one,' he said.

Reuben walked forward and, without warning, slammed his car into the middle of the tower with a crash, leaving just six or seven bricks standing amid a pile of rubble.

Before I could say anything, Tom piped up again, 'We'll just have a small tower, shall we?'

There were more tears when I told Reuben off but, after a few minutes of sniffling, he went over to Tom and gave him a hug. It was his way of saying sorry. He then reached out for another cuddle and kissed me. He may have been loud and rumbustious but he was also extremely loving and winsome. He was also, I noted, still sticky.

By this time I needed a sit down, which became a lie down, and Reuben rested on my front for a lovely cuddle while Tom returned to his beloved Janet and Allan Ahlberg books. I looked at my younger son's rosy toddler face and felt his considerable weight on my chest. It didn't seem like yesterday that he was a tiny, helpless tot.

I stroked his hair. 'Oh, where's my baby boy gone?'

Tom looked up. 'Ingleburn?'

After the joy of *Postman Pat* on TV, where I confused both boys by telling them that Mummy was doing that job and Tom started asking if she was delivering letters to Mrs Goggins, we enjoyed a lunch of boiled eggs and soldiers followed by the bliss of a peaceful half hour where they played quietly.

When restlessness returned, I togged them up in wellies, coats and hats and we headed down the village to the glorious waterfall, our favourite place anywhere. The trees lining the deep rock-cleft were now bare and a layer of damp brown leaves coated everything as we splashed along the path by the side of burbling Buttergill Beck to the point where it fell thirty feet or so into a dark rippling pool of water.

The boys threw in leaves and watched them dance and race away down to the hump of the little stone packhorse bridge. Reuben, as always, wanted to paddle, but there was too much water in the river. Staying away from it would also avoid him falling in, which happened regularly.

'Can we go to the pirate cave?' said Tom, referring to a dark little limestone cavern that the water had carved away down by the bridge.

'The rock will be too slippery, sorry,' I said. 'I'll take you when it's safe in the summer.'

The boys said, 'Aww,' but soon forgot their disappointment as they scurried on to the bridge to play Pooh Sticks.

The walk back up to the house was always slower and Reuben soon ran out of gas, needing a carry. We counted the chimneys around the green, nearly every one puffing small clouds of aromatic grey woodsmoke into the dank air.

Just across from our house, we saw Iris Falconer with her son, Tom's friend, Stewart. Tom waved. 'Can I play with Stewart?' he asked.

'Well, maybe another day. I don't want Reubs to be left on his own.'

'Stewart's going to school now,' said Tom.

'I know.'

'Can I go to school too?'

'You will soon but you're not old enough yet, Tommy.'

'But it's not fair, Stewart goes.'

'That's because he's older than you.'

'Can't I go now?'

'Sorry, Tom, you're not big enough.'

He thought for a moment. 'I'll stand on something!'

I laughed again, took them inside then almost cried when I saw the disarray in which we had left the house.

'Oo, can we do painting now, Daddy?' said Tom. 'Mummy said we could.'

'Hurray,' I said.

'Hurray,' bubbled Reuben through the green dual carriageway now descending from his nostrils.

* * *

At ten o'clock on Monday my class, or rather the remains of it, shuffled into the hall for a practice for the carol service the following day. Six children were absent with the dreaded lurgy and at least five more were sniffling dangerously. I prayed that I wouldn't catch it over Christmas. The chances appeared slim, however: since taking up teaching I had been the victim of regular virus attacks, although Val assured me that I'd build up immunity eventually. It was true that she was never off sick.

'Sit down quietly,' said Joyce, who loved her Christmas carols and liked to ensure that the singing reflected well on the school. 'Quite a few away from Class Three I see, Mr Seed. It's even worse in the infants. Oh well, all you strong children still here will just have to sing with extra gusto.'

I scanned the depleted rows of faces and had never seen such a pale, lethargic rabble of children in my life. Only a handful looked like they wanted to sing and even fewer knew what gusto was.

'Sit up, come on!' said Joyce, trying to sound breezy. A few individuals adjusted their slouches while someone blew a nose with a liquid torrent that none could escape visualising. Hilda sat at the piano with a face like a gravestone.

'Right, anyway, we'd better get started: "Once in Royal David's City" everyone.' Hilda began to poke the keys of the tuneless piano while eight or nine hands went up.

'No questions!' said Joyce, half-singing.

'But we 'aven't any words,' called out Martine.

The music stopped and two children were sent to fetch a pile of tattered carol sheets from the back.

The music started up again amid widespread whisperings of, 'What number is it?'

Eventually, the song was underway and the hall was filled with a discordant droning. Joyce warbled loudly from the front to try to lift the children but improvement was minimal and at the end we knew that this was going to be a long assembly.

'That was *awful*,' said Joyce, looking like she meant it. 'Horrible.' The younger children stared at her nervously as she continued. 'We are performing these carols in the church tomorrow in front of lots of parents and people from the village. They don't want to hear a dirge like that! What will they think of the school?'

We tried 'Joy to the World' next. The singing was slightly improved after the head's tirade but as they performed the children stared forward with ashen faces and glassy eyes.

'That was better,' said Joyce. 'At least most of you were trying, but you all look so miserable. It's called "Joy to the World", not "Depression to the World". Anyone would think this was the season of gloom and despondency. Come on!'

'Away in a Manger' was sung with grim smiles amid the sniffles and coughs but after the next two Joyce stopped everyone once more.

'I think we'll scrub "Ding Dong Merrily on High", Mrs Percival, since the current level of merriment is still hovering around zero. And, Colin Morphet, it is *not* "God Rest Ye Gerry Mentlemen" – I heard that.'

I looked at Val and whispered, 'Perhaps "Silent Night" would be better?'

She grimaced. 'Just be bloody grateful we're not doing the "Twelve Days of Christmas". I think I'd be dead after five.'

The woeful rehearsal continued right through playtime and beyond until everyone faded and it was obvious that to continue would be fruitless. Joyce recognised the signs and looked at her watch, shaking her head. 'Right, well, let's just hope it's better tomorrow. Much better.'

'Why don't we have a solo or two, to break it up?' said Emma, as the staff gathered in a huddle.

'Oh, what a good idea,' said Joyce, regaining some zest. 'Actually we could open the service with one, like "The Nine Lessons and Carols" from King's College.'

Emma looked blank.

'It's on Radio 4 on Christmas Eve,' said Val. 'I think Miss Torrington's more of a Radio 1 person,' she added with a wink.

But Joyce wasn't listening. I could see a plan formulating in her mind while the children sat and waited, still sniffing and coughing relentlessly.

'They always start with a single chorister opening "Once in Royal David's City",' said Joyce. 'Wouldn't it be lovely to do that? Who has the best voice in your class, Val?'

'None of the boys'll do it, I can tell you that now. There's a couple of girls but they're both away.'

Joyce turned to me. 'What about Class Three?'

'Estelle has a lovely voice,' I said.

Joyce called her out and she stepped forward, holding a tissue to her nose beneath bloodshot eyes while the head explained the plan. 'Will you give it a go, dear?'

She nodded and stood next to the piano, while Hilda plonked herself back on the stool with a grumble and hammered out the opening bars.

Estelle, confident as ever, stood up straight and opened her mouth:

'Once in Royal David's City,
Stood a lowly cattle shed,
Where a mother laid her— ATCHOOO!'

Everyone laughed and poor Estelle was relieved of the duty.

'Anybody else?' said Joyce to the staff, looking desperate. I ummed, music not being my thing.

A tall girl from my class stood up and came over. It was Trudy Hammond. 'I'm sorry to interrupt, Mr Seed, but I wonder if you know that Vicky's a good singer. She might not say so but she is.'

Several other children in my class mumbled their agreement and I nodded too, although I couldn't recall hearing her before.

'Thank you, Trudy, that's very kind and sensible,' I added.

'Do you want to give it a try, Vicky?' said Joyce. To my surprise she nodded and stood up. At least she didn't appear to have the virus.

Just as Hilda grudgingly attacked the keys once more, a boom from the back of the hall made everyone jump and the dark, vast figure of Mrs Hyde the dinner lady loomed from the kitchen door, which she'd just thumped open. Without saying anything she started banging and crashing chairs about, making it clear that it was time to set up for dinners. Joyce looked at her watch and reluctantly concurred.

As the much relieved children filed out of the hall Joyce walked over to me. 'Andy, could I have Vicky this afternoon? I'll give her an audition and practise with her if she's any good.'

'Fine,' I said, dearly hoping that, for once, she would rise above plodding.

The following afternoon what remained of Cragthwaite Primary School's pupils sat shivering on the cold, hard pews in the village's large medieval church. As always, the building was packed with mums, aunties, uncles, grandparents, villagers and the inevitable clutch of wailing babies and restless toddlers. For a moment I imagined what it would be like to restrain Reuben for an hour in this echoing stone chamber, full of interesting shiny objects to grab and employ for poking purposes. My mind quickly evaporated the thought and instead I turned to check that my class were all behaving.

Jason was next to me and very grouchy, if quiet, while Martine was on the row in front, within prodding distance if necessary. Dan had been instructed to keep his voice down and Lawrence to try to stay calm. Estelle was away but Vicky was stationed far at the front, standing alone on the raised chancel and looking decidedly worried, despite Joyce's assurance to both her and me that she was the best person for the solo part.

Four tiny, feeble electric heaters glowed red against the fierce December cold but they made barely an impression on the church's refrigerated atmosphere, and clouds of breath vapour drifted across and up into the shadowy oak timbers supporting the building's great roof.

The Reverend Ward, a slim bespectacled figure, nodded to Joyce at the front then fiddled with a microphone before welcoming everybody to the service and saying, as vicars did in every church in the land at this time of year, how delightful it was to see the church full. I watched Joyce, trying to disguise her foreboding with a smile, as she glanced over to Hilda who looked tiny sitting in front of the imposing organ above the choir. No doubt they, like Val and Emma, too, were wondering just how shocking the children's singing would be, especially now that numbers were further depleted by the bug.

The vicar stepped down and Joyce announced the first song, explaining that the congregation would come in for the second verse. While she spoke, tots yelped, children sneezed and the elderly hacked, each sound reverberating off Holy Trinity's cold stone walls and poor Vicky Rushworth trembled in front of the whole community.

At that moment, a remarkable thing happened. Hilda pressed the keys of the pipe organ and soaring notes filled the vast space of the building, as they had done for centuries. The evocative sound soothed the babies and toddlers, the coughing ceased and the sneezes died away before a single, faint tone was left hanging in the air.

Vicky took a long breath then raised her chin. At first I didn't believe that the beautiful, high, ethereal sound was issuing from her person. I wondered whether Joyce had somehow secreted a recording into the service. But, no, it was her; it was Vicky singing in a pure, enchanting, melodic voice that sailed from the choir across the nave, up through the highest beams, filling the church with an eerie spiritual power that took the breath away. Everyone stood perfectly still as she sang the verse and I was so moved that a tear dropped on to my carol sheet as the congregation, forgetting to breathe, barely stumbled into the rest of the song.

I leaned over, desperate to catch Vicky's eye and mouth the words 'Well done' to her, but she stood in a kind of trance, staring blankly forward as she sang, perhaps overcome by the moment. One thing was for sure, though: this time, back at school, in front of everyone, Vicky Rushworth would *not* be short of praise.

Chapter Seven

Gary

Inevitably I caught the cold. I sniffled and sneezed through the rest of the week, dosing myself with hot lemon and sucking menthol sweets continuously.

Barbara despaired at breakfast on Thursday. 'You shouldn't be at school like this, look at the state of you.'

'It's not too bad,' I said with a nasal whine.

'Well, don't blame me if you lose your voice and you're ill over the holiday.'

'I can't be off work during the final week of term – there's just too much happening.'

'Well, I am not going to do Christmas with the boys on my own or drive them round the country either so you'd better get over this soon.'

What happened to sympathy? I wondered, shoving some floppy sandwiches in my bag and heading for the door, only to return as I realised I was still wearing slippers.

At school things were seasonally chaotic, with both Emma and Hilda fretting that the nativity play wouldn't be ready in time.

'You say that every year,' said Val in the staffroom at morning break. 'And it's always ready and it's always brilliant.'

'And there's always a first time,' said Hilda. 'The donkey's got the snots and the innkeeper has no room and no idea.'

'I know how they feel,' I moaned.

Sue looked up. 'Have you gargled with aspirin, Andy?'

'It doesn't help but it gives us all a laugh,' said Hilda.

'Anyway,' interrupted Sue, 'why aren't the juniors doing a Christmas play?'

'Aye,' said Hilda, 'Andy's a shoo-in for Rudolph with that red nose.'

Val smiled. 'Because we're not daft, that's why. We've enough to contend with having a flamin' disco on the last day of term.'

'And we're doing an Easter play,' I added.

'Who's idea was the disco, anyway?' asked Sue.

'Joyce said it was that new PTA bod, whatsisname, Mr Milner, but she could always have said no,' said Val. 'I don't think she has the word in her voca—'

At that moment the door swung open and our headteacher walked in, carrying her usual pages of lists and handouts. She seemed oblivious to the previous conversation but must have been highly suspicious when everyone stopped talking abruptly.

'Everything all right?'

Val smiled. 'Yes, fantastic.'

I barely held a straight face, which was doubly awkward as Joyce then turned to me.

'Andy, oh dear, you look like . . . well, I nearly said a rude word then.'

'I'm not too bad,' I lied.

'You shouldn't have come in today. Anyway, thanks for doing the new post box, love, it looks great. I wanted to ask you a favour there, too. I saw Gary Blacow from your class put a few cards in the box yesterday, but he looked a bit down.'

'That doesn't sound like Gary.'

'I know, so I asked whether anything was up. He said he didn't know why he bothered posting cards because no one ever sends him one.'

'Poor kid.'

'I know, I really felt for the lad. I thought about posting one from me but, well, it would be much better from one of his classmates . . .'

'. . . So, you'd like me to . . . ?'

'Well, ask one or two of the kinder children to send him a card. Just make sure it's someone who'll keep quiet about it, though.'

I wandered back to the classroom thinking about Gary and wondering who on earth to ask. He was a good lad, really, was Gary, but he did suffer from his background. Gary lived with his dad and three brothers in one of Cragthwaite's few council houses and their place was rightly regarded as the village eyesore, presenting the road with a pile of rusty bedframes, soggy rolls of carpet, car parts and old smashed toys, all dumped in the overgrown front garden.

Gary himself was affable and generally did his best but his clothes were scruffy hand-me-downs peppered with holes and rips and, worst of all, he emitted a none-too-fragrant odour. His brown hair was matted and his hands were usually lined with dirt. Baths were clearly not a priority in his life and showers hadn't yet been installed in the terrace where he lived.

The effect of his appearance and unfortunate whiff was predictable. He was shunned by many, called names – 'Gassy Gary' being the most popular – and picked on from time to time, although he was made of tough matter and so usually held his own. I tried, of course, to counter these attitudes and I found that the local Dales families, the farm boys particularly, accepted him and were at least amicable in their behaviour, but Gary had hardly anyone he could call a friend. Ricky had been his closest ally and he had left. The least I could do was to ensure that someone sent him a Christmas card.

Half-way through the late morning Maths lesson, there was a knock at the door and a gap-toothed infant stepped into the classroom clutching a large pile of white envelopes. He came over to my desk.

''Ere's yer class's cards fer today, Mr Seed.'

All the children immediately stopped working and looked over with a buzz of chatter.

'Ooh, can us open 'em now, Mr Seed?' asked Martine as I thanked the boy who scuttled back to Hilda's, grateful that he didn't have to linger in a strange room. I noticed Gary glance at the pile.

'No, it's Maths, Martine, and everyone needs to finish their work. I'll give them out during the lunch break.'

There was a brief wave of grumbling but the children had by now learned to read the tone of my voice and they returned to their worksheet on shapes. I wondered if there was anything for Gary in the big stack of cards, hopeful that I might yet avoid the awkward task that lay ahead but, as always in a primary school, there was a waiting queue of individuals whose demand for attention and help left no time for pondering.

The line was fronted by Lawrence, who held out his page. 'Finished.'

'What, everything?'

'Yep. Was easy.'

'Have you identified all the shapes?' I said scanning the unkempt sheet and trying to blow my nose at the same time.

'Look – quadrilateral four sides, pentagon five, hexagon six, heptagon seven, octagon eight.'

I could just about read his scrawl. 'OK, that's good. And did you come up with a mnemonic for remembering them in order: Q, P, H, H, O?'

'It's on the back,' he said as I turned over. 'Queen Priscilla Has Hairy Organs.'

I quickly turned the sheet back again.

After the midday bell I sent everyone out, despite protests that they wanted their cards, then went over to the large pile of envelopes and began to sift through it. Joyce had introduced the tradition of children posting their Christmas cards to their friends and the staff via the school's home-made post box, with the mail being delivered to each class daily, and it was hugely popular. The teachers also liked to keep the final distribution of cards by children in each class as a reward and it was a welcome incentive to work at a time when there were many distractions.

The frequency of certain names on the envelopes also revealed a lot about popularity. Cards for Estelle were numerous, and Cathy, Anna and Lisa also plainly had no shortage of admirers. Fraser, Stephen and Ian were the most esteemed among the boys, it appeared, but as I reached the bottom of the heap my heart sank as I discovered what I'd feared: once more there was not a single card for Gary.

I went out and called Fraser Garth and Howard Sedgwick over from the playground. Fraser was a farmer's lad from Chapelgarth with wavy golden hair, an uncommonly generous and thoughtful boy. Howard, tall and brawny, was the son of a wagon driver from Skirbridge, a no-nonsense, reliable type who I felt I could trust.

I smiled inwardly when I saw in their eyes the inevitable unease that comes from thinking they might be in trouble.

'Don't worry, boys, you've not done anything wrong. Come and sit down.'

'Phew,' said Howard. 'Ah were tranna recall if ahd dun 'owt.'

'No, nothing like that,' I said. 'I want to ask you a special favour, boys.'

'Oh aye,' said Fraser, his generous face open as always.

'Yes, I've chosen you two boys because you're very sensible and I know that I can rely on you. This is, er, quite a sensitive thing, really.' They waited, intrigued, as I sneezed a couple of times then continued. 'Basically, I'd like to ask you if you'd both be really kind and send a Christmas card to Gary Blacow. Mrs Berry and I noticed that he hasn't received any and, er, he's, well – imagine how you'd feel about that.'

Howard shrugged. 'Wurr'n't bother us – am not much of a robins an' Santas person, meself. But ah'll send 'im one if yer like.'

'I will too; ah don't mind,' said Fraser.

I smiled. 'Thanks, boys, I knew you'd be generous. Please keep it to yourselves and, er, it'll have to be tomorrow because it's the last day of term.'

'I know,' said Howard, looking grim. 'Do we really 'ave ter go to a *disco*?' He said it with such bluff Yorkshire disgust that I laughed out loud.

'Sorry, Howard, I suppose you do since it's in school time.'

The boys walked away and I went to collect my sandwiches, glad that Gary's term would at least end with a little high.

The afternoon was a special treat as the juniors sat and enjoyed the infants perform their traditional nativity. Amazingly, nothing went wrong and at the end the cast of tiny angels, shepherds, animals, kings and miniature parents was given a rapturous ovation by the audience, much to Emma and Hilda's relief.

I saw Gary as we filed out, looking much happier than he had earlier.

'Enjoy that, Gary?'

'It were ace! I love that camel, and the little kid playin' Joseph were a right laff.'

'Are you looking forward to the disco tomorrow?'

'Dead right I am. I allus join in t'dancin' at me aunties' and uncles' weddin's. I've got a new shirt to wear 'n' all – reet snazzy I'll be.'

I smiled and took him to one side, waiting for the rest of the class to pass. I felt that I had to say something about his hygiene if he was going to so much trouble with his outfit.

He glanced at my sore, glowing nose. 'That cold's a good'n, Mr Seed.'

'Gary, if you're getting dressed up for the disco then do make sure you have a good hot bath first, eh? You, er, know why I'm saying this to you, don't you?'

It almost seemed as though he was expecting it. 'Aye, am plannin' to wash me 'air an all.'

'Good lad.'

He nodded and we hurried to catch the class up. I breathed a deep sigh of relief as I went, glad that he had taken it so well; I hated these awkward conversations.

Friday started well. My sinuses began to cease their leaking and at school the children were all in a good mood, bubbling with anticipation as they discussed the afternoon's disco and what they would wear.

Only Howard Sedgwick looked flat but even he, like the others, came in clutching a bag of fancy clothes to change into. I amused myself by wondering if it contained sequinned overalls.

Since the class were all too excited to do much in the way of work, I let them read library books for the first part of the morning before the door opened and once more the school's junior postman delivered the final batch of cards. I gave a little prayer and let Martine and Vicky give them out straight away.

The moment was quietly memorable. Gary sat and waited without any sense of expectation and was genuinely shocked and touched when Vicky handed him a card without any fuss. Another followed soon after and he ripped them open excitedly before, for the first time, joining in the throng of children thanking the senders for their cards.

I blew my nose, almost glad I had the cold as an excuse.

Mr Milner, the Chairman of the recently formed PTA, 'knew a fella' who did discos and from the staffroom I watched this small, rotund individual carrying a square black speaker and various boxes into the hall at the end of lunchtime. I wandered in there just before the start of afternoon bell and said hello as he fiddled with some iffy-looking lights. In fact, the whole set-up looked somewhat on the economy side and the chunky fortysomething DJ certainly wasn't what I was expecting.

In the classroom the noise was riotous as the children changed into their party clothes. Lawrence had a burgundy velvet jacket and bow tie, while Martine sported a quite unspeakable dayglo boob tube with spandex pants that didn't do her any favours at all. I was pleased to see, however, that among the girls from old-fashioned local families there were still a few pretty cotton frocks.

Most of the boys looked uncomfortable in long-sleeved shirts but not Dan, who had somehow managed to find a near-white boiler suit.

'Am goin' fer the full-on *Sat'day Neet Fever* look, Mr Seed,' he announced. I couldn't see it myself and neither could the rest of the class judging by the giggles. But Dan was not the one to truly catch the eye, despite his outrageous appearance, for Gary Blacow was a boy transformed.

From somewhere he'd produced a pair of clean leather shoes to replace his trademark torn trainers, and next up were some smart black trousers, neatly pressed. He wore a clean yellow shirt and the look was topped off with a medallion-man brass neck chain that made him look strangely mature. But it was his face that looked so different: I'd noticed his hair earlier in the morning, shining for the first time ever, perhaps, and seen his pink, scrubbed cheeks, for once clear of grime, but he'd still been wearing grotty clothes; it was only now that he looked like a completely new child.

I gave him the thumbs up and admired various other costumes while the older girls tugged at their hair with brushes.

'Aren't you gerrin' changed, Mr Seed?' It was Martine.

It hadn't even occurred to me. I grabbed an excuse. 'Oh, with this cold I'll not be up to dancing or anything, Martine. I'll just have to sit quietly, you know.' She walked away looking faintly disgusted.

At just before two I sent the prattling children to line up, ready to go into the hall. Jason came up to me, pointing out a very expensive-looking black shirt. I smiled, glad to acknowledge that his recent behaviour had been markedly better since Joyce's intervention.

'What do you think, Mr Seed?'

'Wow, I wish I could afford a shirt as good as that.'

'My mum got it from Harrogate. It was supposed to be for Christmas but she said I could have it for the disco.'

I smiled. 'Actually, Jason, I'm glad you came to talk to me. I want to say well done – your behaviour has been much better in the last week or two.'

'Mrs Berry said if I made a big effort people would like me more.'

'She's right too; good lad. How's, erm, your dad?'

'He's still goes on about the pen sometimes but, well . . .'

At that moment Val's voice boomed for quiet and Class 4 arrived signalling that it was time to party.

In the hall, music was blaring out and the smallest mirrored disco ball I had ever seen shot queasy flashes of purple, pink and blue light around the room, which looked very different with the big curtains closed. Several adults, including the staff and some PTA mums, stood in the corners trying to talk while the junior children were arrayed on the chairs around the outside. I was expecting to see dancing in the middle of the floor but it was completely empty.

I went over towards Val who looked even grimmer than I'd expected.

'I've been here three minutes and nine seconds and it's three minutes and eight seconds too bloody long,' she muttered, not caring if any children overheard.

'At least Hilda's not here to try and make me dance,' I said, speaking too soon as the doors opened and the infants careered in. 'Why aren't the kids from our classes grooving?'

'Too flamin' embarrassed, and who can blame them?'

The five- and six-year-olds poured across the hall floor and started bouncing and shaking to the music right away: apprehension wasn't in their souls. Hilda grimaced at the ugly blare of the cut-price pop music and went to sit next to the school secretary, Eileen, who looked like she was trying to enjoy herself but simply couldn't.

Emma then appeared and was straight on to the dance floor, swirling and whooping in her long cheesecloth garb, then grabbing the hands of various leaping small kids to boogie with them. At least she was in her element.

The one child from Class 3 who looked enthusiastic was Gary. He was moving along the line of boys trying to convince them to get up and dance but this was a step too far for them culturally, it seemed. If I hadn't been so bunged up and weary I would have greatly enjoyed observing the scene.

At long last, the girls from my class began to stand up and dance, encouraged by the wiggling mass of infants who were skidding across the floor and rapidly becoming overexcited. It was the same in Class 4: the girls moved on to the floor, giggled, swayed a little, then began to dance, sometimes looking across to the awkward rows of sweaty boys who sat and fiddled with their shirt buttons.

Joyce came in and asked the balding DJ to turn down the volume in an attempt to get the infants to calm down but they were simply too hyper. She asked for it to stop and made them all sit down before Hilda gladly led both classes, panting, back to their rooms. Emma reluctantly followed but she knew, too, that they'd had enough. The thumping beat and blinking lights then returned and the older girls took the floor once more, swaying only gently, aware that they were being watched.

Two PTA mums dished out cheap fizzy pop and crisps, half of

which ended up on the floor. Val accused a Class 4 boy of possessing chewing gum, and the screeching sound blared on and yet still none of the boys danced.

I kept glancing over to Gary, watching in admiration as from time to time he stood up again and waved his arms for some boys to get up and bop. But it was useless and so were they: the longer it went on, the harder it would be. Mind you, I told myself, I would have been the same at nine.

Then a remarkable thing happened. I was creeping around the edge of the room to find a drink when a cheer went up. The girls on the floor were standing still but a twisting, gyrating figure had joined them in the middle: it was Gary and, having given up on his peers, he was grooving alone, bravely strutting to the music while everyone whooped, laughed and mocked. But, it couldn't be denied, he was actually good, really good and, after a few seconds, the jeers turned to shouts of encouragement and, marvellously, led by Joyce, everyone began to clap. Eventually the girls recommenced their moves but for the next ten minutes, all eyes were on one person alone – the rhythmic, jiving figure of Gary Blacow, Cragthwaite's disco sensation, dancing with abandon in a Yorkshire Dales school hall.

The end of term was welcome indeed, as I motored towards Craven Bottoms in our decaying Alfasud, still snuffling but desperate to tell Barbara about Gary. I prayed that the two Christmas cards would be forever a secret and I pictured his smile as he clutched his prize for 'Best Dancer'. Would he turn up still fragrant and clean next term? If only.

On Sunday evening, we sat in Applesett's snug chapel for the short nativity service. Tom and Reuben were dressed as shepherds and looked adorable, each holding a toy lamb, courtesy of Iris who maintained a remarkable supply of soft toy animals.

I watched, beaming as their moment came and they edged near to present their woolly gifts to the infant Jesus in his rustic crib, then laughed along with everyone else when little Reuben refused to hand over his lamb and fled wailing towards Barbara who gathered him up in a hot fog of tears and mucus.

I sang the evocative songs and relished in the marvellous, simple beauty of the Christmas story, feeling the joy of being back home with Barbara and my boys again. It had been a long and arduous term, and yet one that had ended with two moments of magic. I closed my eyes and once more heard Vicky's pure, sweet voice float through Cragthwaite church, before picturing a small, unlikely dancer drawing whoops and cheers from those who had once turned their backs on him.

Chapter Eight

Stephen

New Year came and went, and Craven Bottoms was unusually hectic as Barbara was only able to have two days off, meaning that most family visitors came to see us since we weren't able to travel. She was still just about in the honeymoon phase with her postal job, although I'd noticed that she was enjoying the windy bite of January rather less than October's autumn sun. The day that she really knew what it was about came on the second Saturday of the month.

The first week of January had seen a fall of snow across Swinnerdale which had begun to thaw after a day before freezing again, making the pavements in Ingleburn treacherous during Barbara's delivery round. But this was only a starter, for on the following Saturday the town experienced its highest recorded rainfall, flooding the surrounding countryside as rivers burst their banks. In the midst of this, Barbara had to tramp round hundreds of houses in a hilly town delivering letters and more.

I sat in the cosy warmth of the living room at Craven Bottoms with Reuben on my knee staring out at the rain pelting down in dark torrents as it had been doing since before dawn.

'Poor Mummy,' I said, 'having to walk about in this.'

Reuben concurred, uttering a sweet, 'Oh dear.'

At midday I was discussing with Tom what special lunch we could make for Barbara to cheer her up when we heard the front door creak open. I turned to look down the hallway and saw a fearsome, mangled, dripping figure that may have been my wife.

'Helllp,' it croaked, as a pool of water accumulated on the mat.

'Is that Mummy?' asked a somewhat alarmed Tom.

Ten minutes later I had wrestled layers of saturated clothes off Barbara's quivering body, throwing them into the bath, while the boys brought towels and woolly socks.

'I need hot tea, pints,' she burbled. 'And a hot water bottle. And two hairdryers.'

While she was attending to her tousled hair, I lit the stove and filled the kettle. Half an hour later, bulked out in multiple layers of winter clothes and sitting inches from the fire, she relived the full horror of the morning.

'They gave me some waterproof trousers but they were too big,' she said. 'And they weren't waterproof. I was wet within five minutes, soaked within ten, then after that everything just acted as a sponge.'

'Surely they give you a decent coat?' I said.

'Well, it's good in one regard: expertly designed to funnel water down your front.'

'Ah, so that's why your jumper and shirt were so wet.'

'But the worst thing is, I'm probably going to be fired for ruining the mail.'

'Eh?'

'Well, they give you this yellow plastic covered bag but the rain got in and everything just turned to a mush. I didn't realise for a while, but I heard a sloshing sound and there was two inches of water in the bottom of it.'

'Oh dear . . .'

'The letters might have survived but the free newspapers didn't fare so well – in the end I was just ladling handfuls of papier mâché through the letter boxes. There's probably all sorts of interesting models being created in Ingleburn at this very moment.'

'What about your boots?'

'Oh yes, they're waterproof. But since the water was running down my body and legs they just filled up. I felt like a deep-sea diver by the end. And my fingers swelled up like prunes then froze.'

'You poor thing,' I said, as kind little Tom gave her a hug.

'Oh I haven't come to the worst bit yet . . .'

'What?'

'Remember I said the trousers were too big?'

'Yes,' I said, preparing myself for an almighty effort not to snigger.

'Well they got wet, unsurprisingly. And as they got wet, they got heavy and they started to fall down. The thing is, I was so cold I'd lost all feeling in my body so I didn't notice. I did half the round with them round my knees.'

'Whoops.'

'Then the only thing I had to secure them with was the red elastic bands.'

'You're not having much luck with trousers at the moment, are you?'

She didn't know whether to laugh or weep, adding, 'And just to make things worse I was bursting for the loo after an hour. I had to stagger round like a drowning drunk held together by bits of rubber.'

We had to laugh and, as usual, Reuben joined in, even though he had no idea what any of it was about.

* * *

Back at school, the continued bad weather had cast a pall over the school, keeping fidgety children in at playtime when they needed to be out, and giving the new term a gloomy start.

Joyce didn't lighten the mood at the first staff meeting, either. 'Right, well, you're not going to be pleased about this, everybody, but the governors are keen to tour each class again and see what's going on.'

'What, all of them?' said Emma, aghast, knowing how disruptive some visitors could be.

'No, erm, just one.'

'Oh well, that's not so bad,' I said.

Joyce hesitated. 'It's Mrs Sykes again.'

'What, that sourpuss bag with the notebook?' said Hilda, putting her teacup down. I felt a shudder as my mind returned to the infamous wasp episode.

'Mrs Percival, that's no way to describe a member of the governing body,' said Val, snorting. 'Anyway, she doesn't bother me.'

'No one bothers you,' said Hilda. 'No one dares.'

Joyce cleared her throat. 'Anyway, on with business . . . I know Mrs Sykes can come across as a little, er, officious, but the governors are entitled to see the school in action and the others are happy for her to report back so that's that. She's in next week.'

I scribbled it in my diary and cheered myself by concluding that the next Class 3 lesson she observed could only be better.

'Now, there's one more thing and this time it's some good news,' said Joyce.

'We can all go home,' mumbled Hilda.

'I've booked a troupe of peripatetic musicians.'

'A what?' said Emma, screwing up her face.

'You know, sort of travelling players,' said Joyce. 'They're called

The Bongo Boys and they bring a whole van of percussion instruments. Bilthorpe Juniors had them in and the deputy head said they were fantastic.'

'Ooh, I like a bit o' bongo,' said Hilda. 'Are they coming to work in each class?'

'No, sorry, we can't afford them for a full day. They're going to do an hour's show in the hall on Tuesday at 2pm.' I jotted in my diary then enjoyed a mental picture of Hilda in tribal costume feverishly slapping a pair of African drums.

'Excuse me, Mr Seed, but my pencil's becoming rather difficult to write with.'

A tall, smartly attired boy waited at my side as I stood up from despairing over Dan's spelling book at his table. I knew who it was right away, even without recognising the voice; only one boy in Class 3 spoke that politely and his name was Stephen Gray.

Stephen was an incomer, the son of one of the small group of professional people who worked at home and had begun to move into the Dales. He was a fresh-faced boy with perfect white teeth and a delightful manner. He was also very good at sports and consequently popular with his peers, despite being very different from the majority of them.

He showed me the problem: his pencil had worn down to a tiny stub barely an inch long. Most children would have abandoned such an inadequate writing instrument long ago but Stephen kept on using his until it was physically impossible.

I went to my desk drawer, found a handsome, brand new Staedtler and sliced off a layer of yellow paint with a Stanley knife so I could write his name on the wood. I had long ago discovered that unnamed pencils went missing much more easily.

'There you go,' I said, not adding the usual, 'Look after it carefully', knowing that he would.

'Thank you, Mr Seed; that feels better. Oh, and can you check my maths page on angles?'

He produced a strikingly neat exercise book with the work headed, dated and labelled precisely. On the page a range of angles had been grouped into acute and obtuse sets without an error or blotch. I ticked each one and wrote *Excellent* in the margin, handing the book back with a smile.

Waiting behind Stephen was the wide, unkempt figure of Martine, who burped quite unaware, scratched her backside then passed over a battered, smudged page, its corners frayed and crumpled. Her writing was hieroglyphic in its illegibility.

'There y'ar, Mr Seed, them's acute and them's obscene.'

She was wrong there: they were all obscene.

The following weekend our friends from York, Doug and Rosie, moved into their new house. I'd offered to help unload the large van they'd hired and also to fill a skip by the road outside with various items of junk and unwanted fittings that the previous owners had left behind.

'Smell that country air,' said Doug as he jumped out of the driver's seat. 'Diesel, rotting sheep and cow jobbies.'

Rosie came over and gave me an effusive hug, her wavy hair blowing into my mouth. 'Oh, it's soooo exciting to be here,' she said, pulling away and looking round. 'It's really good of you to help us, Andy.' She was wearing a curious fat mohair cardigan of around 250 colours and a skirt that looked as if it had come from India and not travelled well. I felt sure that she'd get along with Emma Torrington, if no one else.

They opened the front door and I had my first proper look at the stately old house which had evidently been quite grand for Applesett once but had fallen on hard times, its elderly previous owner, Mr Gill, having let it decline rather alarmingly.

There was a large kitchen with an ancient solid fuel stove and a few grim cupboards. The floor was made from cracked red tiles and the walls were streaked with age and cobwebs. Two unpleasant fly papers hung down, thick with skeletal insects.

Through the door at the side was a huge, magnificent living room with a wide bay window, high ceilings, ornate Victorian coving and a giant black marble fireplace. Again, the walls were peeling and the paintwork was chipped and yellowing but the possibilities were immense.

'Wow!' I could barely conceal my envy.

'Not bad is it?' said Doug. 'We're thinking of deep turquoise for the walls and picking out the decorative plasterwork with gold paint.'

I wasn't sure if he was serious at first, as that rarely happened with Doug, but I could tell from his expression that he was.

Upstairs were three sizeable bedrooms and a remarkably insalubrious bathroom. The house did have almost all its original features but was, undeniably, a monster DIY project. At least Doug and Rosie had no children to 'help'. I thought how difficult it would be to tackle something like this with Tom and Reuben charging around.

We returned to the van and began to unload. Instead of the stacks of large boxes I'd expected, everything was rammed together in a crazy jumble, apart from Rosie's precious nineteenth-century china which was packed in tea chests. I pulled out guitars, paintings, towel rails, a battered vacuum cleaner, old wooden school chairs, a vast ottoman and mounds of hairy clothes in bags, cases and crates.

'Just lob it all in the big room for now,' said Doug.

I returned for more: antique mirrors, toolboxes, more paintings, an enormous metal bed frame, a hat stand, several unidentified objects and a series of weird sculptures.

We stopped for a cup of tea then heaved the large furniture upstairs: painted chests, pine wardrobes and two strange cupboards that Rosie informed me were Chinese. Barbara came over with the boys who enjoyed exploring the house and its mounds of curious items.

'What an incredible place,' said Barbara, and it was obvious that she too coveted its wonderful feeling of space. Rosie then showed us the back garden which was smaller than expected but walled with attractive local stone. It also possessed a magnificent view down the tapering village green and across to the distant northern slopes of Swinnerdale.

Returning into the house we heard a crash upstairs.

'You all right, Doug?' I shouted.

'Yeah, just pulling out some of the dross for the skip.'

We went up and saw him standing on some stepladders ripping down a tacky brass curtain rail.

'May as well get started with this and fill the skip,' he said, clearly assuming that we would help. 'Better to do it before all our stuff's in the way.'

'Oh, right, er, what else is to go?' I asked.

'Those vile kitchen cupboards mainly,' said Rosie. 'It's a big hammer job I reckon.'

I liked big hammer jobs and offered to assist. Barbara suggested that it might not be the ideal habitat for our boys, even though Reuben would have been well at home with some kind of club, and so she left for Craven Bottoms, offering to bring up some food later on.

Doug found me some heavy tools but the old fitted cupboards were surprisingly reluctant to depart the kitchen and after a few minutes of heaving and bashing I went outside to cool down.

Billy Iveson, one of the village's indigenous old boys, was there with his dog, peering into the skip.

'Now then, Andrew,' he said. 'Lendin' a 'and, I see. Looks like a spot o' renovation's underway.'

'Yep, two people we know have moved in from York – I'm just giving them some help.'

'My father's mate, Frank Scrafton, put in that kitchen, tha knows. When 'ud it be . . . some time round 1925 ah reck'n.'

We heard the buzz of an approaching engine and Big Alec Lund came racing down from Town Head Farm on his spattered quad bike. He slowed to a stop, nodding.

'Billy, Seedy. What's job 'ere, then?'

Before I could answer, Doug came out shouldering a pile of battered wood and dropped it into the skip. 'Hello, village elders meeting, is it?' he said smiling.

Big Alec gave him a blank look while Billy nodded a greeting.

'Alec, Billy, this is Doug Burns. They're moving in from York.'

'More townies, eh?' said Alec. 'I 'ope yer less trouble than this youth.' He glanced to me. I could see Doug thinking about a witty rejoinder but he was deterred by Alec's menacing bulk.

Back inside, Doug chuckled. 'Wa-hey, I didn't believe yokels like that still existed – were they real?'

'Oh yes, there's plenty more where they came from too, and they'll all be going past and stopping for a butcher's. They're dead nosey are the locals. Friendly but nosey.'

'Come on, then,' he said. 'Who else will there be, then I can be ready for them.'

'Right, well, there'll be John Weatherall, the resident builder. Good man to stay in with, and a canny lad. Then the rest of the darts team might drop by too: Andy, Vince, Paul, Bri, Dave and Dave – they're all about six foot nine and beefy.'

'Are these all people you know?' said Rosie, joining the conversation.

'Oh yes . . . then you'll no doubt see our wonderful friend Iris from a few doors down – she's not local – but John and Mary Burton are proper Dales folk: they're farmers from Buttergill, just up there, and I have never met anyone more genuine in my life.'

'Are they like the Yorkshire Waltons, then?' said Doug.

'Erm, not really . . . Anyway, the one person who will definitely be here soon is Mrs Dent from the shop – she doesn't miss *anything*.'

We carried on whacking the old cupboards then took some piles out to the skip. There was Mrs Dent, peering in through the open front door.

'Ooh, sorry! Hello, Andy. I was jus' being, er, curious. Are these your friends from York, then?'

'At least she's honest,' murmured Doug before I introduced everybody and Mrs Dent launched into a glowing appraisal of the village shop.

'Do you sell organics?' said Rosie.

Mrs Dent furrowed her brow. 'Oh, you mean that fancy shampoo? No, you'll need to fetch that from Inglebu'n or maybe Hauxt'n.'

'I meant vegetables.'

'Oh, no, we 'aven't anything like that, just the basics.'

'Well I'm going to grow my own anyway,' said Rosie. Mrs Dent duly noted the information then went on her way, stopping five or six times to talk to other villagers.

'That's it,' I laughed. 'Everyone here will know everything about you within minutes.'

'And some of it might even be true,' added Rosie.

Two hours later we'd ripped out the last cupboard and sat down for another tea break. It was now dark outside and the house was bitterly cold.

Doug gave a sigh and wiped his brow. 'Well, at least the rustic busybodies should desist now.'

'Oh, they're all all right really, even Big Alec, though he likes to look and sound murderous.'

'Are there any rural communes round here or workers' cooperatives?' asked Rosie. I said that it wasn't really that kind of place, then sipped my tea wondering how our friends would settle and if both sides were going to manage the culture shock.

On Monday in school, Joyce reminded me that Mrs Sykes was due to be with my class during Tuesday afternoon. I made a mental note to plan some silent basic task when I realised that we'd be going into the hall to see The Bongo Boys at two o'clock. Was that good or bad? I couldn't decide.

A tweed-suited Mrs Sykes arrived in my dingy temporary classroom at five to one the following afternoon and I did my best to look pleased to see her. Once more she maintained a serious, dry expression and produced the same notebook that had damned me four months earlier.

'We're going to be doing handwriting practice first lesson, Mrs Sykes,' I chirped. 'Then at two o'clock it's into the hall to see the musical group.'

She looked nonplussed. 'Handwriting for a whole hour?'

'Yes, er, their letter formation needs a lot of extra practice. I've, erm, been analysing their written work and, well, I'm looking for higher standards.'

She raised her eyebrows and jotted down a note: no doubt my first black mark, even before the children were in. The truth was that I'd chosen handwriting because they could just copy off the board and there was absolutely no reason for idle chatter, stupid questions, spillages, or accidents. The bell rang and, even though it was January, I walked around the windows to check that the room was wasp-proof.

I stood outside the door to ensure that the children came in quietly. They did, having previously been issued with multiple threats. I called the register and set the tone for the afternoon's work, ensuring that every member of the class was looking at me and listening carefully. I'd show this woman.

'Right, Class Three. I've been looking at your books over the past few days and I've noticed that some of you are becoming a little lazy about handwriting. Remember at this school we teach *joined* handwriting and we expect you to form your letters properly and join them. Some of you are forgetting this so we're going to have a good long practice.' Martine began to raise her hand.

'No questions, just make sure you have your pens ready, not pencils, and that you're sitting up well.'

Trudy Hammond, ever alert, noticed that I'd forgotten to give out the handwriting books and quietly distributed them while I glared across the room, daring anyone to talk, make a fuss, fidget or even move. For the first time, Mrs Sykes almost gave the impression that she approved.

'When you have your book, write the date at the top of a new page, and do it carefully, with letters joined of course.'

The children sensed that I was a little tense and they obeyed silently, writing much more slowly and deliberately than usual.

'Now, we are going to practise joining the letter "r" first,' I said, having ensured that everyone was looking to the front again. 'It's actually quite simple to join it to most other letters, like this.' I picked up a stick of chalk and smoothly scribed "ra" on the blackboard, joining the letters carefully.

'Right, everyone write two lines of those, as neatly as possible, joining like I did.'

I toured the room, checking on each child and making comments, ensuring high quality and correcting deviations when necessary. The children worked diligently and I saw Mrs Sykes scribbling in her notebook what could only be admiring remarks.

'All right, stop there, even if you haven't finished,' I said, returning to the front. 'Who can give me some examples of words with "ra" in them? Hands up.'

There was no shortage of examples, although most of them were short like rat and grab. I wrote up some of the words on the board.

'Can anyone think of a longer word containing "ra"?' I asked.

Estelle raised her hand. 'Radiator.'

'Good.' I wrote it on the board. 'Another?'

'Transverse crankshaft,' said Howard. 'Ave 'eard me dad talkin' about 'em.'

'Right, very interesting,' I said, smiling and writing the words transverse and crankshaft before explaining what they meant and thinking that Mrs Sykes would note the vocabulary development.

'One more?' I ventured. Dan put his hand up but I studiously ignored him.

Stephen extended an arm. 'Ragout.'

'Yes, er, good, Stephen. I think that might be French but it's certainly got "ra" in it – do you know what it is?' I hoped he did because I certainly didn't.

'It's a kind of meat stew; we had some last night.'

'Yes, good, that's right.' I lifted the chalk and nervously wrote 'ragut'.

Stephen raised his hand. 'I think it has an "o" after the "g", Mr Seed.'

'Just testing,' I said trying to sound jolly before changing it and trying not to glance over to the hawk-like governor. 'Let's move on. Erm, right, we'll do "rn" next,' I said thinking, *and we won't have any more examples.*

The children wrote two lines of the letter pair then I gave them some words to copy: warn, torn, earned, burn. Control and composure were resumed, although Martine did put up her hand. I signalled for her to put it down but then, gradually, a wave of whispering spread across the room followed by giggles and pointing to the front. I demanded calm but they couldn't seem to control themselves. Mrs Sykes's pen went into overdrive while several children put up their hands, including Martine who was now waggling it furiously.

'What's the matter, Martine? Can't it wait?'

'Mr Seed, yu've wrote bum!'

Before I could say anything, the whole class collapsed into hysterics as if a stopper had been pulled.

'Quiet!' I roared, but they couldn't help it. 'Martine, I did not write bum, that word is burn: b-u-r-n, look,' I demanded, pointing to the board.

'But the way yu've joined the "r" an' "n", it looks like an "m",' said Martine with the class showing their full agreement. 'And now av wrote bum in me 'andwriting book.'

This brought more hoots of glee from the class; I almost wanted to join in.

Handwriting was abandoned and I read a story for twenty minutes before taking the class into the hall to see The Bongo Boys, having first demanded exceptional behaviour. Surely nothing could go wrong here?

Two men stood in the hall, tinkering with a great array of strange musical instruments. One was tall, thin and white-haired, the other more youthful and chunky with glasses. The younger man picked up an accordion. The infants were sitting ready on the floor, most staring up at the two strangers and several picking their noses.

When Class 4 came in and sat down Joyce introduced The Bongo Boys and they went straight into playing fast, melodic folk music without any singing. The older man sat on what looked like a wooden box, beating out an engaging rhythm on its side. The children immediately began to jiggle and sway with some even clapping randomly. It was unimaginably better than the deplorable disco of just a few weeks before.

Suddenly the music stopped and the children burst into applause. Derek, the older musician, introduced his instrument as a cajón from Peru.

'Does anyone know where Peru is?' he enquired.

Dan put up his hand. 'Is it somewhere down Wherndale?'

The other teachers snickered but I didn't, seeing the spectral Mrs Sykes make yet another condemnatory jotting.

Derek explained that he collected percussion instruments from around the world while his partner Joe just played the accordion. Next they launched into a scintillating piece of French Canadian music with Derek playing wooden spoons, before moving on to a tabor and then a whole series of exotic drums.

The children and staff were richly entertained and the pair were very good at adding in little nuggets of information between the music. After half an hour, Derek asked the children if they had any questions and I didn't hold out too much hope that my class would redeem themselves in front of the watching governor-spy. It was always a dangerous move to say, 'any questions', when young children were about, and sure enough the responses were eclectic:

'Is that big thing heavy?'

'I've got a recorder.'

'Do you get much money?'

'How long did it take you to learn the cordian?'

'Where can I get some really cheap drums?'

'How old are you?'

The Bongo Boys did their best to answer patiently then they went into another series of jaunty, varied musical pieces until there were just ten minutes left.

'Right,' said Derek. 'I'm now going to show you some of my favourite unusual instruments which I've collected over the past forty years.'

He picked up a long stick covered with small bells, which actually turned out to be metal bottle tops, loosely nailed on. He gave it a rattle and said, 'I bet none of you know what this is called.'

I looked across with the other teachers and saw Stephen Gray raise an arm. 'It's a lagerphone.'

'Wow! Very good, that's right,' said Derek. 'Also known as a monkey stick or mendoza.'

Next he held up a cylindrical wooden instrument with a series of silver beads wrapped around it. He gave the handle a twist to produce a gentle rolling shake.

'You might know this one,' he said.

Once more Stephen was the only one to answer. 'It's a cabasa.'

I smiled across giving him the thumbs up.

Derek then walked to the back of the hall and pushed forward a curious item that appeared to be a tall, narrow tower made of upturned metal bowls. With a metal beater he brushed the stack and produced a delicate peal of spectral bells before eliciting some sharper, louder rings by striking it hard.

Stephen didn't even wait this time. 'Ooh, that's, erm, a bell tower. It has another name too – an aluphone, I think.'

Derek stopped. 'Well, correct again – that's amazing. How come you know so many instruments, young man?'

'My aunt in London is a percussionist,' answered Stephen confidently.

Nice one, Stevie boy, I thought, glancing over to Mrs Sykes who for once wasn't frowning. My star pupil then went on to recognise the next five instruments too until Derek brought out his last one.

'I don't think even our school genius will recognise this beauty,' said Derek lifting up a most peculiar metal object. It looked like a lidded frying pan into which a row of long, uneven nails had been hammered around the rim, so that they stood up like thin bars. In the middle was a black handle. Derek picked it up carefully then tapped one of the vertical rods with a stick before rolling the instrument slowly from side to side to produce the most magnificently eerie rolling sound like the dying cry of a space dragon.

'Whoah!' purred the listening children. I heard someone say, 'It's like a scary film.'

'That's exactly right,' said Derek. 'This is used for sound effects in the movies. Great, isn't it?' And he tapped and rolled it some more to generate strange ethereal tones which filled the hall.

'Know what it is?' he said, looking at Stephen who shook his head. 'A waterphone. They are very rare and very special. Only one man makes them and you have to order one specially. And they are very, very expensive.'

He left it there but they all wanted to know.

'It was nearly five hundred pounds.'

'Corrrr!' went up the choral cry of amazement. It was clearly more money than most of them could comprehend.

The Bongo Boys received a huge and much deserved round of applause for what had been a tremendous show and for a moment I almost forgot that we were being watched. But then a delightful thing happened. Joe the accordion player thanked everybody, then he held up a hand to ask for a moment's quiet.

'Well Cragthwaite, you've been a top audience but Derek and I have to say that we are very impressed with your musical knowledge at this school – it's the best we've ever come across – and we think there's one more person who deserves a big clap and that's the young man there. What a contribution!' He pointed to Stephen who bashfully smiled while the whole school gave him a cheer.

Once she had put down her notebook, even Mrs Sykes applauded.

Chapter Nine

Cathy

Cathy Lawson was Estelle Wood's friend and the two were inseparable. They were born just a few days apart, lived near each other in Cragthwaite, shared the same interests and sat next to each other in Class 3, being of a similar ability for most subjects. Whereas Estelle was sassy and outspoken, the smaller, dark-haired Cathy was calmer, more sensible and certainly more reserved. They loved each other's company and worked well together but their partnership wasn't without its imperfections, the main one being that they never stopped talking.

Estelle liked to give a running commentary on life and Cathy liked to compare her views on everything while this was happening. They weren't generally loud but simply maintained a low-level prattle, which at times could be very irritating in the classroom. I had observed them while the student Kim Bennett had been taking the class and I noticed how Cathy's eyes craftily followed the teacher everywhere so that when they were under scrutiny they would instantly cease their babble only to start up again when the coast was clear.

At times I enjoyed the battle of wits, catching the girls out by pretending to look away before quickly returning to them, but there were days when their constant chatter became too much. One of these occurred in late January.

Vicky Rushworth had written a poem about winter. It wasn't good. In fact, it was shocking. But one thing had pleased me: for the first time ever in Class 3, Vicky had volunteered to read something aloud. I had been trying to develop the children's speaking skills for some time, ever since discussing with a teacher friend how pupils from private schools always seemed to talk with such confidence, expressing themselves in a clear, eloquent way which was far removed from the average Cragthwaite kid's mumbled drawl.

I didn't want to try to change their wonderful Yorkshire accents, or for them to lose the dialect words I enjoyed so much, but rather I was keen for my children to be able to communicate well, to be clearer and more articulate: there was plenty of room for improvement and so when Vicky put up her hand I was delighted to be able to encourage her to speak well. Perhaps her great success in singing had given her more confidence? Anyway, she stood up with her English book and began to mutter:

Winter is cold,
Sometimes snowy,
Sometimes not.
But not hot.
Cold.
I wear my new coat,
The blue one with the poppers and the fur round the collar
That mum got me.
Thanks mum.

I feared that there was going to be pages more but I had to stop Vicky anyway because someone had been talking during her reading. It wasn't difficult to guess who: the low hubbub from the back gave it away. That and the hunched, conspiratorial postures of Cathy and Estelle. Guilt was written all over them. Normally I would have given them a ticking off but this was the third time it had happened that day and it was putting poor Vicky off – junior doggerel or not – at a time when she needed to be encouraged.

'Cathy and Estelle this has to stop!' They were noticeably taken aback by the force of my interjection. 'I am really pleased that Vicky has volunteered to read her poem and she's doing her best but you two girls are spoiling her efforts.'

They stared at me, Estelle looking somewhat unremorseful but Cathy was blushing for all to see. I decided to drive home the point.

'It's one thing chatting when we are all working on something but it is never acceptable to talk when someone else is speaking to the class: it is actually very rude. Do you understand?' They gave reluctant nods. 'Right, no more or I shall have to go and tell Mrs Berry that we have two extremely rude girls in Class Three and she might suggest splitting you up.'

This appeared to do the trick and they sat quietly for the rest of the session, although no other children offered to read their poems following my outburst. Perhaps, if Vicky's ode was anything to go by, it was just as well.

On Sunday morning Adam Metcalfe from wild Reddle was the visiting lay preacher at the chapel next door to Craven Bottoms and, as previously, he gave an understated but challenging talk. After the service, Barbara went to speak to Adam's wife Ruth, who was busy keeping a check on her four rosy-cheeked children, while I headed over to see Adam who was laughing heartily with the bull-like Jacob Burton. I was often magnetically drawn to male company after spending most of the week in the female-dominated domain of Cragthwaite Primary.

'Now then, young Andrew. How's thee, lad?' said Jacob, with a pat on the back which left me wheezing. As soon as I'd answered he glanced at his watch and said he had to be off to attend to a 'badly tup'. 'Mek sure Adam tells thee about t'septic tank.'

He hurried away to find Mary while I congratulated Adam on his sermon.

'Oh, and what's the septic tank thing?' I added.

'Ah, it's a story about a neighbour o' mine, Frank Suggett. He farms at Moss Bank.'

'Is that what you were laughing at?'

'It would be hard not ter laugh . . . he had a problem with his drain from the house to the septic tank. It was blocked somewhere so he tried rodding it but got nowhere so decided on emptying the tank using his slurry tanker – it has a pump attached for fillin' up, y'see.'

I nodded, picturing the tractor-drawn metal tankers that were often seen spraying slurry over the fields in spring.

'Well, it was all connected up but nothing was coming through and Frank was gettin' really frustrated, seeing as he 'ad plenty o' jobs to be on with. It was obviously a really bad blockage so Frank decided to take drastic measures and reverse the pump to blow the obstruction out.' I watched Adam's sharp blue eyes, moist with the enjoyment of the tale as he continued. 'So he puts the tanker on full power pressure, as if he wa' spraying slurry, and he hears a big noise and can tell that it's done the job, so he switches the machine off and heads inside for a brew. Well, he only gets half-way to the house when the door bursts open and his wife runs out waving her arms and shouting, "Frank, what 'ave yer done to the toilet!"'

Adam exploded into guffaws as I pictured the scene and tried to imagine its full horror. He wiped his eyes and shook his head. 'They can spray stuff thirty yards those tankers so yer can imagine what 'appened in the toilet. It was all over the ceiling, the walls . . . everything completely clarted.'

'Good job his wife wasn't on the throne at the time,' I said wickedly as Barbara, Ruth and the children came over to see what we were laughing about.

'I can guess which story that is,' said Ruth, raising her eyes.

'Is it the poo one, Daddy?' asked little Robert, pulling at his dad's trousers.

Barbara looked confused. 'I'll tell you it later,' I said to her.

'Er, to change the subject,' said Barbara looking at Adam. 'We should be inviting you for lunch, but I'm afraid we don't have any food in the house.'

'Oh, no worries; we've been invited over by Iris Falconer,' he said. 'I think it's roast chicken.'

'Wow, you'll have a feast there,' I said enviously.

Tom looked up, his eyes wide with disquiet. 'Do we really have no food, Mummy?'

'Oh, we'll find something for lunch, don't worry, petal.'

Back at home we soon discovered that Tom was right to be worried. Barbara and I delved through the cupboards and fridge with a dark sinking feeling.

'A can of peaches in here, and half a pack of stale Ryvitas. Oh, and some stock cubes,' I said, wondering how we'd come to this.

'Sorry, I just haven't been to the shops for a while – this postie job has thrown my usual schedule to pot. I thought we had some bread, though.'

'The boys and I had toast for breakfast – since there was no cereal.'

'Well, you could have gone to Ingleburn yesterday,' she said. 'Didn't you notice the lack of food?'

'I didn't realise it was this bad. There must be something in the fridge.'

'Yes, one egg, some cheap ham with a best before October date, a few jars of manky jam and the remains of that thing you made last week which nobody liked and now has green fungus on top.'

'What about the freezer?'

'Remember, I defrosted it last weekend and we had to use up the contents. We had that nice curry and fish finger slop.'

'Mrs Dent's is closed . . . We could get some sandwiches from the tea shop in Chapelgarth . . .'

'It's shut on Sundays in winter. We can't take the kids in the pub, either.'

At this point Reuben toddled in and made it plain he was hungry.

Half an hour later we were pushing round bowls of grey porridge with egg and marmalade.

'What are we going to have for tea?' enquired Tom.

'Good question,' said Barbara looking at me. But I wasn't listening; my mind was at Iris Falconer's picturing a steaming chicken dinner with fat sausages, crisp Yorkshire puddings and rich gravy.

Reuben was in a grouch for the early part of the afternoon and even placid Tom was irritable, so I unfolded the pushchair and took them out to give Barbara a little peace.

'I know, we'll go to see the football farmers,' I said, remembering that the local team, Hubberdale United, were playing on the flat fields down beyond the bottom of the village. Several members of the darts team were in the side and the rough-and-tough matches were usually quite entertaining.

Reuben soon dropped off to sleep in the pushchair, as planned, and Tom enjoyed being out in the crisp air. It took us some time to reach the little bridge over Hubberdale Beck from where we could see the pitch marked out in the corner of a large field and, as usual, there was a straggly line of trucks, four-wheel drives and small sporty cars parked along the road. The match hadn't yet begun and two lofty figures were hanging up nets while most of the players got changed by the wall.

There was no clubhouse here, and in a typically rural scene which summed up the Dales, Big Alec Lund was on the pitch shooing off the resident sheep to another corner of the field while John Weatherall and Dave Whiterow from the darts team wandered about flicking turds off the playing surface. The grass was none too even, either, and there were even a few thistles in one corner.

The match, against local rivals Kettleby FC, was soon underway and, amid the bluff shouting of players and the calls of the few hardy spectators along the edge of the pitch, Tom began to bombard me with questions, as he always did when seeing something new and interesting:

'Why does that man wear a different colour?'

'Who is winning?'

'Which team do we want?'

'Why did the whistle blow then?'

'What did that man fall down for?'

'What was that word that big man used?'

I sidestepped the final query and enjoyed the game, which was a classic 1980s British encounter of long-ball hoofing interspersed with little cameos of skill by the best players before they were scythed down by brute defenders. Within twenty minutes every man was smeared with mud and bits of grass and the field was furrowed by sliding tackles. Hubberdale took the lead with a thumping header, only for the beast-like upper-dale lads to square the game after a missile of a shot from a short, wide fellow referred to as Dunny by his team-mates.

Reuben woke up and was anxious to join in with the game so I diverted him with one of the spare balls next to the wall. He and Tom had great fun trying to boot a proper football against the wall then hurling themselves down on to the grass pretending to be goalies.

By half-time the sky was already drawing a curtain of gloom across the valley and the boys had had enough: they were hungry, thirsty and cold, and I was in severe need of a cup of tea. We wandered slowly back to the village then up the long green, past the waterfall and towards the swings and slide, where the boys found a second wind for playing. I put each one on a swing and gave them a push.

'Wheeee,' went Reuben.

'Is that what you need?' I said.

'Higher!' called Tom.

'Hiya,' I said, waving.

He giggled. 'No, higher!'

'Hiya!'

'No *higher*!'

'Hiya!'

I lifted them off the swings, still chortling, and we headed for home. We passed the butcher's shop, with its big colour picture in the window of steaks and roast pork, then walked past Mrs Dent's shop where we could see apples and chocolate bars and cheese and packets of biscuits. Silently we drooled as we climbed the last part of the green near The Crown. This was the worst place of all: the kitchen extractor fan wafted warm aromas of meaty stew and hot pies right up our tortured nostrils.

'I'm starving,' said Tom.

Reuben patted his tummy. 'Hungreee!'

'Me, too, boys,' I said dejectedly as we crossed the grass to our barren house. Just for a moment, I wondered if Barbara might have discovered some cache of hidden tins or perhaps ventured up the green to beg Doug and Rosie for a few potatoes to bake but when we stepped inside, the longed-for smell of cooking was absent. Barbara, however, was sitting in the living room smiling.

'Have you found something in the house?' I asked with a sudden surge of hope.

'Not a sausage.'

'Have you borrowed some food?'

'Nope.'

I shrugged, aghast. 'Then why are you smiling? The boys and I are nearly passing out!'

She tittered mischievously. 'You'll find out soon. I'll make you a cup of tea and get the boys a drink, anyway.'

I followed her into the kitchen. 'What is going on, we need to eat . . .'

'Just be patient. You shall be eating, I promise. Something hot and yummy, too.'

'What? You're driving me bonkers.'

'I'm not going to spoil the surprise. At quarter to six, a meal will be served.'

The strong Yorkshire tea did at least revive me and quell my torment. Tom and I tried to work out what was going on while Reuben went for a change of nappy. We just couldn't solve the mystery.

Darkness fell on the village and Barbara simply pootled about for the next hour, avoiding the kitchen altogether, adding to the puzzle. Then, at half past five, she put on her coat and sidled out of the door without saying a word. Tom and I ran to the window and watched her hurry down the road.

'Where's she going, Daddy?'

I watched her slip out of sight in the gloom. 'I don't know.'

'Is she bringing something to eat?'

'I hope so.'

Fifteen long minutes passed before the door clicked open and in came my wonderful, brilliant, beautiful, clever wife. Cradled in her arms, like a delicate newborn child, were three packages, swathed in shiny foil. And there in our house was the glorious, the magical, the unmistakable smell of fish and chips.

Her face was alight with triumph. 'The pub!'

'Since when have they done takeaways?'

'They don't.'

I looked at her doubtfully, my mouth drooling. 'Then how?'

'I popped in there when you took the boys out and told Dennis that we had no food. He went into the kitchen and offered to make this later.'

'I love that man.'

We gorged, we feasted and, though it was widely acknowledged that The Crown's fish and chips portions were not the largest and that the mushy peas were an odd colour, it was then and still is to this day, one of the finest meals I ever ate.

The staffroom at Monday lunchtime was cacophonous. Val was talking to Sue about the best place to buy tyres in Swinnerdale, Hilda was complaining to Emma about one of the children in her class, while I was trying to ask Eileen the school secretary about ordering some drawing pencils.

'My Dave says that Stan Foster's aren't good value because they're such poor quality,' said Sue.

'Well, he's overweight, that's the problem,' said Emma, 'But I wouldn't have dared make him do PE in his undies.'

'Is it the hard or the soft ones you want?' said Eileen.

'My neighbour gets his from Bilthorpe,' said Val.

Hilda shook her head. 'I'm sure you need a licence for pants that large.'

'Soft, either B or 2B, but not the ones with rubbers on the end,' I said.

Emma brushed crumbs off her yellow trousers. 'What a mouth as well.'

'You mean at the back of the library?' said Sue.

'Why not rubbers?'

'That child thinks he could bring kippers back to life.'

'No, next to the pet shop.'

'They pick bits off them and flick them.'

'Mother never disciplines him, though.'

'Oh, Fast-Fit.'

'I'll get four boxes, then.'

None of us noticed the door open and Joyce walk in.

'Sex!'

Instantly the clamour ceased and we all turned to the headteacher who was coolly smiling.

'Yes you did hear me right and I did say "sex".'

'Are you sure there's time? The bell's going to go in a minute,' laughed Hilda.

'It's the governors again, I'm afraid,' said Joyce, disregarding the previous remark. 'They've been discussing sex education.'

'I can't imagine Mrs Sykes and old Arthur Fawcett bringing up that topic,' said Val, eyebrows raised.

'No, it was the two new parents, and Mr Milner surprisingly. Apparently one of the Class Four girls has been asking her mother what she called "embarrassing questions" and the upshot is that the mother thinks the school's sex ed provision should be covering this and, well, the two parent governors agreed.'

'Ooh, what were the questions?' said Hilda, rubbing her hands. 'I have a few of me own.'

As usual, Joyce ignored her and carried on. 'So, while you're all here, I just thought I'd warn you that we're going to have to revamp what the school does.'

'Er, what do we do?' I asked.

'Good question,' said Joyce. 'Well, at the moment from what I can gather Nurse Michaelis speaks to the top juniors – girls and boys separately – for about seven minutes using a load of unhelpful euphemisms.'

'I don't think we need to bloody bother,' said Val. 'The farm kids know what's what – we should just take the rest across to Sunters' shed at tuppin' time.'

'There seems to be widespread agreement that poor Nurse Michaelis is just confusing matters, anyway,' said Joyce. 'They want the lower juniors to be involved too.'

'So what are we supposed to do?' said Emma, looking at the clock as it approached five to one.

'They want us to show a film.'

* * *

That afternoon while the children were busy designing jigsaws in Design and Technology, I wondered what on earth my class would make of a sex education film. I had no idea what kind of teaching material was out there since my college training course had avoided the subject altogether. I was trying to recall what happened at my own primary school when two children came up to me with design drawings. Colin Morphet was first.

'Done it, Mr Seed. It's a tractor.'

'I can see that, Colin. The drawing is good but have you remembered who the jigsaws are for?'

'Erm . . . a friend?' It didn't surprise me that Colin hadn't listened as he rarely took the trouble to do so.

'It's for a young child aged two or three. And how many pieces does your design have?'

'About a hundred.'

A slight giggle came from Cathy, standing behind. 'You're supposed to have eight pieces at the most,' she said.

He groaned and walked back, muttering that the task was boring, while I scanned Cathy's own delicately sketched plan. It was for a simple flower with each petal and leaf a different piece.

'That's good; I like the way you've colour coded it too.'

'Can Estelle and I work together?' she asked, giving one of those inflated smiles so beloved of junior girls.

'You know this is an individual project, Cathy. Anyway, you also know what happens when you two work together . . .'

'We won't talk all the time, honest. Well, we'll talk a bit but we won't be rude and interrupt others.'

'Well at least you remembered what I said but, sorry, this time you need to work on your own. Anyway, you don't need Estelle's help here – your jigsaw's going to be brilliant.' She skipped away, her disappointment more than offset by my encouragement.

The following week's staff meeting was the strangest and certainly the most entertaining in my time at Cragthwaite Primary. Joyce, in her usual brisk fashion, had managed to obtain four sex education videos labelled as suitable for the 7–11 age group and it was the staff's task to select the one deemed most appropriate.

The staffroom's red curtains were closed and the TV trolley had been wheeled in, making the already cramped space even more uncomfortable. While Joyce brought the videos to the front, Hilda cranked up her non-stop tide of cheek to almost unbearable levels.

'Four!' she cried. 'My delicate constitution's not ready for that much filth.'

'Where did you get them from?' asked Val.

Joyce fiddled with the temperamental VHS machine. 'Three from the Health Authority Resources place in Bilthorpe and one from the BBC.'

'The BBC!' whooped Hilda. 'Are we going to see more of Angela Rippon's you-know-whats? Well as long as it's narrated by David Dimbleby we'll be fine.'

Val turned round. 'Hilda, it's bad enough having to sit here and watch this stuff like a bunch of dirty old men without you jabbering on.'

'Sorry, Mrs Deputy Head, but my mother warned me about mucky movies and I can't help it if my nerves get the better of me.'

Joyce stood up. 'Please, everyone, let's be grown up about this. It's not "mucky" – we have a duty to provide sex education so let's at least choose the best material.'

'What's the first film called?' said Emma.

'*Confessions of Nit Nurse*,' whispered Hilda. She simply couldn't help herself.

Joyce looked at the box. '*Where do I come from?* And, Hilda, do not say Rotherham.'

She pressed play, sat down and Emma dug me in the ribs as the school's decrepit television shuddered into life. The film was a brief animated piece that was full of confusing diagrams and advanced vocabulary. It looked like it had been written by a group of lab biologists who had better things to do.

'What do we think?' said Joyce.

'Didn't like it,' said Val. 'Too technical and, well, cold.'

'It was awful,' said Emma. 'I didn't know half those words.'

Joyce turned to me. 'What did you think, Andy, bearing in mind that the governors want your class to watch this as well?'

'Far too difficult for my class – they won't have a clue.'

Hilda's arms were folded. 'Are the ice creams here yet?'

The second video was American and everything about it was irritating: the vacantly smiling actors, the whiny narrator, the script that somehow managed to avoid mentioning parts of the body altogether. We all gave it a resounding 'no'.

The third film centred on animals and had clearly been made on a shoestring budget in the early fifties and later transferred to tape. The posh, clipped tones of the voiceover had us giggling straight away and as 'Mr and Mrs Bunnyrabbit' appeared and started sniffing each other, we began to snort. When about fifty tiny baby bunnies abruptly materialised the jolly commentary gave no explanation of the matter and Joyce switched off the tape before the end.

'Awww, we'll never know what happens now,' laughed Emma.

'The Celia Johnson rabbit goes back home, I think,' said Hilda.

'At least it was in the context of a loving relationship,' said Val. 'On the other hand, I think he was just after her carrots.'

Even Joyce guffawed at this point and it was some time before we all calmed down enough to view the final offering.

'I need another cup of tea first,' I said.

'I need a fag and a lie down,' said Val.

Hilda got up to put the kettle on and pretended to look under the table. 'Mrs Sykes isn't in here making notes is she?'

After our short break, Joyce picked up the fourth cassette and looked at it. It was clearly much newer than the others. 'Well, this is the BBC one. It's just called *Sex Education*.'

'Well, let's hope it's better than the other cr—rubbish,' said Val.

The video was completely different. For a start it was a straightforward documentary-style film which showed a normal-looking British family at home: a mother, father and two young children. The script declared that it was going to reveal how people have children.

'Stopping them would be handy 'n' all,' said Hilda.

None of us was quite prepared for the next scene: bath time followed by bedtime. The first part was fine but when the two parents undressed and then walked towards the camera stark naked, even Hilda was dumbstruck. After this unequivocal clarification of the differences between the genders, the video then moved into a realistic animated sequence which showed the process of reproduction with clarity and a full explanation. Finally, we saw real footage of a baby being born. There was not a euphemism, prevarication or fluffy bunny in sight.

After fifteen minutes, the video ended and we all sat for a moment.

'What certificate was that?' said Hilda. 'Even I'm not old enough.'

Emma blew out her cheeks. 'Well, it's certainly the most educational; I learned a few things, anyway.'

Joyce stood up and opened the curtains. 'It didn't mess around, did it?'

'What will the parents think?' I said. 'Mind, they wanted something different.'

'I thought it was good,' announced Val. 'It told it straight and it's five hundred times better than the other ones. Even if that man did have a funny willy.'

Hilda made one last gag about her glasses steaming up and then we agreed to use the BBC version for Classes 3 and 4.

'In fact, let's show them the video this week, while we've got it on loan,' said Joyce. 'Then perhaps the governors will be able to move on.'

On Friday afternoon Nurse Michaelis was drafted in to show the film to my class along with Val's, and to answer any subsequent questions. It was agreed that the teachers should stay out of the hall, and Val and I were delighted to get a bonus 30 minutes of non-contact time in which to mark some books. We also thought it would be a good idea to let the children go out to play afterwards, thinking that there would be too much understandable chatter in the classrooms for any serious work to be achieved.

At two o'clock I walked on to the damp playground and waited for my class to come outside from the hall. The back of the school was eerily quiet and I surveyed the cold, brooding hills of Swinnerdale that hemmed in the village, each one shrouded in curtains of mist. A few sheep drifted about the field next door searching for sustenance among the faded grass.

I looked at my watch and wondered if there were lots of questions. How had Nurse Michaelis managed with the explicit film? Just then, the door from the school swung ajar and out streamed the junior children, most of them running to get a ball or find a friend. Some were laughing, some looked pale and most were talking excitedly. Last out of the door were Estelle and Cathy, locked in their usual tight nattering knot, their eyes wide as they came up the path, their voices more animated than ever.

Rather than heading out to the yard they headed straight for me. Estelle spoke first. 'Mr Seed, I can't believe people do *that*!'

Cathy looked me in the eye. 'And you told *us* not to be rude . . .'

Chapter Ten

Trudy

It started in early February, just before half-term. Vicky Rushworth returned to the classroom from a visit to the loo one Tuesday morning and instead of sitting back down in her place, came over to me.

'Mr Seed, there's stuff on t'ceiling in the girls' toilet.'

'Stuff? What do you mean?'

'I don't know wharrit is. It's white sort of lumps, like.'

'On the ceiling?'

As Vicky nodded, Martine – never one to overlook an opportunity to eavesdrop, especially during an exercise on adjectives – confirmed the story. 'She's right, Mr Seed, ah've sin 'em. Someone's been chuckin' screwed up bits of bog roll on t'ceiling.'

I frowned. 'Martine, please don't use that word – it's toilet paper. Anyway, how do you know it's that?'

'It is, yer can tell – they wet it, like, and it sticks.'

By now the whole class was listening. 'You said "they"; do you know who's doing this?' It was highly suspicious that she knew so much about it.

Martine shook her head. 'Could be someone from Class Four.'

I turned to the class and put on a serious voice. 'Does anyone know who's throwing wet toilet paper in the girls' toilets?'

There were a few whispers of 'euurrgghh', and several pairs of eyes involuntarily flicked over in Martine's direction but no one offered information.

'Right, well, I'll go and look for myself at break and we'll sort it out later; we've already wasted enough lesson time.'

Estelle put up her hand. 'Mr Seed, you can't go into the girls' toilets!'

'Don't worry, I'll send someone sensible in first to check it's empty.'

'Ooh, I'll do it,' said Gary, causing widespread rumpus and putting back Class 3's understanding of adjectives even further.

As the children filed out of the room for playtime I called Trudy Hammond over for a word. She was a willowy, athletic girl, one of the oldest members of the class and an individual I'd found to be reliable. She came from a respectable horsey family that rented fields and stables on the edge of Cragthwaite, and showjumping was the great passion of her life. I found her mother rather domineering but Trudy herself was an agreeable, cheerful character.

'Trudy, would you do me a favour and come and check that there's no one in the girls' toilet, so I can see what's been going on?' I said.

She nodded. 'I've not seen anything so it must have been done recently.'

'Right, and have you, er, heard anyone talking about it?'

'No.' As always, she sounded dependable.

We walked into the main building and through to the junior cloakroom which was, as usual, a jumble of coats, bags, PE kit strewn across the floor and an unpleasant-looking leak from somebody's lunch box. Trudy went into the toilets and re-emerged after a few seconds.

'All clear, Mr Seed; Vicky was right, too.'

I ventured into an alien domain and noticed two things straight away. One, there were no paper towels on the floor as there always were in the boys' and, two, the ceiling was peppered with small crusty lumps of white toilet tissue. Some of them appeared to be still damp.

I left the room quickly, thinking back to the dark days of the previous head, the dour, long-serving Howard Raven, when the children had to contend with the cold crinkly sheets that were universally referred to as 'tracing paper'. One of the first things that Joyce Berry had initiated as the new boss was to give the children the same lavatorial privileges as the staff. It appeared that this was now being abused – but by whom? That was the question.

Trudy Hammond was still there when I emerged. An idea came to me.

'Trudy, you're a very sensible, trustworthy girl so I wonder if I can rely on you to do something for me?'

'Yes, Mr Seed?'

'Martine seems to know an awful lot about this, so, in the classroom, next time she asks to go to the toilet, will you come over and ask me if you can go as well? Then, er, you can follow on half a minute later and, erm, see if you, well, notice anything. Do you understand?'

She nodded with a serious mien. 'OK, I'll try and notice when she asks.'

'Oh, yes, right,' I said. 'Don't worry about that – if necessary I'll, erm, let you know.' I glanced around the cloakroom, wondering if some furtive child was listening in on this clandestine deal. The coast seemed to be clear and I sent Trudy out to play, asking her not to tell anyone about our conversation.

After break, the children's concentration on their maths exercise was sporadic at best. I could detect a scatter of whispered dialogues across the room as the girls, in particular, discussed the Great Toilet Mystery. I'd noticed that every girl in the class had a desperate need to visit the loo at the end of break and no doubt they were all speculating on the culprit, having seen the evidence. Cathy and Estelle were in overdrive.

Since the level of work was feeble anyway, I decided to stop everyone and address the class about the toilet issue to appeal once more for information, having now been confronted by the extent of the crime. In many ways I found the showing of stern disapproval for this type of prank exceedingly difficult, having been no angel myself when at school. Being a responsible teacher now, I shuddered, thinking back to the excess of wayward stunts that I had instigated as a youngster, albeit mainly in the secondary phase: lobbing water bombs from high windows; rubber-bung wars in the chemistry labs; the placement of plastic doggy-doos in French and worse. But it needed to be done.

I clapped my hands together briskly. 'Right, Class Three, everyone stop there. Put your pens down, close your books and look this way.' Their rapid obedience signalled that I had set a sufficient tone of authority. 'I have seen the ceiling of the junior girls' toilet and it is a disgrace. Someone has been flicking wet tissue paper on to it and it's a mess. I just hope it isn't anyone from this class.' I scanned the room, attempting the kind of laser eye-contact that I'd seen Val Croker employ to draw out the truth from even the most recalcitrant offender.

It didn't work. Instead of the type of frightened stares I'd hoped for, the children's eyes revealed a continued amusement at the nature of this jape. Only Trudy looked serious, her expression acknowledging our secret understanding. I soldiered on anyway.

'Does anyone in this class know anything about who might have done this?'

They shook their heads slowly.

'Well, it must be *one* of the girls in the school.'

Gary put up his hand. 'It might be Mrs Rudds; she goes in there a lot.'

'Gary,' I screeched. 'I hardly think that the school caretaker is going to mess up the girls' toilet since she is the person who has to clean it each day!'

The force of my response to Gary's inanity shocked the children and for the last twenty minutes they worked quietly. Then, at five to twelve, Martine's large, dishevelled figure stood up and shuffled over to where I was helping Jason.

'Mr Seed, cannus go t'toilet?'

I very nearly said, 'Oh Martine, it's almost lunch break, can't you wait?' but I just managed to stop myself, glancing at Trudy as I did so. She had her head in her maths book, concentrating hard.

'Er, yes, all right, Martine. Off you go.'

I dropped Jason's exercise book, confusing him considerably, and sidestepped swiftly to Trudy's table, grabbing her book, much to her surprise.

'How are you getting on, Trudy?' I said, swinging my eyes towards the door where Martine was departing, and jabbing my head in a kind of Basil Fawlty style, a motion which the rest of her group plainly found disconcerting. She twigged just in time to see the chief suspect slipping outside. With great calmness she put up her hand and asked to go to the toilet.

I very nearly blew her cover, wanting to give her a big thumbs up and nod vigorously but appreciated that this might arouse unnecessary suspicion, and so I quietly said, 'Yes', before casually sauntering to the window to watch my top spy tail her target down the path.

The shrill midday bell rang before they returned and I sent the class out quickly, anxious to pick up my agent's intelligence about the mysterious Cragthwaite Dunny Chucker. Martine didn't return at all – did that signal guilt? – but a minute later Trudy skipped up the steps into the room, looking around her. She was clearly a pro.

'Well?' I said, exhibiting rather too much excitement.

Trudy took a deep breath. 'It's not her. Well, I didn't see her throw anything.'

I tried not to sound disappointed. 'Oh, well, er, did she act suspiciously in any way?'

'No, she just went to the loo.'

'Do you think perhaps she noticed you and that put her off doing anything, erm, else?'

'I don't think so, because I'm sure she didn't see me follow her down the path and I watched her go in then I waited outside the door listening. I heard her go in a cubicle so I stayed there until she came out and a few seconds after that I went in.'

Wow, she was good. 'Clever idea, that was very smart. But she wasn't holding any loo paper?'

'No, nothing.'

'OK, well, thanks for helping, Trudy. I'm glad that it doesn't seem to be Martine.' I tried to smile.

'Mr Seed, there *was* one thing I need to tell you.'

I leaned in. 'Yes?'

'She didn't wash her hands.'

* * *

After school, I went through to Val's room to let her know what was going on.

'They're doing *what*?' she said, looking as ever like she was desperate for a smoke.

'Wetting loo paper, scrunching it up and throwing it on to the ceiling. It sticks surprisingly well – I, er, tried it myself.'

'Daft buggers. Anyway, you've no idea who it is?'

'No, I had a suspicion but I've since changed my mind.'

'Right, well, my class will be grilled about it tomorrow. I'll sort it out.'

I knew that if ever there was someone to solve a mystery like this, it was the school's formidable deputy head. In the four years I'd been at the school I'd seen every type of child melt before the heat of her fiery temperament.

'Does Joyce know about this toilet business?' she added.

'Not as far as I know.'

'OK, well, we'll get to the bottom of it.'

I needed Hilda to do that one justice.

I went home earlier than usual that afternoon, having promised to help Barbara get Tom and Reuben ready for the pirate party they'd been invited to at four-year-old Billy Morphet's down the bottom of the village. We'd spent the previous weekend making costumes and creating props and it had been enormous fun. When I arrived, Barbara was struggling to get our rowdy younger son into a pair of torn trousers.

'I'd swear he gets larger by the hour this lump of toddler,' she said. 'Keep still, Reuben!'

Not wriggling was a foreign concept to him. 'Daddeee!' he called, seeking to be carried.

I took over the task, realising that we hadn't taken either his nappy or walloping pot belly into account when selecting the pants. Finally, I heaved them on and let him free for a cuddle.

'What else do we need?' I asked.

'Else do we nee!' said Reuben.

'Good boy,' I laughed.

'Well,' said Barbara looking around. 'Tom's got his costume on but he needs his parrot fixing to his shoulder – that's your job – and I still think that cutlass needs blunting more, and I don't know where the treasure chest is. Unfortunately Reubs here discovered my cache of choccy doubloons earlier and ate half of them.'

'Yeah,' said Tom, in a splendid Blackbeard costume, 'he should be Wide John Silver.'

We both laughed. 'That's very good!'

Reuben went into a grouch, however, realising that he was being teased.

'I need a hook too,' said Tom. 'And an earring and an eye patch.'

'Oh, right,' I said, disbelieving at how much we'd taken on at short notice. 'Anything else?'

'Yes, my telescope. And a beard.'

Twenty minutes later, after convincing Tom that a peg leg for Reuben might not be an ideal addition to the buccaneer garb, our two small sons were ready and they looked magnificent. The corrugated treasure chest, somewhat squashed when raided, had been located and next to it were two pint-sized scowling sea-dogs posing for photos.

Reuben wore a green headscarf and spotty neckerchief over an old T-shirt. His torn trousers looked very odd with wellies and he insisted on scything around with the foil-covered cardboard cutlass, which was now bent in four places.

Tom was resplendent in a wide, black skull-and-crossbones hat. He wore a huge DIY earring and his face was transformed by a stylish eye-liner beard and eye patch. His costume consisted of a chopped-down lacy white blouse, broad silk belt, black trousers and a huge pair of leather boots borrowed from Iris Falconer. In one hand was a comedy red eyeglass and in the other a hook fashioned from a coat-hanger. Our painted origami parrot, Cap'n Flint, had alas not made it, being the victim of Reuben's earlier cutlass-testing programme.

'Let's go!' shouted Tom, wiping his moustache on to his cheek with a white sleeve. We were only half an hour late.

It was dark outside and gusty. Tom's hat blew off straight away and Reuben went three steps before wailing that he was cold. Bloodthirsty adventurer or not, he would need to be carried most of the 700 yards. I picked him up and he dropped his sword. Tom couldn't walk in the big boots. We forgot the treasure chest and Billy's birthday present.

After recriminations about who had it, we were finally off. When we reached the pavement outside the shop I had to put Reuben down. Mrs Dent came rushing out.

'Well, look at you two. Little pirates! Yer look wonderful. Let me get me camera.' She dashed back inside and we heard her exhorting the three customers inside to go and see the miniature sea-dogs. Barbara used a tissue to try and rescue Tom's face. His beard had been washed away by a river of mucus and his eye patch was over his nose. Reuben turned to the fruit stall outside the shop and attacked a banana.

We finally got away when the boys' babysitter, Holly Weatherall, appeared outside Billy's house. The wonderful girl had offered to take care of them at the party and bring them back.

She threw back her head and laughed. 'Boys, you look amazing!' Tom held out his hook and Reuben growled.

'Are you sure you're OK to do this, Holly?' said Barbara. 'They're both quite overexcited.'

'They'll be fine,' she said, straining to pick up Reuben. 'Come on, Tom, let's go in – the party's started and there are lots of other pirates in there to meet.'

She opened the door of Billy Morphet's house, releasing a riotous hubbub into the Dales night. We turned and scurried home, anxious to make the most of two hours' peace and quiet.

At seven o'clock Barbara and I were lying against each other on a settee in front of a blissful wood fire in our stove. We'd enjoyed an excellent meal and a rare moment to catch up. My eyelids were already heavy when the front door handle clicked and a rush of noise burst into the house. It was over. We stood up and went into the hall where a haggard-looking Holly was grappling to remove Reuben's wellies while he sobbed and twisted. Tom had a new full-face beard of chocolate. Their costumes were in tatters.

'How did it go?' asked Barbara.

'You don't want to know,' said Holly, shaking her head. 'You honestly don't want to know.'

Pat Rudds wasn't happy. Come to think of it, I'd never seen her happy, but the morning after the pirate party, back at school, her mood was particularly dark and I didn't have to guess why.

'I shouldn't be going up ladders wi' my ankles, it's norron,' she said, dropping her galvanised bucket with a deliberate crash.

'Did you manage to get all of the paper off the ceiling, then?'

'Well, eventually, but it took me until nearly six o' flamin' clock.

I 'ad to scrape it off wi' a wooden ruler in the end – sticks like concrete that ruddy stuff.'

'I'm sorry, Pat. Val's going to make sure it doesn't happen again.'

'Well she better 'ad do, cos next time I aren't going up a stepladder.'

It didn't take Val long at all, and at morning break she marched into the staffroom with a satisfied grin.

'Jess Iveson and Yvonne Collier,' she said.

'I prefer Morecambe and Wise, meself,' said Hilda.

Val took no notice, but turned to me. 'Our perpetrators in the case of the flying toilet paper. They're outside the head's office now, awaiting sentence.'

'Really?' I said, astonished. 'How do you know?'

'One, they confessed, and two, they were seen doing it.'

'Case closed then,' said Emma, who had found the whole affair most amusing.

I raised my eyebrows and sighed. 'Well, I am glad that for once it wasn't my class.'

'How did you find out so quickly, Val?' asked Sue, passing round a tin of sorry-looking digestives.

'Oh, I have my means . . .'

Hilda tutted. 'Torturing children is illegal, Valerie. Well, apart from upper Wherndale where it's still encouraged.'

'Come on, Val, we want to know your secrets,' said Sue who, being a teaching assistant in the infants, had never ventured into Class 4.

'Yeah,' I added, just to be cheeky.

'Oh, all right,' said Val.

'Well?' said Emma.

'I shouted at the buggers.'

No more explanation was needed. We'd all felt the walls of Cragthwaite Primary shake in the past.

I went to search out Pat Rudds the next morning to reassure her that her ankles were safe and that the toilet mystery was solved. There had been no more flicked paper the previous day and Joyce had warned the whole school that if it happened again, girls or boys, there could be a return to the dreaded 'tracing paper'. That wouldn't stick to anything.

I also sought out Trudy Hammond in the playground at morning break.

'Yes, Mr Seed?' she said, looking slightly concerned that I might be sending her out on another hazardous mission.

'Don't worry, Trudy, I'm not going to ask you to, er, watch anyone or anything like that. We know who was responsible for the toilet ceiling mess now, so that's all over.' Her shoulders relaxed as I continued. 'I do want to ask you to keep quiet about Tuesday, though, when you followed Martine.'

'Oh, right.'

'I think it's very important that Martine doesn't find out that, erm, this happened. She could be quite upset, you understand?'

She nodded gravely.

'Good. I know I can trust you, Trudy: you're such a reliable, sensible girl. Thanks.'

She walked away and I returned to the classroom, safe in the knowledge that there would be no more fallout from the affair. I'd already had sufficient parent trouble this school year.

The rest of the week passed off quietly and by the following Monday the strange episode had almost been forgotten. I busied myself with the on-going battle to get eight- and nine-year-olds to remember their multiplication tables, to use commas and full stops in the right places and to understand the difference between 'allowed' and 'aloud'. At times the fight was dirty and brutal but I refused to be defeated by a load of kids.

Tuesday afternoon was a more serene affair. Everyone in the class was enjoying an art lesson based on the playful line patterns of Paul Klee. I barely noticed when Cathy asked to go to the toilet, simply nodding before returning to my admiration of Lisa's charming picture. Five minutes later I felt a tap on the shoulder. It was Cathy. She spoke almost in a whisper.

'Mr Seed, it's started again.'

'Pardon? What has, Cathy?'

'The paper on the girls' toilet ceiling.'

This time I didn't mess around but sent Cathy straight across to the main building to tell Val and Joyce. I thought about stopping the art lesson to challenge my class about it, too, but felt that it was more likely to be Class 4 again, although I found it hard to believe that Jess Iveson and Yvonne Collier, or indeed any of their classmates, would dare to cross the fearsome Miss Croker in such a fashion.

After school I went straight to her room. Joyce was there, too.

'Is it true?' I asked.

'I'm afraid so,' said Joyce. 'I checked myself. There are only three lumps of it but someone has clearly done it this afternoon.'

'It's not Yvonne and Jess, then?'

Val shook her head. 'I'm sure it isn't. I had a word with each one separately and I could see it in their faces. They actually looked quite surprised.'

'Any other suspects, then?' I said.

Joyce frowned. 'Not at the moment. Which girls from your class went to the toilet this afternoon, Andy?'

The question stumped me. 'Er, well, I don't think there's any way I can remember them all. Er, well, Cathy did, of course, but I can't believe she'd do this. Er, Pamela, I think . . . maybe Vicky and, erm, two or three others. I really can't remember.'

'Well, not to worry for now,' said Joyce. 'We'll get all the girls from Classes Three and Four in the hall tomorrow and I'll give them a proper rocket. We can't have this.'

'It could be a boy, of course,' said Val.

'Oh, you mean snuck into the girls' loos and just threw the stuff?' said Joyce.

I nodded. 'It's possible.'

Joyce sighed. 'Right, I'll have all of Classes Three and Four in the hall after assembly.' She turned and marched out looking decidedly frosty. Val ran a hand through her wiry ginger hair and raised her eyebrows.

'Well . . . I'm going out too – I need a cig.'

The mystery was back on.

Barbara and I talked about the cheekiness of children that evening and wondered whether our own boys were going to perpetrate such crimes when they reached school.

'You never know,' I said. 'Reuben's a bundle of mischief but he's still very little and basically he's a good boy. He just can't sort of stop himself.'

'Oh, he's a lovely boy really and so is Tom, despite the pirate debacle.'

'But what about this school toilet thing? You like crime fiction and whodunnits. How would Miss Marple solve this?'

Barbara smiled. 'I think if it was in an Edwardian boarding school catering for the sons of landed gentry she would have your villain, but Cragthwaite Primary School? Out of her league.'

We laughed and I wondered if the next day would bring any answers.

At twenty to nine the following morning the door of my sagging mobile classroom opened and in walked Trudy Hammond. She looked very serious. Perhaps she had some information about the case?

'Mr Seed, I know who did it.'

'You've seen someone or just heard about it?'

'I've seen them.'

I waited in suspense. 'Well, who?'

'It was me.'

I opened my mouth but no sound emerged. She continued.

'I did the toilet paper on the ceiling yesterday. I didn't do it before, though. That was Jess and Yvonne.' She looked up at me with big eyes for a moment, then cast them down in shame.

'But, Trudy, why did you do it?'

She hesitated. 'I don't know . . . Well, I do know.'

'I think you'd better tell me before Mrs Berry and Miss Croker ask you about it.'

She nodded and gulped. 'Well, I—I've never been in trouble. I just wanted to find out, well, what it was like to do something naughty.'

I could still barely take it in. 'Oh, right.'

'I've always been really good, at home and at school and . . .' Her words tailed off and she started to cry.

I don't know how it happened but somehow, ridiculously, having wasted valuable time, caused ire among the staff and made extra work for the cleaner by her actions, Trudy Hammond had gone up in my estimation.

Chapter Eleven

Ian

Some children take to academic work and some do not. There are those, usually the ones whose parents have encouraged them from an early age with talk and books and educational games, who learn to read quickly, enjoy letters and numbers and grasp the opportunity that writing gives to express themselves on paper. Then there are the strugglers, the uninterested and those of erratic disposition whose attention span is barely a blink.

Working in a country school in the Dales, I soon discovered that there were a lot of children in this second category. They were mainly boys, often the sons of farmers, who loved practical work and being outdoors but who found sitting behind a desk for several hours each day, confronted with paper and pen exercises, to be a mean slog – a sentence to be served until they were released into the world of fields and beasts and engines and stone walls: the things they understood.

Occasionally there were children whose interest in numbers and words was curbed for different reasons: they were not so much lacking in brainpower or even equipped with a practical nature; instead, they were destined for other things. Ian Tattershall was one of these.

I'd first become acquainted with Ian when he'd joined the class the previous year. He was unobtrusive in the classroom, a lean, fair-haired boy who got on with everything quietly and stayed close to his friends. Yet it soon became apparent that Ian was exceptional.

I could recall the moment clearly, in September of the previous year, when a dry, warm spell had given an opportunity for some outdoor team games on the field during PE. After a brief throwing and catching practice I'd organised a game of rounders, and Estelle was batting. She hit the ball quite well and ran to second base. Jason Fisher, a capable player, stepped up next and gave the ball a mighty crack, sending it high into the air. His team gave a roar as he set off sprinting for what appeared to be an easy rounder. But my eyes were not on Jason, nor even the ball, but on a blur in the outfield – the shape of a boy scorching across the grass to take an incredible one-handed catch.

'Whaaat!' cried Jason, hurling his bat down in disgust. But, again, no one was watching him because Ian Tattershall had not stopped running. He plucked the ball from the air without breaking his stride then bulleted on to the pitch, like a peregrine falcon in for the kill, glancing it against fourth base before a dumbfounded Estelle, travelling at full pace, reached the post.

'Two out!' he declared, leaping with triumph. I stood with my mouth open, then joined in the clapping. I'd never seen anything like it.

It soon became apparent that he was good at all sports. In cricket his rocket-powered bowling gave no batter a hope; in hockey nobody could get near him; and he was unbeatable at all forms of athletics. His speed and coordination were mesmeric and most of the class, if landed on the opposite team to Ian, simply gave up before starting.

Yet Ian wasn't interested in these games. Nor tennis, nor rugby, nor basketball, nor gymnastics, nor any of the other sports at which he was accomplished, because Ian had one love and one love only: football. He talked about the game all the time and played at every opportunity, whether at playtimes, after school or weekends. Ian lived near Cragthwaite Primary and when I drove home in the evening I would invariably see him, along with his two younger brothers, blasting a ball into a home-made goal in their small back garden.

Ian was also captain of Ingleburn's Under-10 team and played for the Cubs in West Doddthorpe. I wasted no time in putting him in our school team, even though he was younger than the boys from Class 4 who usually made up the eight players we used for matches.

As always, our problem was finding opposition: there was no organised school league in this rural area and so we ended up playing mainly tiny village schools, most of whom travelled to us because they didn't possess a pitch. Ian would frequently score six or seven goals against these minnows and I sometimes had to substitute him to save our opponents the ignominy of a double-figure defeat. Even against our deadly rivals from up the dale, Kettleby Primary, he was simply unstoppable, dancing around the lumbering farm lads to notch a first-half hat trick in a 6–1 win. He could even score from free kicks and bullet headers, something I'd never before seen from a player so young.

'Can we play Ingleburn Juniors next, Mr Seed?' asked Ian, coming over after the last victory. 'I know some o' their players. They'll give us a really 'ard match.'

'Well, maybe,' I said, thinking back to the one previous encounter I'd arranged against this much larger school. They'd insisted on playing eleven-a-side on their big, sloping field, and my poor team at the time had been simply overwhelmed, going down 12–0. Perhaps this time, with Ian, we'd give them a decent game but I was still short of other players.

'There is a problem, Ian. We've only got nine players who are really good enough and interested, but Ingleburn will only play us if we have eleven.'

'My brothers'll play, Mr Seed. They're good – better than some o' the lads in Class Four.'

'But Scott's only seven and Robbie's still in the infants. The Ingleburn boys will all be ten or eleven.'

'Oh, go on, Mr Seed. It'll be good – it dun't matter if we lose.'

The following day I made a special point of watching the boys play football while I was on playground duty. It was a dank February morning, with the muddy field out of bounds and so the school's quad of tarmac was crowded with children. One half was taken up with huddles of girls, some playing clapping games, others chasing around with the little ones, while the far side, as always, was the domain of the footballers.

About thirty boys, crammed together and sweating in their jumpers and long trousers, mobbed after a half-flat plastic ball, shouting and rushing, most barely receiving a touch. Ian stood in one of the goals by a tacit agreement that it was simply unfair to have him as an outfield player. As I expected, he was an outstanding goalkeeper and rarely did anything find a way past him. He had the ball in his hands as I watched, darting a quick throw to his brother Scott, almost a clone of his elder sibling. Scott controlled the ball on his instep, swivelled and dinked a pass inside to a team-mate who hoofed it upfield. Scott ran on and demanded a cross.

It came via a deflection but he adjusted his body athletically and scythed a volley towards the goal. The keeper never moved as it flew past him.

'Wow,' I said to myself, looking out for the third Tattershall, Robbie. He was a lot skinnier and smaller than his brothers, and consequently was knocked off the ball by older boys with some ease, and yet I saw something in his spirit: he was a fighter and, even if his control wasn't anything like that of the two older boys, he still helped to dominate the little game, playing accurate passes, tackling decisively, running into space, telling others what to do and never tiring. These boys were born footballers. I decided there and then to phone Ingleburn Primary.

Doug and Rosie Burns had now been in Applesett for six weeks and were working every waking hour on their house. As ever with old dwellings, a season of renovation had uncovered all sorts of unexpected problems, ranging from damp and rotten wood to uneven walls, which made adding tiles and fitting cupboards a trial. They also discovered that their new home was not fully uninhabited when they moved in; just as we had learned, the resident mice held on to their rodent squatters' rights with fierce determination. One Saturday morning, Rosie came round to seek our advice.

'They're everywhere: in the living room, kitchen, bedrooms. None of the floorboards or skirting boards fit tightly and I think they're just coming up from underneath,' she said, running a hand wearily over her paint-speckled face.

'We had the same problem when we moved in here,' I said. 'They ate most of my notes from university.'

'So how did you get rid of them?'

Barbara intervened. 'Don't ask him, whatever you do. He nearly burned the house down trying, didn't you dearest?'

Rosie appeared to think it was a joke and carried on looking serious. 'So how do you get rid of mice in a place like this?'

'Lots of poison, traps and get a cat. Then block off all the holes,' I said, trying to sound authoritative.

'Ugh! I couldn't poison a living creature – that's cruel. And I don't want to kill them anyway. We just want to get them out of the house.'

'Hmmm, you've got a problem there,' said Barbara. 'I was a bit like that at first but they are such a destructive pest and they're so unhygienic. We resorted to chemicals and Tom and Jerry traps, I'm afraid.'

'I just don't think I can bring myself to kill an animal like that.'

'You're going to have to get used to dead beasties in the Dales, Rosie. It's part of life here,' I said. 'We all hit pheasants accidentally in our cars, then there are myxi rabbits everywhere, dead sheep on the hills and farmers shooting crows or catching moles.'

'Oh, I know, I've seen their poor little bodies hung out on barbed wire – it's barbaric,' said Rosie, cringing.

'Wait till you meet the hunting brigade,' said Barbara. 'You'll love them . . .'

'So, anyway,' I said. 'What have you tried with the mice?'

'Doug went into town a few days ago and bought four of those humane traps but so far we've only caught one. I let it go down by the river. But we've got to do something – there are piles of droppings everywhere and they've nibbled into our food and even through some electrical cable.'

'You could try a stick and box trap,' I said.

'Uh-oh, sounds like one of your crackpot schemes,' said Barbara shaking her head.

'What is it?' asked Rosie.

I reached for some paper and a pencil. 'You know, one of those jobs where you prop up a box on the floor using a stick with string attached to it.' I sketched the simple device and Rosie twisted her mouth doubtfully.

Barbara simply laughed. 'Don't be daft, Andy. For a start it'll never work and secondly, they'd need to wait for hours watching each time – if there are lots of mice they'll breed faster than you can catch them. Silly boy . . .'

I was a little hurt by this dismissal, even if there was some logic in the argument. 'But they do work,' I said. 'I got the idea from Sam Burnsall who used it when he was a kid.'

'Is that the ancient flat-capped gent who lives next door to us?' asked Rosie.

I nodded. 'I talked to him in the pub once about what the village was like when he was young. He was born in the 1890s, you know.'

'Oh wow, I used to be involved in an oral history project in York,' said Rosie. 'What did he tell you?'

'Oh, all sorts. There were no cars, of course, and there used to be a sheep fair on the green here and the waterfall froze once. But the thing that really sticks in my mind was that he was always hungry as a lad so a group of them used to go round catching anything they could eat. He caught spuggies with a box and stick trap, he said.'

Rosie looked bemused '*Spuggies?*'

'Sparrows.'

Barbara laughed again. 'Oh yes, you told me this – they roasted them over a little fire.'

Rosie stuck out her tongue. 'Euurrgghh, gross.'

'Anyway,' I said. 'I bet you a pint of beer I can catch a mouse like that. Promise I won't bake it, though.'

'Come on,' said Barbara. 'Let's take him on.'

I wasted no time that afternoon, heading into my den in the garage to find a suitable box and to rig it up with a piece of kindling and string. As always, Tom and Reuben wanted to help, so I assisted them in making their own mini-traps too. Reuben insisted that his string should be tied to the box so that he could drag his teddy along but Tom's version worked well and so did the larger one that I constructed. A quick tug on the string pulled away the stick propping up the box, which came down rapidly. It was simple and foolproof.

That evening, with Holly Weatherall installed at Craven Bottoms, Barbara and I walked up the village to Doug and Rosie's house carrying the trap.

'This is going to be a fun night out,' said Barbara with more than a hint of sarcasm. 'I can't believe we've paid for a babysitter so that we can stare at a box.'

'Oh ye of little faith,' I said. 'The main thing is, is there enough money for my pint?'

'You don't seriously think it's going to work, do you?'

'Yes. Maybe.'

We knocked on the door and walked into a scene of disarray. Doug and Rosie's kitchen was much as we'd left it on the day they moved in, except that there were open boxes everywhere and crockery, pans and packets of food strewn about. There seemed to be an extraordinary number of greasy jars containing strange beans and pulses. Unwashed dishes abounded.

'Welcome to the Somme,' said Doug, kicking aside a sack of wholemeal flour so that we could walk through to the living room.

This at least was in some kind of order, even if they were half-way through painting it. There was a long black Chesterfield sofa in the centre and Rosie quickly emptied it of newspapers and yoghurt pots.

'Cup of tea?' she said. 'I've got some nice herbal stuff somewhere or this amazing Cambodian infusion that's supposed to cleanse the blood.'

'Erm, no thanks,' I said.

Barbara held up a hand. 'I've just had one, ta.'

'I see you've brought your contraption,' said Doug. 'It's not at the cutting edge of technological innovation, is it? A box, a stick and some string.'

'Are you joining the scoffers?' I said.

'I never pooh-pooh at this time of night.'

Barbara intervened. 'We'd better set it up, anyway, since it's going to take several days to work.'

'What's the best bait?' said Rosie.

We all agreed, having been brought up in the golden era of cartoons, that cheese was the only suitable lure, and so Doug disappeared and clattered around in the kitchen before eventually producing a disreputable-looking lump of Double Gloucester.

'Where do you want the trap set up?' I asked.

Rosie looked around. 'Well, we all need somewhere to hide . . . er, probably in here – we can all crouch behind the settee.'

I walked to the back of the room and noticed trails of small unmistakable droppings on the dust sheets by the wall. I cleared a space, placed the cheese on the floor and carefully set up the box to a chorus of sniggers and wisecracks from the sofa.

'The mice are probably watching this and killing themselves.'

'Does it do rats too?'

'The mice in here are bigger than that box.'

I finally arranged the stick and string satisfactorily, then crept back to the couch, telling the rowdy spectators to shut up.

'It'll never work if we're noisy,' I said, draping the string over the sofa.

'It'll never work in fifty years,' hissed Barbara, crouching down. We all did the same, kneeling on the cushions and peeking back to the box.

'Hang on,' said Rosie, and she switched off the main light, allowing just a muted glow to enter from the open door to the kitchen. 'That's better.'

'Come on meece,' whispered Doug. 'Mickey, Jerry, Mighty – nothing to fear.'

'Cork it,' I muttered. 'That box would be full by now if you were quiet.'

We laughed again and then managed a whole minute before more jokes and remarks. Barbara started running fingers along my back when I thought I saw a movement in the gloom of the corner by the window.

'Wait. I think it's a mouse.'

'Really?'

'It's the mouse of desperation,' hissed Doug.

'No, I can see it!' said Rosie, pointing. And there it was, up on its back legs sniffing the air before moving warily. At first it scuttled away from the trap, bringing groans from the crouching stalkers, before reassessing the source of the curious odour and scampering rapidly across towards the cheese.

'Bloody Norah,' said Doug. 'It's falling for it.'

We all watched, amazed, giggling like three-year-olds as the small, nut-brown rodent scurried under the box and on to the bait. I yanked the string and the box dropped with a clatter. Did we have it? None of us saw an escape. I ran round and put my ear to the cardboard. There was the unmistakable sound of a panicking mouse.

'I do not believe it,' said Barbara. 'I simply do not believe it.'

I stood up, smiled and looked at my watch. 'About fifteen minutes. Not bad. Shall we head for the pub now?'

Doug slid a sheet of card under the box and we deposited the quaking mouse near the beck at the bottom of the village before walking to The Crown where, with much ceremony, I was awarded my triumphal pint. I refused to let a welter of teasing from the darts team detract from my moment of glory, nor the fact that the trap never worked again.

Ingleburn Junior School was a square brick building on the edge of the market town which stood at the gateway to Swinnerdale. I parked my car and unloaded the quartet of apprehensive young footballers each ready-changed in a faded yellow kit of the cheapest polyester.

'It's a big school,' said Jason Fisher who I'd selected as a replacement for an absent Class 4 boy.

'It's big for Swinnerdale, yes, but the children are the same size,' I said, trying to sound reassuring. Just ahead in the car park I saw Wendy Tattershall with her three sons who were peering across to watch Ingleburn's team warming up on their pitch.

'They're massive!' said Scott.

Two more parents' cars arrived from Cragthwaite with the rest of our side and I gathered the shivering boys together after greeting the opposition's teacher and coach, the affable Eric Brown.

'Remember, lads, this is eleven-a-side, not eight, so stick to your new positions. That does not mean that the defenders just stand at the back like statues, though. Keep your passing simple, don't try and just boot it, and, well, just do your best.'

Little Robbie put up a hand. 'Shu'n't we just give to Ian?'

'Well, that might not always be possible, and I want everyone to have a touch and be involved in the game anyway.'

Eric blew his ref's whistle and the Cragthwaite boys turned and jogged across the pitch to their positions. I heard Victor Wood from Class 4 clap his hands and shout, 'Right, come on, lads – just pass it to Ian.'

A numbing wind blew across from the west and my team's players looked tiny as they spread out across the large sloping pitch. I pulled my coat a little tighter. At least the boys would warm up once they were running round.

Ingleburn's players knocked the ball about stylishly. They had been well coached and they understood the value of keeping possession. My boys, on the other hand, just weren't used to this. All our matches, even against Kettleby, were kick and rush affairs, with a brainless swarm always chasing the ball with no understanding of the value of space. Ingleburn, on the other hand, were spread out and calm, calling names, pointing and telling each other what to do.

For three minutes we couldn't get a touch and I feared for a repeat of the previous drubbing. At least they hadn't scored: Ian Tattershall had dropped back and was flying about, blocking any attempts at a shot. Then one of the opposition's midfielders played a loose pass back to a defender. Ian saw a chance and surged forward. The Ingleburn boy looked certain to reach the ball first but Ian knew what to do and launched himself into the air at speed before slicing through the slimy pitch surface like a beached torpedo and scooping the ball away from his opponent with a seven-yard sliding tackle which threw up flecks of grass and earth. His momentum upended the other boy spectacularly but the ball had been won first and the referee held back his whistle.

'Go Tatts!' screamed a Cragthwaite voice as Ian flipped up on to his feet in a rapid movement and stormed down the wing towards the Ingleburn goal. His back and side were coated with a great smear of mud and I heard a parent mutter, 'Glad he's not comin' back in ma car.'

Ian's break produced panic in the Ingleburn defence. The opposition knew only too well what he could do and four boys immediately surged around him. He looked up and nonchalantly flicked the ball over them and into the path of his brother Scott who, calmly running forward, poked the ball ahead into space. I thought he'd made a mistake at first as no one was there but then Ian, with astonishing pace, exploded through the crowd of markers, charged on to the ball and with a first-time shot cannoned it into the top corner of the goal from fifteen yards.

The Cragthwaite parents arranged along the touchline joined me in leaping and cheering, while Ian's team-mates mobbed him like puppies.

'What a goal,' I heard one of the Ingleburn dads say. 'That lad is something special.'

From that moment on, Ingleburn lost their composure and started to argue among themselves, blaming each other for allowing Ian through on goal. Their slick passing of earlier disintegrated and my team's confidence grew. Every time Ian touched the ball there was alarm in the home side and sometimes as many as five or six opponents closed in on him. Rather than trying to beat them all, Ian wisely played smart passes into the spaces that opened up, allowing Cragthwaite to keep the ball. Little Robbie ran round making remarkable tackles while Scott marshalled the defence like a veteran general. I just stood there and watched in awe with a stupid grin on my face.

The game remained 1–0 until two minutes from the end when Ian slalomed round three defenders and won a corner. Victor swept the ball across from the flag into the box and Ian sprang upwards, as if trampoline-powered, and nodded in a deft header. That was it. The whistle went and Cragthwaite's players gambolled and punched the air before once more crowding around their hero.

Eric Brown strode over to me and hid his disappointment cheerily. 'Well played, Andy. Your lads deserved it. We knew that we couldn't give Ian any clear chances but the lad's just too good; he's brilliant.'

'Well, it was a bit better than losing twelve–nil.'

'I tell you, with those three Tattershall lads you've got a chance against anybody. Are you entering the Bilthorpe five-a-side competition?'

'Erm, actually, I'd forgotten all about that. When is it?'

'Two weeks on Saturday. We're going but you should get a team in, for sure.'

I thanked him and walked back to gather together my team. On the way to the car I heard yet more local parents talking about Ian.

'Ah've 'eard thes a scout comin' ovver from Leeds 'n' that to see 'im play fer Under Tens.'

'Aye, he could go far that youth.'

Bilthorpe was the nearest large town to Swinnerdale and a fifty-minute journey from Cragthwaite. It stood on low, flat land in the Vale of York and boasted all of the facilities that were unavailable in the Dales, from a hospital and supermarket to a sports centre and bookshop. The local college hosted the annual primary schools' five-a-side tournament involving over twenty schools from a wide area and as we stood and looked across the vast playing area we couldn't believe the scale of the event.

Wendy Tattershall had once more brought her three talented sons, while I'd brought the three best players from Class 4: Oliver, Victor and Lee. It had been a difficult decision to select the two young brothers of Ian ahead of some of the older boys but they had played so astonishingly well in the match against Ingleburn that I simply couldn't leave them out. While the six lads warmed up I used the opportunity to talk to the stocky Mrs Tattershall, one of those rare people who always appeared to be cheerful, whatever the circumstances.

'I thought your husband might be here today,' I said.

'Well, he'd love ter be but he works until one. Might be down later if we're not back.'

'I heard someone saying that scouts might be coming to watch Ian.'

'Aye, when he plays fer Ingleburn lads' team. There 'as been a fella or two watchin' 'im, aye.'

'Wow, how exciting – you must be a proud mum.'

'Oh aye. Well, they're football mad these three. It's all they ever talk about and do. Just as well they're good at it.'

I pondered this for a moment. 'I find it quite hard to get Ian to concentrate on his school work sometimes because he's always talking about football. Er, do you worry that he might put so much time and energy into the game that he, well, might neglect other things in his life?'

'Oh, I aren't worried about that, Mr Seed. I know he's not one of the smartest in the class but he's 'appy doing his sport and he's determined to mek it to the top.'

'You mean become a professional one day?'

'Oh aye, he talks about it all the time. Man United he wants.'

'Well, might as well aim high . . . It's good to have an ambition in life.' I said the words but underneath I wondered whether such an outlook could only lead to disappointment.

In the distance a tinny squawk from a loudspeaker mentioned Cragthwaite and our boys came rushing over excitedly to find out which pitch they were on. I looked at my piece of paper, which indicated that our first game was against Hemford Primary. At least it was another village team and not one of the big schools.

Our five enthusiastic lads lined up with Scott and Ian over the ball, and Lee as substitute. The playing surface was tight with small, low goals. On the other side of the pitch the Hemford boys looked nervous.

The whistle blew and Mrs Tattershall bawled encouragement. Scott touched the ball to Ian who shimmied one way then flicked the ball past the first approaching opponent. A second followed swiftly but our star man was already gaining momentum and cheekily pipped the ball between the lad's legs before jinking past the last two outfield players with ease. The burly goalkeeper came out to close him down and Ian pulled back his leg as if to unleash a rocket. The goalie ducked, instinctively covering his face and Ian deftly chipped the ball over him into the net. One–nil and we'd been playing for seven seconds.

The match only lasted fifteen minutes and we won 8–2, with Ian scoring five. I felt sorry for the opposition who gave their everything but had no answer to Ian's pace and skill. Twice he dribbled round the entire team and by the end of the match he was sensibly taking it easy.

Word soon got around the tournament that Cragthwaite were

good and their blond lad up front was special. For our second match, against Hauxton Park Primary, quite a crowd of spectators had gathered. This was a much larger school and our opponents this time included a couple of bruisers: tall, hefty lads with the clear intention of intimidating the other side. They obviously knew all about Ian and straight from the off the two big boys tried to kick him into submission, surprisingly egged on by their teacher, an aggressive bearded man by the name of Gough.

Little Robbie had a tough time, in particular, being half the size of some of the Hauxton players and yet several times his football brain allowed him to get the better of them by anticipating passes or using his ability to turn and twist in tight spaces. Once more Scott Tattershall, too, showed that he wasn't too far behind his elder brother: he wasn't as fast or skilful but his reading of the game and courage were immense.

At half-time it was 0–0 and Ian came off red in the face, wanting to complain to the referee. Robbie too was almost shouting with rage at their tactics.

'Just calm down,' I said. 'We only have one minute. Have a drink and rest. Listen, Ian – I've had an idea. I want you to drop back and swap with Oliver. Oliver, you go up front and keep those big lads occupied – run around and draw them out of position. Ian, if you get hold of the ball at the back you'll have more time to pick up speed and you'll be facing the right way so you can see who's coming.'

'Good idea,' said Scott. Ian looked a little doubtful but nodded. I let Lee come on for Robbie who looked desperately disappointed.

With four minutes to go, one of Hauxton's players took a long shot which Victor, our keeper, caught easily. He rolled the ball quickly to Ian who was immediately faced by an opponent. Ian exchanged passes with Scott and he was away. He danced past the first midfielder and just had the two big lads left. He played to stop and the first boy made a lunge for the ball. Ian flicked it over his foot and simply swayed past the last defender who fell on his bottom as Ian ripped a left foot drive into the bottom corner of the goal.

'Yesss!' screamed Mrs T, who felt that justice had been done. The game finished 1–0.

The next three games were comfortable victories and, before we knew it, Cragthwaite Primary was in the final. The opponents were Bilthorpe Juniors, the local favourites who had huge support. My boys were now tremendously excited and convinced that they were going to win. Ian had scored twelve goals already.

'Same formation, Mr Seed?' he said, jogging on the spot to stay loose.

'Yes, but drop deep if you're marked too tightly.'

'Do you think we can beat them, Mr Seed?' asked Scott.

'Of course I do,' I said, patting him on the back. I was nearly as excited as they were.

I zipped up my jacket, feeling for the first time a sharp breeze that had been absent earlier. The announcer called the players on to the pitch and the spectators lined right around the edge cheered and clapped eagerly.

We kicked off again and I saw Ian look up just before Scott tapped the ball to him. Taking everyone by surprise he launched a shot from the half-way line. Bilthorpe's goalkeeper, who had strayed a few yards forward, peddled back furiously but could only watch as the ball sailed over his grasping arms. It pinged against the crossbar and dropped behind the goal as the crowd gave a deep gasp. Only Ian could have attempted something so spectacular in the final.

The game then fell into a pattern. Our opponents had done their homework on our best player and effected a massed defence, all five boys holding back and blocking the route to goal. Ian saw plenty of the ball but there was no way through so many bodies in a tight space and nor was there any opportunity to use his blistering speed. What's more, from time to time Bilthorpe launched a dangerous counter attack, catching our team all forward. On the third occasion this happened they scored and the chilly home crowd erupted.

'Plan B, boys!' I called and Scott nodded before going over to tell his older brother.

'Good idea, Mr Seed,' said Mrs T. 'Ian's getting frustrated.'

I was aware of another frustrated figure too, as little Robbie Tattershall hopped about on the touchline, desperate to be involved again. I thought about bringing him back on but he was just so young.

The pattern of the match changed again with our tactical switch and Ian picked up the ball from defence and started running at Bilthorpe. Sometimes he beat two and occasionally three but he just couldn't make it past the fourth to face goal. Time was now running out and to make matters worse, Oliver went down with cramp. He tried limping on but it was no use.

'You're on, Robbie,' I said and he ripped his tracksuit top off and burst on to the pitch as poor Oliver limped off. 'Come back!' I yelled into the wind. 'I need to tell you where to play!' Laughter abounded from the Bilthorpe parents and some stared in disbelief that we were bringing on someone so young.

Robbie's sheer enthusiasm made an immediate impact and with two minutes to go he found a big space on the left and called for the ball, which Scott then fed him. Two Bilthorpe players hounded over to block his route to goal and this opened up a channel for Ian. He scorched through from the back and Robbie scooped the ball into his path. Ian took it on his chest and slid it past the next defender. He was now through on goal but the last Bilthorpe outfield player was closing in fast and their huge keeper was also rushing out to close the angle. A collision appeared unavoidable but somehow Ian found one last superhuman surge and flicked the ball up high so that it missed both players who crunched together painfully. Ian himself hurdled the mêlée and watched the ball bounce slowly towards the open goal. As it reached the line he turned and whooped, jumping in the air. Our other players mobbed him, with a joyous Robbie climbing on to his back.

'Look! What's going on?' said Mrs T pointing to the goal.

I had been so busy celebrating and watching our boys do the same that I hadn't noticed that the game had restarted. The Bilthorpe keeper had recovered and had the ball in his arms. He rolled it out to a defender.

'What's happening?' I shouted. 'It should be a kick off!'

Our players turned too and pointed, then Ian ran over to the ref. I couldn't see what was said but saw the thin, angular man cross his arms as if to signal no goal. Robbie and Victor rushed over to him to protest while Scott chopped down the boy who had the ball with an ugly tackle. I ran around to hear what was being said while the referee blew on his whistle.

'It was a goal!' called Ian. 'I didn't foul anybody.'

The ref shook his head. 'The ball didn't cross the line.'

'That's not fair, we scored!' It was Robbie, his eyes wide, unable to control his outrage at such a perceived injustice.

'But surely it was a goal?' I appealed to the linesman.

'Sorry, the wind blew the ball back before it crossed the line.'

Robbie stamped and twisted round. 'We scored a goal. You've cheated us!'

The referee's face twisted and he pulled out a yellow card. 'I will not be spoken to like that. Any more and you're off!'

Scott pulled his little brother away and Ian reluctantly withdrew after one last protest. I saw tears falling from Robbie's cheeks.

Bilthorpe had a free kick and they kept possession for the last few seconds before a shrill blast of the whistle killed off our hopes and brought a tumult of roars from the home crowd. My five boys stopped and stared. They then trudged slowly off the pitch, their faces disconsolate.

The journey back was long and quiet. Even Ian's 'Player of the Tournament' medal brought no consolation. The six young footballers of Cragthwaite had been utterly convinced that the big trophy was theirs and they felt that their heroic efforts counted for nothing.

Fifteen years later, this day would be all but forgotten. For Ian Tattershall stepped on to another, larger pitch in front of a crowd of twenty thousand: his debut as a professional footballer. And, remarkably, a few years later Scott followed, making the League himself, before little Robbie, now a strapping six foot three, also walked out in a grand stadium. Both Ian and Robbie played in the top division but for the younger man, who had cried as an infant when his hero brother's goal had been disallowed, an even greater honour awaited and a little corner of Yorkshire would always remember the day when, with great pride, he pulled on an England shirt.

Chapter Twelve

Howard

Every primary school in the land takes on a task each year that is repetitive, wearisome and seemingly never-ending: the teaching of multiplication tables, or simply 'tables' as we called them. For us, the process began in the infants and was, hopefully, completed at the top of the school, but as the teacher of lower junior children most of the burden fell on me.

Over the few years that I'd been in the classroom I'd tried various strategies to help Cragthwaite's next generation learn the 100 maths facts that the government had recently dictated were essential. Class 3 had chanted, written them out, taken them home to learn, played number games, done tests and challenges. At one point I'd even tried a cassette which put the tables to music. Some of the children liked it but it made me nauseous.

I was determined to find a better way to help children retain their learning and I found one following a stroke of luck. A special needs adviser had given me a simple card game for Ricky Dawber, when he'd been in the class, to help him learn some key words for reading. There were ten words written on small cards which were spread out face down and mixed around. The adult turned over a random card and Ricky attempted to read the word. If he was correct, he kept it and if he was wrong, the card stayed with the grown up. At the end, the process was repeated with the adult's cards until Ricky had all ten. The cards were used on several successive occasions until Ricky got all ten first time for three days in a row.

It occurred to me that we could use this system for times tables. I took home a pile of card, a marker pen and a paper trimmer one weekend and set about making hundreds of small cards each with a simple multiplication: 3 x 4, 9 x 6, and so on. There were multiple sets of cards for every number from two to ten, each colour coded and held together with rubber bands. The children started with the 2x cards and played the game in pairs; when they were certain they'd learned their twos they came to me for a test. If I was sure they knew them thoroughly I marked this on a wall chart and gave them the 3x cards.

The system had been going for several weeks by early March and the class used the cards each day. The natural mathematicians had reached the nines while those for whom numbers were evil foes still dawdled on their threes and fours. The majority of the class, however, were battling on the sixes, sevens and eights, with the result that these sets of cards were running out.

Estelle Wood stood at my desk, with Howard Sedgwick behind her. She was jiggling slightly.

'Mr Seed, I really, really do know my sevens now, honest – please can I have another test?'

I looked her in the eye. She had been close last time, I had to admit. 'OK, Estelle, give me the cards, then.'

'Oh thanks, Mr Seed, you're the best.' I knew she was only saying this because her competitive nature demanded that she didn't fall behind Cathy in the chart.

On my desk I shuffled the small purple cards, now dog-eared, and inwardly groaned that I'd have to spend hours making yet more, despite having covered the last batch with sticky-back plastic à la *Blue Peter*. I turned one over at random. It was 8 x 7.

'Right,' said Estelle, her fingers spread with tension. 'I know this. It's fifty . . . six!'

'Hmmm, you're supposed to just come straight out with it if you've learned them properly, Estelle.'

'I have, I have, really – please carry on.'

I noticed the big, phlegmatic Howard glance at his watch. I turned over another card. It was 1 x 7. Estelle answered this and the rest without hesitating and I had to give her a 'pass'. She punched the air as I put my thumbs up.

'Can I have a set of eights now?'

'Yes, if we have any.' I reached for the sectioned wooden tray but there were no green 8x cards left. I flipped through the other piles in the box just to check.

'Sorry, Estelle, they're all being used. You'll have to wait until someone's finished.'

'That's not fair; Cathy's going to overtake me now. There must be some eights I can use.'

'Nope, I checked.'

Howard leaned forward and looked into the box. 'Just gi' 'er two fours.'

I smiled then laughed, shaking my head. It was typical of this big, bluff boy's wit. 'Howard, I have to say that was very funny.'

'Good, can I 'ave ma go now?'

Estelle, however, refused to budge easily and made another desperate appeal. 'Can I go on to nines, then, Mr Seed? There's some of them in the tray.'

'No, you have to do them in order, that's how it works.'

'Oh, go on – I won't tell anyone.'

'Estelle, no. You'll just have to wait for some eights to be returned.'

'But I can't wait.'

'It's Howard's turn now. Stop making a fuss and go back to your place and read.'

She stomped off, muttering, and Howard came forward, holding out a set of 5x cards in his chunky, oil-stained fingers.

'I don't like fuss neither, Mr Seed.'

I smiled at him again. He was an archetypal no-nonsense Yorkshireman in the making, all right. But he was also dependable and immensely practical. Standing tall and woolly haired, he waited for me to arrange the cards. A minute later he was done and walking away with a set of sixes.

Val, Hilda, Emma and I sat in the staffroom waiting for Joyce to begin another staff meeting. She was often late, delayed by the phone or a parent wanting a word.

'Were we supposed to prepare anything, because I haven't,' said Hilda.

'Probably,' grumbled Val, blowing on her pint pot of coffee.

'No doubt there'll be seven or eight new initiatives from the Education Department to put into place,' said Emma, who appeared to be gradually taking on the two senior teachers' bearing of cynicism and grouchiness.

Hilda folded her arms. 'Oh aye, because we're always short of things to do, aren't we?'

'Anyway,' I said. 'I want to complain about something else.'

'Ooh what?' said Hilda. 'Are we going to have some fireworks with the head?'

'It's assemblies,' I continued.

'Oh, well, I know Miss Croker's talks can be a touch tedious but I don't think this is the right forum to discuss them,' needled Hilda.

'I don't care if they're very boring,' said Val. 'As long as they're short.'

'No, it's the music when we come in,' I said. 'I've been at this school for a while now and every single week we've had "The New World Symphony". It was good for the first two years but if I hear it again I am going to die. I don't even like Hovis.'

Emma nodded. 'Totally agree, and the record is so scratched it should be chucked out.'

'We used to have "Peer Gynt" before you came, Andrew,' said Hilda, 'but it got left out in the sun and warped – sounded like it was being played by the Grimethorpe Colliery Band in an earth tremor.'

At that moment there was a bump against the door and Joyce reversed in, carrying an ominous pile of handouts and documents once again.

'So sorry I'm late – it was Pat Rudds complaining she's run out of grit.'

'What, for her cage?' said Hilda.

'No for the paths – oh stop it, Hilda, I've no time for jokes or anything else – we've loads to get through so let's crack on.'

I sighed, knowing I'd be consigned to the 'New World' for the rest of the term at least.

'Right,' announced Joyce, putting down the pile and pressing her long red-tipped fingers together. 'Some good news first: the PTA want to buy us a video camera.'

'A what?' blurted Hilda, whose familiarity with technology ended at the radiogram.

'It's like a big film camera to, er, film things,' said Joyce.

'Why would we want to film things in school?' said Val. 'I see enough of the bloody place as it is.'

'It doesn't have to be school; we can take it on trips, record performances, take a video round the village to use for geography – that kind of thing.'

'Ooh,' said Emma, rattling her beads, 'I think it's a great idea. We can make a video of the nativity plays.'

'The children can write and perform adverts and sketches and those sorts of things too,' I said, thinking back to when we'd tried one at college. 'It's good for developing speaking and drama.'

'There we are,' said Joyce. 'Lots of ideas and, best of all, it's free for the school. Andy, since you're our technical bod, will you find out how to use it when it arrives and then give us all a demo?'

'Er, right, OK,' I said, fighting hard not to imagine what it would be like trying to get Hilda Percival to operate such a machine.

'How big are these cameras?' said Emma. 'I've never seen one.'

'Mr Butterfield showed me the brochure – they are quite big and heavy but we'll get a tripod with it. Anyway, we'd better move on to the next item: swimming.'

Hilda leapt up in mock joy. 'Hurrah, the PTA want to buy us a pool. Can they stretch to a lilo?'

'I'm afraid it's all a bit more serious, this one,' said the head, deadening her tone.

'What's up, are we doing it all wrong?' said Val. 'Is Keith Joseph insisting on doggie paddle?'

'It's the parents – well, some of them – I've had more complaints about them having to pay for the coach to go to Hauxton ever since we put it up to 40p.'

'Why don't we get the PTA to subsidise that instead of getting a video whatsit?' said Val.

'Well, actually they do subsidise it a little already but I have been thinking about changing the arrangements for swimming anyway. The problem is that it takes up a whole afternoon for Classes Three and Four and the curriculum's coming under more and more pressure. They want us to teach all these new things like computers and, well, I just can't justify a whole afternoon out any more.'

'Are we going to drop swimming, then?' I said, truly surprised.

'No, we're still supposed to do it as part of PE.'

'So how are we going to teach it, then?' said Val. 'Hauxton's the nearest baths.'

'Well, that's not completely true. It's the nearest public place, yes, but there is a twenty-metre pool in Twissham.'

Hilda's eyes were huge. 'What, at the mental hospital, you mean?'

Joyce tried to sound calm. 'It's a psychiatric residential home, Hilda.'

'Well, I've always called it the mental hospital and so does everyone else round here. It's the one in the old hall.'

Val put down her coffee. 'It's actually a secure psychiatric unit. There are dangerous people in that place – a friend of mine used to work there – we can't take kids swimming there, surely?'

'Well, Twissham Primary do,' said Joyce. 'They've been going for a year now and there's been no problem. I spoke to the head last week and she said the pool's lovely and the changing facilities are much nicer than at Hauxton. What's more, it's free – the bosses are trying to improve relations with the community.'

'It's still got a dirty big security fence round it,' said Val.

Emma put up a finger. 'But even if we took the juniors there we'd still need a bus and it would still be in lesson time, wouldn't it?'

'It's much nearer and so the PTA will be able to cover the cost if they do a couple of big fundraisers each year like the fair. And I'm proposing that we take the children after school.'

There followed a brief silence. Val looked at me and we both turned to Joyce who held up her hands. 'I know it's more hours for you two, which is why I'm just saying it's a proposal at the moment. If you want to think about it, fine.'

I was surprised at Val's response. 'Well, I do actually think swimming's important so if this is the best way I suppose it'll have to be done.'

Joyce looked at me. I shrugged. 'I don't mind – it's nearer and if the pool is good I think we should at least try it for half a term.'

'Very sensible, Andy,' said Joyce, nodding. 'And thank you, Val. That's sorted. Right, next item: nits.'

The video camera was about the size of bulging suitcase and weighed roughly twice as much. It arrived in a huge black bag just a fortnight after Joyce had first mentioned the PTA's idea and I was really excited to get the thing working. I unzipped the case and saw the big Japanese device enveloped in plastic, with its prominent bulbous microphone. There was a manual nearly as thick as a church Bible and lots of cables, along with a paperback-sized square plastic box which I realised was the VHS tape. It was clearly going to take me a while to drive this beast so I decided to take it home for the weekend.

On Saturday, after an hour of fiddling with the camera and an unsuccessful attempt to read the manual with Tom and Reuben jumping on me, I began to assemble some lunch when Barbara walked in, an hour and a half late.

'Sorry,' she said, unzipping her bulky Royal Mail coat. 'It was Ethel's cats again.'

'What about them?'

'I had to get some flea powder from the vet's for them again. Poor old dear was itching like a monkey.'

'And that took an hour and a half?'

'No, I also had to mend Prue's Hoover and help a flustered chap who was going to a funeral and had a flat tyre.'

'What's happened? You're turning into social services. Well, that or the RAC.'

'I didn't change his wheel – I just went round to someone who I knew would do it right away.'

'Don't the Royal Mail mind you doing this on your round?'

'I don't do it on my round – I just chat to people as I'm delivering and then I sort them out after I've clocked off. The old ladies sort of rely on me now.'

Tom and Reuben came thumping downstairs from playing in their room and demanded mummy hugs. 'Hello, my gorgeous boys,' she said, squeezing them hard. 'So, what's the big news here?'

'Daddy's got a big film video camera,' said Tom. 'He's gunna make a film of us like on telly, when he gets it working.'

Barbara laughed, putting down a protesting Reuben to take up a much-needed cup of tea. 'Oh, this is the school one you told me about.'

'It's enormous – wait till you see it. But anyway, I've had a fab idea.'

My wife lowered her face. 'Yezzzzzz?'

'No, you'll like this one. We've got the camera for the whole weekend so why don't we film the boys?'

'We?'

'I.'

'Oh, you mean a few scenes of them playing, that sort of thing?'

'No, it'll do a ninety-minute tape. I was thinking more along the lines of *A day in the life of Tom and Reuben Seed of Applesett.* You know, like a documentary of their whole day from waking to sleeping.'

'Wow, that *is* a great idea. If . . .'

'If what?'

'If you can get it working.'

On Sunday morning, much against my better judgement, in the blackness of five-thirty, I thumped the alarm and dragged myself out of a gloriously warm bed. The house was glacial and I blundered around for warm slippers and a dressing gown before heading to the kitchen for something to keep me warm and awake. Barbara groaned and turned over as I left the bedroom and clicked the door tight shut.

After a hot drink and the briefest of washes, I sought out the big video camera, lifting it on to my shoulder like a side of beef, and ascended Craven Bottoms' wonky stairs towards the boys' room. Gently I pushed the door open. It was just before six and I wanted to capture their waking moments.

In the sparse light from the landing I could see that Tom had completely disappeared under his covers and was curled up in a little ball, still sleeping. Reuben on the other hand was always hot and I wasn't surprised to see that he had kicked off his quilt and was spread-eagled on his back like a starfish, an arm and leg hanging out of the bed, his mouth agape. I switched on the camera which whirred into life then I pressed the record button.

Once I'd opened the curtains, the boys moved and blinked into life, pulling themselves out of bed with hot ruby cheeks and croaking about drinks. I passed Reuben his favourite plastic beaker with the spout and started filming again. On the floor were two 'jumper men': warm clothes we always laid out flat the night before, for the boys to slip straight into for playing.

'Hey, I'm on video,' said Tom, and he immediately started larking about like a chimp, diving on to his jungle-themed bedclothes and making irritating noises.

Reuben, as usual, copied. 'Ba-na-na-uhh!' they both chanted as I groaned, thinking that I'd have to edit several hours of this.

Tom started to get dressed while Reuben tipped his drink over, then pulled down his pyjama bottoms, standing with his legs apart to inspect a droopy yellow nappy. 'Lotsa wee-wee,' he accurately assessed.

Once dressed, Tom moved to the dressing-up box and attached a pink flowery cape to his shoulders, announcing that he was Superboy. He jumped off a low blanket box to show his powers, the least masculine hero in Yorkshire. Reuben, meanwhile, insisted on trying to get dressed himself even though he couldn't manage. The back of his hair was in a giant mangled frizz, while the front was the usual pudding-bowl arrangement that represented the mobile hairdresser's default.

After fifteen minutes of filming they still hadn't left their room but eventually they tumbled downstairs and asked to watch telly – a Sunday morning treat. I made some warm oat slop, their favourite, for breakfast and put a curved plastic bib on Reuben to stem the overflow. Barbara wisely had a lie in.

I was now getting the hang of the zoom on the camera and moved around while they played with Lego on the carpet after breakfast. I heard a tinkle of glass outside.

'Ooh, boys, the milk is here. Who wants to get it?' Outside in the gloom I saw the lights of the delivery Land Rover go by. The boys jumped up and went to the front door. It was raining. A lot. The single milk bottle was just out of reach on the low wall by the door. Tom strained but couldn't make it. They looked at the damp step outside then down at their socked feet.

'We'll get wet,' said Tom. Callously, I said it was all right and continued filming. Tom gingerly stepped out on to the wet path but Reuben was not one to be left out and he ran outside into the rain and grabbed the bottle before Tom got there. They both had wet socks. Reuben dashed in lifting the bottle up in triumph before the camera caught his expression abruptly change to alarm.

'Can't hold!'

I dived forward and caught the glass bottle as it slipped out of his grasp. Sadly, the replayed footage just showed bare wall, even if the audio caught the full panic.

Getting dressed properly, a painfully drawn-out procedure, was then recorded, followed by brushing teeth, during which time I gathered hard evidence that Tom's method was to hold the brush still and waggle his head, while Reuben simply ate the toothpaste then rinsed his brush.

More Lego followed with the established routine of Tom making a good model and Reuben needing a piece of it, usually at the bottom. He wailed and grabbed it, as always, and I told myself that as a neutral journalist I was powerless to intervene.

Somehow we had now reached ten o'clock, although it felt like I had been filming for days. I made a snack, inveigling them into the consumption of carrot sticks by pretending it was an indoor picnic. The next bout of playing featured their favourite role play where they took on the characters of 'Daddy' and 'Baby'. As far as I could tell, the game involved emptying every container in the house on to the floor and mixing up the contents.

The afternoon featured some video highlights: Tom as an egg-box-clad spaceman, Reuben cheating at a matching card game, inevitable tears when plans for tower-building became over-ambitious, and a spectacular session of nose-mining from Reuben while Barbara shared a book with them. The rain stopped eventually and I sent them out in coats to play in the sandpit, which had turned into a water pit. They made a mess, argued and came in.

There was more wailing when it came to 'putting everything away' time: a mammoth operation which was beyond the scope of our film project, but this was followed by a happy bathtime featuring lots of botties and boats.

Getting ready for bed was going quite well until Tom randomly declared that he was, 'The new boss in town', which for some unfathomable reason was a signal for them both to go wacky, rushing round and diving on beds. Toddlers, I'd learned, just did this.

Reuben inevitably became overexcited and launched a mouth-first attack on his brother, caught in gruesome detail by the camera.

'He chewed me,' moaned poor Tom.

Barbara took over the filming for bedtime story as it was my turn and she failed to keep the camera still, jiggling with amusement as Tom inevitably selected the excruciatingly long *Thomas the Tank Engine* anthology once again and Reuben arbitrarily grabbed a German picture book. I did my best but we all faded during the tedious tale of Mavis the naughty diesel. At least we were all cheered up when the camera operator's inadvertent bottom burp was captured by the mic.

After kisses and drinks and tucks and one last attempt by Reuben to play, we switched off the light and the camera too. The result was hardly Oscar material, but it became a treasured family archive.

The school bus coughed and trundled along the twisty Swinnerdale Road towards the large village of Twissham. It was more like a small town in reality, with a miniature cobbled square, three ancient pubs and rows of fine Georgian stone houses. But the place was dominated by the ruins of a giant castle, formerly home to kings, sitting high on a mound, its once glorious towers crumbled and poignant. The coach slowed as we passed a group of lithe race horses waiting to cross the road; the village had several stables and many of the local school's children were the sons and daughters of jockeys and trainers.

It was our third visit to the swimming pool at the psychiatric home and the first two had passed off quietly. I sat next to Val and we discussed the merits of the place as the children of Classes 3 and 4 babbled excitedly behind us.

'I have to say it's better than Hauxton in a lot of ways; a lot less echoey for a start,' said Val.

'The pool's a bit small when they're all in but like Joyce said the changing rooms are positively luxurious.'

'I still think it's odd that we're taking kids into a place where they lock up you-know-whats.' Val looked round to check that none of the children were listening.

'Twissham Primary seem happy, anyway.'

'Well, yes, but I saw one of the teachers, Carolyn Thorp, at Ingleburn market last week and she said that the alarm in the hospital goes off now and again when they're at school and they have to rush all the kids inside and lock the doors.'

I furrowed my brow. 'What's the alarm for?'

'It means someone's escaped, you pillock.'

We heard the bus's growly diesel engine change gear and saw the elegant three-storey country house that was Twissham Hall appear behind tall railing gates. At the back of it were various modern extensions with residential blocks, treatment rooms and the greenhouse-like swimming pool building. It was at least an attractive environment for the patients, who suffered from a variety of mental illnesses and learning disabilities.

The security man waved us through the entrance and the children whooped as they saw the steamy glass of the pool.

Val stood up as the bus parked. The children instantly hushed. 'Make sure you've got all your things and line up quietly in pairs outside.'

I walked around to the side of the building and pressed a buzzer next to the entrance to the changing rooms. Instead of Phil, the affable gym instructor who usually let us in, a young woman dressed in a blue uniform opened the door with a slight look of panic then hurried towards the pool, apologising for her rapid exit. I wondered what was going on but it soon became apparent as the children filed through into the pool area. There, being assisted out of the water by Phil, was one of the patients, a pale young man with emaciated limbs and a twitching face. I held out my arms to stop the children who couldn't help but stare.

'Really sorry!' called Phil. 'Just lost track of time. Come on, Kevin.' He hustled the lurching man through a door, wrapping a towel around him. 'All yours now.'

Val pushed through. 'Hang on – I'll check the changing rooms just to be sure.' She disappeared into the female area then the male one while the waiting juniors whispered excitedly behind me clutching their bags.

Once the children were in the water, the episode was forgotten and the awkward business of trying to teach youngsters to swim was underway. Val stood at the side of the shallow end with the beginners, while I worked with the large and noisy group of confident and improving swimmers at the deep end.

'Come and hold the side,' I called. There were several arguments about who was next to who. 'I'm waiting.'

'Stop arsin' about, you lot!' It was Howard Sedgwick, who was an excellent swimmer and wanted to get on with improving his strokes.

'Er, thank you, Howard, but that's not the type of language you should be using.'

'Sorry, Mr Seed. Ah meant stop mekkin' a fuss, that's all.'

After five minutes of breaststroke we used floats to practise backstroke leg action. To maintain interest, I ended this session with a race. Each child grasped the polystyrene board to his or her chest then lay back with a fury of flapping legs. It was only a width and yet everyone went flat out, transforming the pool into a cauldron of bubbling, splashing eruptions.

'Oi, you lot!' called Martine from the shallow end, after a wave swept over her head as she took a few tentative waggles with her feet off the bottom.

The race was not a success: not only did I end up being soaked from the splashing but, without any circling arms to feel their way forward, two boys cracked their heads on the side and Lawrence lost all sense of direction, veering away down towards a greatly amused Val. The rest of my group had a huge argument about who won.

'Calm down! Now, are you all right, boys?' I looked towards the two lads who were rubbing their skulls hard. One of them was Jason Fisher and I immediately envisaged his father storming into school to complain.

'It's a good job it's only plastic,' he said.

'What, yer head?' said Howard.

'No, the side of the pool.' I smiled, glad to see that Jason had taken the joke well.

Once order was restored, we went on to the stroke that most children found the hardest to master: front crawl. A couple of Class 4 girls were competent but the only other one who knew how to move and breathe properly was Howard. I asked these three to demonstrate, then told the others to swim two widths. It was the usual mayhem of straight flapping arms, heads lolling from side to side and virtually no legwork. I asked Howard to hold on to the side of the pool with his arms out and demonstrate the leg action to the others who were gathered round. In his enthusiasm he kicked a little too hard and once more my clothes were doused with the stink of chlorine. At least the children enjoyed it.

'Oh, sorry, Mr Seed. Don't know me own strength.'

He was right there. Once we'd practised the arm action, I paired the children up with a float between them and set them off having 'push of war' contests using front crawl leg action to try to force each other backwards. They loved this and demanded to swap opponents after a go. I noticed that the Class 4 children were far better, although none of them beat Howard. With their pride upset, the older boys pushed forward their champion, Oliver, and demanded that he take on Howard.

Everyone stopped and watched, even the learners at the far end of the pool, as the two boys set themselves opposite each other, grasping the float. I gave a short blast of whistle on my Acme Thunderer and once more the water was churned madly as the two large lads gave their all. Initially, neither moved forward and I could see Oliver gritting his teeth as he thrashed his legs in a frenzy. Howard used slower, larger movements and breathed steadily. He was clearly less tired and after a few seconds he edged forward, building momentum, until the older boy was forced back and knew he was defeated. The Class 3 children roared and Howard waved a fist.

Val took her group out of the pool and lined them up by the side.

'Right, this'll help you if you're still a bit nervous about the water. I want you to jump in the shallow part first, then climb out and go to the back of the line. Second time, jump in half-way down the pool, here, where it's deeper.'

'Urrhh, I don't like look o' that,' said Martine, still evidently anxious.

'Don't worry,' said Val. 'You can still put your feet down here, just.'

My group were distracted by the jumps and asked if they could practise diving.

'All right, but you can only dive from the deep end,' I said, recalling the potential danger. They cheered and pulled themselves out of the water before lining up.

Lawrence went first and performed an outlandish belly flop which had the children creased up with mirth. It also doused my clothes for the third time.

'You did that deliberately, Lawrence,' I said. 'Please take this seriously.'

'I didn't, Mr Seed,' and to my shame I realised that he wasn't kidding. I drew attention away by giving advice about how to perform a successful dive. The next two were much better and I moved away down to the side of the pool to avoid more soakings.

Next it was Howard's turn and he held up a hand.

'Hang on.' He turned to the wall and picked up a pair of crusty goggles, pulling them over his eyes. 'Where am I?' he said, before crouching at the pool's edge and performing a surprisingly graceful dive with barely a splash, despite his heavy frame. I was watching the divers intently and didn't notice the beginner's group across the other side of the pool, now jumping into the middle. I didn't notice them, that is, until it was Martine's turn. Still unsure, she held back till last and stood, staring at the water, her large, plump form shivering with fear and cold.

'Oh, come on, Martine,' called Val. 'Stop faffing about and jump in.'

Seeing her classmates now jeering, she stepped back two paces, closed her eyes and charged forward at pace, yelling like a banshee. That's when I noticed her. But it was too late to move; she launched her huge figure into the air and splayed out her arms and legs in panic.

'Arrrreeeeuuurrrghhhh!'

It was as if a Greenland glacier deposited an iceberg into the North Atlantic from altitude. The splash detonated outwards, completely saturating my clothes and Val's too. But I hadn't counted for the tidal wave that followed, sweeping across the pool and over the side, filling our shoes with a cold chemical stench.

There was only one way to react and both Val and I threw back our heads and laughed long and hard. Martine, meanwhile, was bouncing around in the half-empty pool. 'I did it, I did it!' she shouted.

Time was running out and after uselessly dabbing myself with towels for the fourth time, I set the children to swimming underwater for as long as they could before resurfacing. Once more, Howard outshone everyone; he really was impressive.

'Can we swim through each other's legs again, Mr Seed, like last week?' It was Estelle.

'Go on then, but be careful. Get a partner and take turns.'

They enjoyed this for two minutes, one person standing in the centre of the pool with legs akimbo while the other dived underneath, until it was big Howard's turn to swim through Gary's legs.

'Ooh careful, you're tickling me meat 'n' two veg,' said Gary, nearly falling over.

For the final five minutes we let the two groups have a free playtime in which they messed about with plastic balls, floats and hoops. The best swimmers took turns to retrieve a heavy rubber brick from the bottom of the pool while others did handstands or simply splashed about.

Trudy climbed up the ladder and came over to me.

'Mr Seed, Vicky doesn't feel well – I think she's swallowed a load of water.' With Gary having cleansed himself of ancient dirt in the pool this was probably a bad move.

'Vicky, you'd better get out,' I said. She did look groggy. 'Trudy, would you be kind and go and sit with her in the changing room?'

The two girls disappeared while I went to tell Val. The rest of the children continued to splosh and holler. After a minute Trudy reappeared.

'Vicky's gone a really funny colour now.'

Val sighed. 'All right, I'll go in there and see what's what.'

When she opened the door I walked down to the shallow end to keep an eye on the learners. Dan Alderson was keen to demonstrate to me his outstanding ability to sit on the bottom of the pool where it was a metre deep. He couldn't swim but he left me in no doubt that he was exceptional at sinking.

I was just about to blow my whistle and call time up when I heard a strange gurgling sound and looked across. It was Martine. In her new-found confidence she had somehow waggled over to the deep end of the pool and was now out of her depth, and in real trouble. I immediately rushed along towards her, ready to jump in, thinking that it wouldn't really make my clothes much wetter, when a shadowy shape slipped through the water from the other side and scooped her up, swiftly and safely pulling her into shallow water.

It was Howard Sedgwick. He had spotted the danger and dived in. I recalled reading in his written News one Monday that he had achieved a Life Saving certificate. Martine stumbled over to the side of the pool, coughing and spluttering, her eyes wide and red. I checked she was all right then ordered everyone out of the water. Finally, I turned to her rescuer, breathing a heavy sigh.

'Howard, that was smart and brave; well done for thinking so quickly.'

He shrugged. 'It were nowt really.'

'Oh, come on, it was, Howard, everyone saw it. I'm going to tell Mrs Berry and your parents.'

'Steady, Mr Seed; I told yer, I can't be doin' wi' fuss.'

At the following staff meeting Emma asked how the swimming at Twissham was going.

Val glanced at me. 'Well, apart from Vicky being sick in the changing rooms last week and Martine nearly drowning, it's going well.'

'You forgot the psychiatric patient being in the pool when we arrived. And our shoes being filled with stinky water,' I added.

Joyce opened the school diary. 'Well, that's all been dealt with, so let's move on. Now, I wrote down for us to do something today and I can't remember what it is.'

'I can,' I said, pointing to a giant black bag in the corner.

'Is there a body in there?' said Hilda. 'Another swimming victim?'

Val folded her arms. 'No, it's the bloody video camera.'

'That's right, and Andy's going to show us how to use it,' said Joyce.

Ten minutes later the huge camera was on its tripod and Hilda was looking through the viewfinder and having trouble with her specs.

'What am I supposed to be seeing? A film?'

'No, the wall,' I said.

'It's that exciting, is it?'

'We're just trying it out, Hilda. You can film Val if you like.'

'Oh, we're going for horror, are we?'

'Careful, Mrs P,' growled the deputy head. 'I haven't had my go yet.'

'Have you pressed record, Hilda?' I said.

'Where's that again?'

Val looked upwards. 'The red button, like we explained. Twice.'

'I can't see a red button, just the wall.'

'That's because it's on the outside of the camera, Hilda,' I said, trying not to snort.

She stood back, shaking her head. 'Well how the fiddlesticks am I supposed to be able to see the inside and the outside at the same time? I'm too old for this modern electronical nonsense – I've only just mastered the abacus.'

We laughed gently and Joyce asked Hilda to have one more try. I stood up and showed her the red button.

'It's there, Hilda, OK? Now look through the viewfinder and press it.'

'I've lost it again,' she said as she squinted through the machine once more.

'Feel for it,' said Emma.

'I am flippin' feeling,' she said. 'Feeling a right nelly.'

She poked about with her finger, while we willed her to find the target. Finally, her digit landed on the red button and we all called, 'Yes!'

'Hang on,' said Hilda. 'Something's flashing. What do I do?'

I stood up and took over the viewfinder.

'The battery's flat.'

'Thank heavens for that,' she said.

Hilda Percival never did use the school's new video camera but the staff heartily agreed that it was just as well; like Howard, we just couldn't be doing with the fuss.

Chapter Thirteen

Barry

'Just be careful you don't fall off!'

Barbara called across to Tom and Reuben who had climbed up on to the stone steps of the old cross on the village green.

'They'll be fine,' I said, stretching out on the wooden bench by the swings. It was a Saturday afternoon in mid-March and we had made the familiar short walk from Craven Bottoms. Green daffodil shoots swayed in the damp wind and there was a fresh green life to the grass that had been absent for months.

'I can't wait for the weather to improve,' said Barbara.

'Yeah, come on, spring – make more effort. I could do with a proper long walk or a bike ride to blow away the cobwebs. These slow toddles to the swings don't do it for me, and this term is getting to be really intense with this play we're doing, as well.'

'Never mind, it'll be Easter soon and you can have a proper break; you could go for a decent walk with Adam. I'll be slogging away through the rain again nearly every day.'

I put an arm around her shoulders. 'Yeah, poor you. I can't believe how wet this winter's been.'

'At least the postie job has kept us afloat financially. I'm still having to watch the spending but we can just about manage – well, if we keep eating economy soup and special offer pie.'

'Just think, in twenty years we'll be able to afford a new boiler and get the roof fixed.'

The whine of a straining car engine behind interrupted Barbara's answer and we turned to see Doug and Rosie's mucky 2CV pootling down the road. They waved and pipped the horn as they went by.

'I wonder where they're off to,' I said.

'I think it's Hauxton to get wallpaper.'

'They seem to spend more time out of the dale than in it.'

'Hmmm, I think they're finding it tough to adjust to the rural life.'

'Not enough hairy vegetarians in Applesett.'

At that moment, a familiar wail rose up from the far side of the stone cross.

'Reuben's fallen off,' called Tom.

The unmistakable twang of a wooden ruler rent the air. After a short burst of sniggering, the classroom briefly entered a rare state of silence as I stood up and surveyed the twenty-four faces to determine the perpetrator.

'Who was that?'

No answer.

'I know it's a funny sound but it has caused *everyone* to stop working, so it's just not on. Someone must know who did it.'

I scanned the children's eyes searching for traces of guilt or giveaway glances. I also registered who had a wooden ruler on the table, although if they had any sense they'd have dropped it on to a lap as I used to do.

'Well?'

Whoever did it was really holding out. I folded my arms and scrutinised each expression again. It was hard to avoid turning to the usual suspects in these cases: Martine, Jason, Gary and Colin. But there was one other person I was drawn to: Barry Caygill.

I shouldn't have suspected Barry; he was a good lad, really – neat and tidy and generally sensible – a local boy with no history of mischief. But, at the same time, it couldn't be avoided because poor Barry had a countenance that was undeniably shifty. He just always gave the impression that he was up to something. 'Sitting on marbles' was how Hilda Percival described it.

I looked at him now, his eyes flicking from side to side and his face twitching ever so slightly. But there was no ruler on his desk and he'd never done it before. Instead of making accusations I went for an old ruse.

'Right, well Class Three, it's the third time it's happened this week and if I don't find out who it is before playtime then everyone is going to stay inside.'

This was met with a muttered 'Awww' of protest and some whispering and pointing before a hand was raised by Estelle.

'It was Martine, Mr Seed. I saw her.'

Cathy nodded. 'I did, too.'

I turned to the accused. 'Well, Martine?'

For a moment she held out her hands and opened her mouth. 'I didn't do it the other times, like.'

'Why did you do it this time?'

'Fer a bet.'

I looked at the clock. 'We've wasted enough time; everyone back to work and, Martine, come and have a little chat at break, please.'

When the bell rang, the offender was saved from interrogation by the arrival of a stern-faced Val Croker in the classroom. Martine scuttled out with a warning while Val parked her broad bottom on the corner of a desk.

'There's a problem with the Easter play. Peter's decided he wants out.'

'I didn't know you had a Peter in Class Four,' I said.

'Peter the disciple, you nut case. Mervyn was supposed to play the part but he's now decided he can't handle it.'

'Isn't there anybody else who can take over?'

'Not among the boys in my class. There were only three keen ones and they've all got parts. We'll have to look at your lot.'

'Well, I've a few actors and comedians, that's for sure.'

'What about Barry Caygill?'

'Barry? Well, he's never really struck me as the dramatic type, although he does do a very good impression of a dodgy dealer.'

'Eh?'

'Well, he just always has this shifty expression, haven't you noticed?'

Val shook her head. 'All bloody kids look shifty to me. They're always up to something.'

'So, anyway, why Barry?'

'I just made a note when we did the auditions a fortnight back. I thought he was quite good.'

'Well,' I said, raising my eyebrows, 'all right then.'

A few days later Classes 3 and 4 were sitting in the hall fidgeting and yawning while a rehearsal for the Easter play went ahead. This production was a departure for Cragthwaite Primary. For as long as anyone could remember we'd performed some kind of drama at Christmas time only; the infants with a nativity or story about Santa, and the juniors with a musical or pantomime or seasonal show. It was the vicar who'd suggested doing something about the Easter story and Joyce had concurred.

'It'll take some of the pressure off with everything else going on at Christmas,' she'd said.

'And add more work in spring . . .' Val had grumbled. But we'd agreed to give it a try and so a commercial script with music had been purchased entitled *The Man from Galilee*.

Four children were standing at the front of the hall with scripts while Val barked at them.

'Come on, you've just seen your closest friend arrested, the person you believe is the son of God. He's been dragged away by soldiers and you're just standing there like you're in a Post Office queue!'

They shifted uneasily. One of them was Barry Caygill, playing the part of lead disciple, Peter.

Val continued. 'Right, we'll do that again and put some oomph into it!'

The quartet of boys glanced at each other and one stepped forward putting his arms out.

'What shall we do now?'

A second boy lifted the script to his face. 'They've taken him to the High Priest.'

'I'm going to follow them,' said Barry, his voice strangled by fear, before walking to the side.

Val held up a hand. 'Right, stop. Well, it was a bit better but still as wooden as a coffin from some of you. What's next, Mr Seed?'

'It's the song, "Who Do You Think You Are?"'

The audience were told to stand up then Mrs Henderson, a parent helper, plonked away at the piano while the children attempted to sing the song. It was grim. I often wondered at these early stages of rehearsal how a play would ever succeed but somehow, every time, things came together at the last moment, despite the obstacles.

'Well, I didn't think it were possible,' said Val, 'but the singing was actually worse than the acting. Anyway, we'll do the songs again in assembly. Let's go on to the next scene.'

I flicked through the script. 'This is back at the meeting room. Peter returns to tell the disciples what he's seen.'

'Come on then, if you're involved,' said Val. A group of anxious boys and girls shambled forward, each clutching a paper. It included Lawrence and Estelle from my class. I recalled how several children had been desperate to secure one of these minor roles when the play had been announced.

Val signalled for action.

'Look, it's Peter!' said a Class 4 girl pointing to Barry.

He stepped forward, panting. 'They've kept Jesus at the High Priest's. They beat him and spat on him. It was terrible.'

The girl playing Mary turned to Barry. 'Couldn't you do anything?'

He shook his head. 'I only jus' managed to escape my self.'

'What?' It was Val, almost laughing. 'That was actually much better but, Barry, that last line came out all wrong.'

The boy looked nonplussed.

'You read the words on the page,' I said, 'but it sounds like you escaped from yourself.'

He just stared and shrugged.

Val glanced at the script. 'It says, "I only just managed to escape *myself*." Have another go.'

Barry viewed the line on paper then looked up. 'I only jus' managed to escape my self.' Three or four of the older children giggled.

'It's *myself*,' said Val, working hard to remain patient. 'One word. Can you say it?'

'My self,' said Barry, unable to comprehend the problem.

Val shook her head. 'We're getting nowhere here. Mr Seed, would you please spend a bit of time with Peter helping him with that line?'

I nodded and Val ordered the actors to move on.

At lunchtime the following day I called Barry in to see me for some one-to-one drama coaching. He was a short, unremarkable boy with straight mousy hair and brown eyes.

'Have you been learning your words, then, Barry?' I asked, smiling to encourage him.

''Ave been tryin' but there's quite a bit to learn.'

'What about the "escape" line?'

'Well, I know it but I dunno if I'm sayin' it right.'

'Let's see.' We flicked through the script to the scene in question. 'I'll be Mary,' I said. This time he smiled. 'Let's go from here.'

'Couldn't you do anything?' I said, wisely avoiding any female impersonation.

'I only just managed to escape my self.'

'Right, let's stop there,' I said, fearing that I could say goodbye to the rest of my lunch hour. 'I think I see the problem now. Imagine I was, say, doing something messy like, erm, using clay to make a model.'

Barry looked at me and half nodded, unsure where this was going.

I continued. 'Well, when I'd finished I might say, "Now I'd better go and wash myself." Or, if I was chopping vegetables with a sharp knife and it slipped I might say, "Oh dear, I've cut myself."'

He clearly thought I was potty but I persisted. 'After a swim I might dry myself. All those make sense but no one would ever say "I need to *escape* myself", do you see?'

He didn't.

I moved on to a different approach. 'Can you hear the difference between "escape, *myself*" and "escape my self"?'

At this point his eyes betrayed some understanding so I repeated the pair.

'How can a person escape from himself? That's what it sounds like you're saying.'

He half-nodded again.

I smiled. 'Right, come on, let's have another go.'

We turned to the script and again I read Mary's line. 'Couldn't you do anything?'

'I only just managed to escape my self.'

I silently screamed then took a deep breath. He understood it but couldn't say it.

Twenty minutes later, at five to one, with the bell imminent, I had a brainwave.

'Right, Barry; you're not leaving a gap between the word "escape" and the word "myself" so after "escape" I want you to stop and in your head count to two, then say "myself". All right?'

He looked doubtful but had a go. 'I only just managed to escape . . . . . . my self.'

'That was a long gap. Can you count to one?'

He nodded just as the bell rang.

Later in the week, I sat in the staffroom with Val discussing the play.

'I still think half the problem is that they find the Easter story confusing,' I said.

'That's because they don't know it well enough. I presume you read it to your class?'

'I read it, we discussed it, and I also used your idea of getting them to write it as a story in their own words.'

'How did that go?' she said, stirring three sugars into her coffee.

'It was very revealing. As you said, they are confused about the story; I had bits of Christmas in there, "angles" guarding the tomb and they *really* had trouble spelling Gethsemane.'

'Oh aye, mine were the same: Ponchus Pilot, Judas has Carriot, Mary Mad the Lame . . . it's a goldmine for gaffes.'

'My favourite was written by Gary Blacow. He was describing the bit where the women find the empty tomb and he put "Peter, Peter, come quickly – the load has risen!"'

It was rare to see Val Croker laugh but she threw back her shoulders and roared. The door opened soon afterwards and Hilda, Emma and Sue hurried in.

'What's going on, Valerie? We heard that from the infants,' said Hilda. 'Has Mrs Hyde announced her retirement?'

'You'll have to tell them, Andy,' said Val, wiping a tear.

After they enjoyed the tale, we spent a joyous ten minutes exchanging recent howlers and calamities in our classes.

'Have you told them what happened in Art yesterday, Emma?' said Sue.

Emma closed her eyes and shook her head. 'Oh, Hilda's heard this but not Val and Andy. I set the Reception group off painting portraits of the person opposite, then I went to check up on the older ones. When I got back little Adam and Robert's faces were covered in blue and green. I said, "What happened?" and Adam said, quite innocently, "You told us to paint each other."'

We hooted again before Hilda slapped her knee and held up a

finger. 'Hey, wasn't it Adam who you found sat on a desk on his first day?'

Sue started shaking with giggles. 'That's right; Emma said, "You go and sit on that table, Adam," so he did.'

Emma covered her face with her hands then looked up. 'I'd forgotten all about that. This sort of thing happens about fifteen times each day in my class.'

Val grabbed a pile of books and stood up. 'As long as the buggers are sorted out by the time they reach Class Four . . .'

Cragthwaite School's small, high-ceilinged hall was crammed with well over half the village, expectantly waiting to see the evening performance of *The Man from Galilee*. Large square farmers were wedged on to little plastic chairs, toddlers squirmed and grannies pointed as they caught glimpses of children in costume through the half-open doors. At the back, Mr Milner from the PTA fiddled with the school video camera on its tripod. At the front a low stage, borrowed from Swinnerdale's lone secondary school, stood in front of a broad painted backdrop of hills, palm trees and what the children of Class 4 took to pass for the type of buildings found in Palestine at that time.

A huge quantity of tea towels and old curtains had been requisitioned for costumes and the children wearing them stood anxiously waiting to go in as Val and I dashed about making last minute adjustments and checking that necessary props were present. I went over to Barry Caygill, who stood with his eyes shut, his lips silently working over the lines he would shortly have to say. My mind was on one line only.

'Are you all right, Barry?'

'Er, yeah.'

'You know what to do?'

He nodded.

We heard Hilda play the opening bars of the introductory music and the children in the choir, some giggling nervously, filed into the overcrowded hall. I gave a thumbs up to the waiting actors then went to take my seat at the front, keeping a firm grasp on my script for prompting purposes. I caught Joyce's eye as I sat down. She was smiling, loving as she did the chance to show off her school.

The children sang the opening song beautifully and this set the tone for the evening. The play was strangely moving; there were no humorous lines like we always incorporated at Christmas, and the audience was noticeably quiet, even the tots at the back.

Sue Bramley, our multi-talented assistant, had created all the special costumes, from Roman guards to the High Priest's showy garb, and the children on stage looked resplendent. Once their initial nerves had been overcome, the actors began to rise to the occasion, too, and everyone watching was drawn into the sorrowful story. More than once I had to surreptitiously wipe an eye as the disciples listened to their master, never understanding what was to come.

The songs were lyrically more sophisticated than the children were used to but the music was excellent too, and so the show was carried along powerfully. I felt the strain build in my body as we moved to the moment of Jesus's arrest, and I prayed that Barry would hold himself together and not break the spell of the drama with an unwanted moment of comedy.

After the next song the act was upon us with the cheerless disciples pretending to whisper in small huddles as the breathless Peter broke in on the scene. He explained what had happened to their leader, speaking clearly in his broad Dales accent.

Mary then stepped forward. 'Couldn't you do anything?'

For the hundredth time, Barry shook his head. 'I only jus' managed to escape . . . myself.'

There was no laughter, no sniggering from the choir, no loss of atmosphere. In fact, no one in the audience noticed.

He had done it.

I felt an elbow from Val as I clenched a fist and let the tension drain from my insides. *Barry Caygill, you are a genius and I never doubted you for a moment.*

Adam Metcalfe stopped to admire the view: the folding sweep of hills around the high market town of Kettleby. Scraggy sheep and tiny cotton-wool lambs dotted the fields all around, the landscape held together by a latticework of dark stone walls that followed the soaring contours of the land. Two oystercatchers screeched above a clump of naked trees.

'It's great to stretch the legs properly,' I said, delighted that we'd finally managed to get together for a good long walk.

'Aye, it is now it's finally stopped rainin'.'

'What's that bridge down there?' I pointed to a narrow stone arch that carried a lonely track over a dark, rushing beck in the gill below.

'They call that Scabba Wath Bridge.'

'Really? I think you made that up.'

'No, it's real. There's all sorts o' funny names o' places round Kettleby. See that bank over there?' he said pointing to a dark hillside beyond the town. 'Just at the back o' that there is Cobscar Rake. Then on the top of the moor behind us is Lingy Rigg.'

'Do you know the names of all these places, then?'

'No, just the ones me old dad taught me. His favourite was a little rock outcrop on the road to Millscar called Thorny Grave Nab.'

We dropped down into the valley below and drew near to the River Swinner, which was swollen and brown from the continued recent downpours. Adam cut across a field and pointed to a stile at the far side, beyond which was a tight cluster of trees.

'It's nice down there – we take the kids sometimes in summer, lots of wild flowers.'

'Barbara would like that – she loves the orchids and cranesbill round here.'

'In that case you need to get yourselves to the special wildflower meadows in Wherndale in June.' He explained where they were and I made a mental note to take the family.

Inside the little wooded valley which led on to the main dale were joyous signs of spring. Steep banks of broad-leaved wild garlic pushed up through the moss and beech leaves. Tall dog's mercury and shiny celandines lit up the shadowy clefts between trees and fallen rocks. Great swathes of ivy were draped over the banks and the remnants of old walls.

'You're right, it's beautiful,' I called, but Adam didn't hear me, my voice drowned out by the crash of the beck surging down from the hills. The path then veered out of the woods and we climbed again towards a jumble of mounds and small crags, with pockets of ash and sycamore hiding weathered field barns.

'How are things on the farm?' I asked now that we could walk side by side again.

'Oh, could be better. A lot better really.'

'I suppose the rain's been even worse up Reddle?'

'Aye, it's bin the wettest winter and early spring for ten years, probably. The grass still isn't growin' and it's costing me a fortune in feed fer the sheep. Not to mention the foot rot.'

'Any lambs yet?'

'No, we start next month – we're always last in the dale.'

'Don't you just get fed up with all this?'

'No, I have a bit of a moan now 'n' again but then I remember what it was like for me granddad. He had ter keep horses on top of everything else and had virtually no machines. I just hop on me quad bike when he 'ad to walk. So, thinking on that makes me thankful.'

We crossed a steep field and I noticed small springs trickling out of the ground, as if the colossal weight of the hills were squeezing the water from their rocks. The land opened up further as we ascended on to a ridge and the wind picked up force unhindered by the thin pines on the crest. Rabbits bowled away and once more we stopped to scan the great sweep of the dale in the distance with dark moors rising behind and grey villages tucked against the valley sides beneath the scudding sky.

'See that farm down there?' said Adam, pointing to a jumble of sheds, tyres and broken tractors surrounded by a sea of churned mud four fields away below. 'That's Len Sunter's place. He's an old fella now, Len, and a bit of a character.'

I saw my friend's eyes light up as he recalled another little tale.

'I suppose he's related to the Sunters who farm in Cragthwaite?'

'He most likely is, but ahm not the person to ask about that.'

'So, how do you know him?'

'Oh, I see 'im at the auction mart and out and about. The local NUF man, Jack, told me a story about 'im, too. He'd claimed that some sheep had been stolen so Jack went round to look into it. Everything was in such a mess that Jack had a right job of it. He was trying to check Len's stock and he pointed to a sheep and asked him about it. "That's a redchested yow," said Len. Well, Jack 'ad never heard of that breed in all his years, so he said to Len, "It looks like a Swardle to me – what did you say it was?" Len said, "It's a redchested yow. Aye, 'ad it redchestered at Kettleby last year."'

Adam laughed with me then looked up at some brooding clouds overhead. 'Come on, I don't want to get wet. We'll take a shortcut back.'

We hurried down the hillside and through a couple of gates towards a narrow track which wound its way back towards the town about two miles away. Adam then veered off across another field, over some tumble-down walls and through a boggy stretch of ground near the valley bottom.

He indicated ahead. 'There's a beck runs across just down here but if we skip over that it'll save about twenty minutes.'

The stream soon came into view but it evidently wasn't the narrow dribble that Adam expected. A ribbon of peat-black water charged down from the hills behind and then wound through the folds of the long field. It was at least ten feet wide and twelve or more in places, with deep water surging with menace and power.

'Good grief, never seen it like this,' said Adam.

'Is there a bridge anywhere?' I asked hopefully.

'Nope. We'll just have to follow it and hope it narrows further along.'

'What if we can't cross it?'

'Then it's a much longer walk back . . .'

We squelched along the banks of the raging beck for several hundred yards, studying its speed and depth. It didn't look hopeful.

Adam stopped and stuck out a finger. 'I think just in here there are some big rocks we could've used as steppin' stones.'

I could see the gushing brown flow rising up in mounds over the submerged boulders. 'I don't fancy that. Not only would we definitely get soaked but if we fell in we could end up in the North Sea.'

'It's not quite that bad, Andy, but you'd be very cold and wet, alreet.'

We carried on but the river gave no indication that it would allow us to cross. I looked at my watch and knew that Barbara would start to worry if we had to turn back and go the long way round.

'It's a bit narrower yonder,' said Adam as we came to a place with higher sides where the water had undercut the banks. 'It's about nine feet here. Think you can jump it?'

'Probably . . . possibly.' I was wearing heavy boots plus several layers of clothes and a thick coat. While I was still considering the likelihood of success, Adam dropped back a few yards and charged at the river, aiming for a clump of grassy earth that projected out on the far bank. He sailed across and landed with a thud on the little mound, diving forward with his momentum before scrabbling up on to two feet.

'There y'are, not so bad,' he chuckled.

That was it. I looked at the clump which had half-collapsed under the tall farmer's weight. At least it was still there to aim for. I stepped back a few paces then a few more, checking that there was nothing loose in my jacket pockets to fly out.

'Come on,' he called. 'I need a brew.'

Sucking in a full breath I stormed towards the churning water, straining to remove the graphic picture of the consequences of failure that my mind had been playing in full sensory big screen mode. Alas, I misjudged the take-off point badly and left the near bank a foot before the edge. For a moment, as I soared above the icy mountain water that would be only too glad to wash me away, I concluded that I wouldn't make it. Adam, however, clearly not enamoured with the idea of fishing me out, leaned out over the far bank and extended a long arm.

I hit the clump with my leading foot and felt it collapse into the torrent. My boot pressed through it and I hit the bank, jarring my progress. For a ghastly moment I felt myself falling back into the roaring beck and prepared to swim when a stout hand clamped around my arm and yanked me up out of the gush. I flopped on to the grass and we both laughed long and hard.

'Easy,' said Adam.

The adrenaline in our bodies returned us to our cars in minutes and within the hour I was back at home, gobbling a piece of warm flapjack in front of the stove.

'How was the walk?' said Barbara.

'Good,' was my considered reply, but there was only one thing that I really wanted to say: *I only just managed to escape myself.*

Chapter Fourteen

Susan

'How's the house coming along?' I asked Doug Burns as we bumped and rolled along the country lane to Skirbridge in his tinny, temperamental 2CV.

'Oh, not bad. In about five years it'll all be done.'

It wasn't easy to get sense out of Doug most of the time; he liked to joke about everything but on this occasion I wasn't going to object since he was giving me a lift to work on his way to the secondary school at Ingleburn where he taught CDT.

'Actually, the kitchen's just about finished now,' he continued. 'Rosie told me to tell you so that if you wanted us to look after your boys sometime we could at least feed them. I'm not sure who to, though.'

I forgave the gag. 'That's really kind, Doug, thanks. At the moment we've got Iris Falconer and she loves having them when we're both working but if she's ever away . . .'

'Erm, actually, Rosie saw Iris yesterday and she did say that she was finding Reuben quite hard work. Hmmm, I probably shouldn't have told you that.'

'Oh, right, I see. Iris hasn't said anything to us.' I sounded a little surprised but I shouldn't have been, knowing our excitable younger son.

For once his tone became almost staid. 'So, well, mention it to Barbara and think about our offer. Rosie's always wanted kids but, well, you know, it hasn't worked out.'

I was just wondering what to say when he continued, as if a small flood gate had been opened. 'We've thought about fostering and adoption but it's a big thing and with the house move and new jobs it's probably too much at the moment.'

'It's quite a long, involved process adopting kids, isn't it?'

'Yeah, it's a right to-do.'

'What sort of age would you go for?'

'Rosie wants a baby but I think I'd be happier with a brat a few years older.'

'You're not into babies, then?'

'I'm not sure I'm into kids at all, to be honest, especially having been a teacher for a few years now. And with adoption you just don't know who you'll get – it could be the next Charles Manson. Or even worse, a Young Conservative.'

Didn't think the serious approach would last I said to myself as we rounded a corner and drew up behind an old slow tractor pulling a long trailer of muck. The driver's mirrors were obscured by the huge load so there was no way he would pull over.

'Damn,' said Doug, veering out as far as he dared. 'I've got a pile of stuff to get ready this morning, too.'

'There's a straight section a bit further on,' I said, doubting whether the ancient Citroën's feeble engine possessed sufficient power to pass anything.

'This thing needs a two-mile downhill stretch with a following wind,' said Doug, gripping the wheel tightly and once more swinging the jalopy into the middle of the road. 'Even then, it'll only take a full milk float.'

'I could get out and push,' I joked but Doug wasn't listening. He stared ahead, determined to look for an opportunity to overtake.

'Hang on,' he said, spying about eighty yards of empty tarmac with only a minor twist. I did hang on. Doug pressed down on the flimsy pedal and swerved out as the car's food-mixer-sized motor let out a squeal of protest at being issued such an unreasonable challenge. We drew up alongside the smelly trailer, gaining perhaps 3mph on the tractor. The tight bend in the road ahead drew near. Doug's eyes, already spookily large in his glasses, gawped forward and his knuckles turned white. I closed my own eyes and prayed.

At school, the teachers of Cragthwaite Primary witnessed the end of an era. For over a hundred years every classroom of every educational institution across the land possessed one piece of vital equipment. It was awkward to use, messy, difficult to clean properly and decidedly primitive: the blackboard.

My own example was a shabby dark green item, full of irritating pits and shiny areas which proved endlessly resistant to the application of chalk. The dog-eared board rubber provided simply spread dust across its surface and writing on it required patience, intense concentration and a hand as steady as an assassin's. I washed it clean with a damp cloth three or four times a day but all that did was to ruin the surface further.

Val and Hilda had chalked on theirs for years and were used to them but Emma and I hated blackboards and we had mounted a campaign to get Joyce to replace them with the glossy new whiteboards that we'd heard about from colleagues in more enlightened establishments.

'I agree,' Joyce had said to our delight over a year ago. 'But they're horribly expensive. And the marker pens cost much more than chalk.' She had seen our faces drop and taken pity. 'Perhaps the new PTA could take it on? They're planning various purchases already but I'll have a word.'

Thirteen months later I stood in my classroom and stared with wonder. The dilapidated old board had been unscrewed from the wall and in its place was something square and brilliant white and shiny and marvellous.

I went for a closer inspection just as the classroom door opened. It was Val.

'Sixty bloody quid each, these things,' she said. 'I could have done all sorts with that dosh.'

I touched the flawless surface. 'Yes but look: it's clean and smooth. Have you got a pen for it?'

'There's a box on your desk. Just make damned sure you don't use permanent marker by mistake.'

I went over to my table and took out one of the chunky dry-wipe markers before writing my name. The tip of the big pen glided over the surface like a skate on ice.

'Wow, that is beautiful,' I said standing back.

'Still not flamin' straight, though . . .'

'I don't care. It's easy to write, clear to read and there's no dust. Erm, how do we clean it?'

'You need an old cloth,' said Val. 'Here, try this.' She threw me a screwed-up tissue. I wiped off the writing and laughed at the simplicity of the new board.

'It wobbles a bit, though, Val,' I said. 'Is it not fixed to the wall?'

She stepped forward. 'No it's not, but even I have to admit that this bit's clever.' She reached out and to my astonishment lifted the board off the wall before swinging it around. 'Double-sided, look.' She almost smiled. 'We can write up double the work for the buggers.'

'Wow.' I studied the simple design: there was a twin-hooked piece of aluminium attached to the top of the frame and this simply sat on a long upturned bracket fixed to the wall. 'So, even if one side wears out in time you've still got the other.'

'Aye,' said Val, reaching into her bag for a cigarette and heading for the door. 'No doubt we'll soon wonder how we managed without them.'

I had another play with the board then remembered that the children would be arriving soon and so started to organise my first lesson, on spelling. The children had a group of words to learn each week based around a familiar letter pattern such as 'ough' and were given a short test each Friday. Today was Monday and I needed to give out the books.

Half an hour later the children were inside, having admired the new whiteboard on their arrival and I was handing out the books, making comments on the previous week's performance in the test.

'Three out of ten, Martine,' I said, trying not to sound too depressed as I slid her grey, crusty book across the desk. 'Do you actually try to learn them at home?'

'It's 'ard, Mr Seed. Either t'babby's mewin' or dogs 're yappin' or me mam's 'aving a ding-dong wi' me brother. I can't concentrate on 'owt.'

When she'd finished I just caught a whisper from the table next door. '*She's just thick, that's the problem.*'

I turned and the four girls on the table looked down with stony faces. But I knew who it was. I passed the offender an immaculate, neatly scribed book, deciding that this was not the time to mention her spiteful insult.

'Well done, Susan; ten out of ten again.'

She held out a hand. 'I always get ten.'

I couldn't deny that it was true. Whatever the task, whether a maths exercise, a history quiz or some English homework, if it was made up of closed questions or was a practice activity, Susan Bell always scored full marks; you had to admire her consistency.

She was a prim, petite girl, pale with tightly curled carroty hair and cool grey eyes beneath those winged specs that librarians always used to sport. She was always turned out in old-fashioned skirts, cardigans and floral dresses. Her shoes were permanently spotless and gleaming and her possessions, especially her school books, unblemished and mechanically neat. But the feature that made Susan most distinctive for me was her mouth. It was tiny and generally twisted tightly closed with concentration because Susan was ferociously competitive.

She certainly had rivals who could match her ability and intellect, such as Estelle, Stephen and the professor-like Marcus, but none of them was willing to pour their all into achieving faultless results at every single occasion. She was proud but only respected, not liked, in the class. But she didn't care about that, as long as she was top.

As I walked away she spoke again. 'Mr Seed, you've forgotten to write the date on the new board.' It was true. In my excitement over the upgrade I'd neglected this daily ritual. I went over, uncapped the chisel-tipped black pen and took great pleasure in scribing *31st March*. It occurred to me at that moment it would be April the following day.

When I arrived home Tom and Reuben were playing dens under the dining table so I snuck into the kitchen to talk to Barbara.

'Good day?' I said giving her a kiss.

'Not bad; I took Bert his eightieth birthday cake, tracked down the people who'd left their front door wide open and arranged to visit old Margaret's sister in hospital. At least it didn't rain. How about you?'

'Well, I nearly died when Doug overtook a tractor round a blind bend this morning but I don't care because I've got a new whiteboard.'

'Oh, yes, Doug . . .' she said, disregarding both my near demise and new toy. 'I had a chat with Iris when I picked up the boys.'

'Don't tell me: she's finding Reuben hard going.'

She eyed me suspiciously. 'How did you know? Anyway, it took her an age to say it – you know what Iris is like and she does love the boys – but, yes, our younger son is proving troublesome. He's just so . . . physical, and she's got all those valuable china things all over the house.'

'So, let me guess . . . Rosie has offered to have Reuben in the mornings.'

'Doug's obviously told you but, yep, that's what we need to discuss.'

'Well, how do you feel about it? He can't really wreck their house because it's already wrecked,' I said, wickedly.

'It's all those sacks of food they have in the kitchen just lying open I'm concerned about. What if he gets in the mung beans?'

'Well, we have to do something with him. Perhaps we should go over and make a few suggestions to avoid mishap then give it a trial run.'

'OK,' she said, looking unsure. 'They've never had kids, have they? But it is very kind of her and she's a lovely person.'

We talked for another five minutes before the boys realised I was home and careered into the kitchen with demands that I play.

Tom turned and pulled at Barbara's trouser leg. 'Mummy, have you asked Daddy about the animals?'

'No, I haven't had time, darling, sorry.'

'What animals?' I said, picking up the weighty Reuben.

'Well . . .' said Barbara. 'Tom was at playgroup this morning as usual and apparently they were talking about their homes and they were counting things, you know, like how many brothers and sisters and so on.'

'What's that got to do with animals?'

'Well, poor Tom was the only child in playgroup who doesn't have a pet.'

'He's got Reuben – you can't get much wilder than that.'

'Yes, but joking aside, it would give them something to care for.'

'Hang on, you know as well as I do that ten minutes after getting a rabbit or hamster it's the parents that end up scraping poo and filling water bottles. Then a couple of weeks later the things are dead anyway.'

Tom started pulling at my trousers now, ripping out some leg hair. 'Can we have a pet, Daddy, can we, can we?'

Reuben bounced around too, while Barbara grimaced. 'The problem is we don't have much money at the moment, boys,' she said.

'And Daddy doesn't really like to see animals in cages,' I added.

'What about a horse?' said Tom. 'They don't go in cages.'

'Horseee!' called Reuben, doing a jockey impression.

'You could ride it to work,' laughed Barbara. 'It would be quicker than Doug's 2CV.'

Tom looked up with his big eyes. 'Sam Bentley has two horses, five goats, a pig and ten million billion chickens.'

'Sam Bentley lives on a farm,' I said.

'And is stinking rich,' murmured Barbara.

Tom had clearly been thinking. 'Well what about a duck? It could live in the sand pit.'

I held up a finger. 'I'll tell you what, boys. Mummy and I will have a talk about it tonight when you're in bed and see if we think an animal is a good idea.'

Reuben wriggled down while Tom ran along the hallway jumping. 'Yahey, we're gunna get a pet!'

'Oh joy,' I groaned.

At half-past eight the following morning I walked into my classroom and was once more taken by surprise at how different it looked with the sparkling new whiteboard at the front. I picked up one of the dry-wipe pens and went over to it to write the date:

1st April

At that precise moment a naughty idea entered my head.

It was usually handwriting practice on a Tuesday morning and so I took out the book we followed before carefully penning up the next set of cursive letter patterns on the board. I filled up the whole of the surface and included some of the trickiest letter joins on the last line to ensure that everyone would be challenged. I smiled; there was no danger they wouldn't.

At five to nine the first children drifted in and then after registration I asked the class to retrieve their handwriting books and pens.

'Right, Class Three!' I called, waiting for everyone to settle. 'It's handwriting as usual today but the session is going to be very different so listen carefully.'

Even the fidgeters appeared intrigued as I continued. 'Now, you may be aware that the government is making all sorts of changes in schools at the moment. A few years ago we started the National Curriculum and now we have tests for eleven-year-olds and lessons in new subjects like Design and Technology.'

A bit of shuffling started so I got to the point. 'Well, they have just sent a letter to all primary schools in the country saying that they are very concerned that children can only use one hand for writing. Imagine if you are left-handed and you fall off your bike and your left hand has to be bandaged up. Well, you won't be able to do any written work. Or if you sprain a wrist or dislocate a finger on your writing hand then you're going to be stuck.' They stared at me, agog. 'So, what they've decided is that from this week every child in the country must learn to write with both hands, equally well. Now, that means, Class Three, that today you are going to do handwriting with your weaker hand. Everyone must practise so that you can eventually use both.'

The children burst into a babble of noise and questions.

'That's not fair!'

'I can't write wi' me left, it's useless . . .'

'Do Class Four have to do this 'n' all?'

'Me ordinary writin's bad enough!'

I held up two hands. 'STOP! Quiet now, everyone. We've wasted enough time already. Turn to the back of your books and copy the letter patterns on the board now, using your other hand. In silence.'

Amid grumbling and the scrape of chair legs as several individuals contorted themselves into odd postures, the lower juniors of Cragthwaite Primary began a brief and hysterical new chapter of their lives. I fought like fury to keep a straight face as my young charges tackled this tortuous new skill with profound inadequacy.

The results were many and varied, ranging from comically huge letters to ghostly wobbles and eccentric leans. Most individuals looked flustered or bewildered but I didn't let up.

'Make sure every letter is joined properly. It has to be like your ordinary handwriting.'

Strangely, a few seemed to be enjoying the task.

'Ay up, mine's better'n me usual,' I heard Dan whisper to Lawrence.

'Snot as 'ard as ah thought,' said Vicky.

'Quiet please!' I called, not wanting the ruse to be broken just yet; I intended to tour every table first and there was one child I looked forward to seeing in particular.

Ever since she had started school, Susan Bell's writing had been immaculate. Even as a new infant her letter formation was textbook, then as she learned to put sentences together, her handwriting was the epitome of neatness and cursive flow. No comma, no hyphen was out of place: her pages shone with a kind of scholastic perfection rarely seen in an eight-year-old. Until today.

I could see from a distance that Susan was agitated. She twisted her body and writhed in her chair trying to obtain an angle that would somehow give her wobbling left hand a chance of success. But it was not to be. Leaning over her book, I could see her locked in a vicious battle: her right hand hovered over her pen, desperate to wrest control while the beleaguered left flapped around underneath, producing mangled approximations of the letter patterns on the board.

She saw me and threw down her pen. 'Mr Seed, I can't do this. It's a stupid idea and my book is spoiled now.'

'Susan, first of all, you're writing in the back of your book so no one will notice. Secondly, you shouldn't speak to teachers like that and, thirdly, I'd like a word with you at break.'

She sat, stunned. 'About this?'

'No, about how you talk about other children.'

I walked to the front, knowing that I'd put the class through enough tribulation for the day but also ready to deliver the final and most anticipated part of my ruse.

'Right, stop there, pens down,' I said. 'Most of you have actually done very well but the government thinks this is so important that we need to keep practising, so I'm afraid there's another whole side of words to copy on the other side of the board.'

The groan almost took the roof off the classroom but I ignored it, turning instead to lift the whiteboard off its bracket and swing it around. There were actually only two words on the reverse:

APRIL FOOLS!

There was a curious moment of stunned silence followed by bawls of protest, delight, confusion and relief. Then, along with me, Class 3 lapsed into laughter. Well, all except one.

At playtime I called Susan over to my desk and warned her regarding using offensive words about other people. She stood in sour-faced silence knowing that she had been found out.

'I won't take this any further, Susan,' I said. 'As long as it doesn't happen again. After all, you'd hate to hear someone say something like that about you.' She gave the faintest of nods. 'Now,' I said, 'bring over your handwriting book.'

She passed me the crisp yellow exercise book and I opened it at the back while she watched. I opened my desk drawer and pulled out a craft knife, ruler and cutting mat. With great care, I placed the mat under the ugly page of scrawl that defaced her proud book then, using the knife, I cut it away tight to the staples so that there was no trace left.

'There, no one will know about this page. I don't want it to spoil your work either – it's beautiful and I really value the care that you take.'

She let out a low sigh of relief and her tight-lipped mouth opened. 'Thank you,' she said.

I smiled. 'Right, Susan: this is my side of the bargain, now keep yours, OK?'

And as far as I was aware, for the rest of the year, she did.

On the way home in the rattling 2CV I shared my April Fools stunt with an envious Doug then told him that we'd be delighted for Rosie to look after Reuben in the mornings when Barbara was at work, adding that they would need to child-proof their home considerably.

'Leaving power tools out is a no-no,' I said. 'In fact, anything that could be deployed by a desperate, freedom-fighting toddler who's dedicated to testing the limits of acceptability in all things.'

'Right, it sounds like it's going to be a barrel of laughs.'

'No, I'm embellishing a lot. He's very loveable and loyal – if Rosie keeps him active and gives lots of cuddles they'll both be fine.'

We pootled along beside Applesett Green and Doug pulled up outside Craven Bottoms. I shot out, desperate to tell Barbara about the Great Handwriting Hoax.

As it happened, I didn't mention the prank for several hours that evening. As soon as I opened the door, I could tell that something had changed. There was a big rumpus in the living room and a slight delay before Tom, tomato-faced, came rushing into the hallway to see me.

'Daddy, Daddy! Come and look, come on!' He dragged me through into the lounge where Reuben was lying on the floor laughing like a drain. Standing on his tummy, shaky and suspicious, was a tiny, mottled-brown furball. A kitten.

Chapter Fifteen

Helen

'He's called Alfie!' shouted Tom as the little fluffy kitten pounced on to Reuben's feet causing him to screech in mock pain.

'What's going on?' I said, as Barbara entered the room, looking somewhat sheepish.

'Before you say anything, yes, I have remembered that you're allergic to cats.'

'Then why—'

'Hang on. This little one is just on loan – it's a trial to see if you survive.'

'It'll certainly be a trial for me,' I said. 'I could lurch into spasm at any moment.'

'Oh don't be ridiculous – they only make you sneeze a bit.'

'Well if my throat locks up and I turn blue you'll have to explain to these boys where Daddy went . . .'

'But it's so *cute*!' cried Tom, overcome with excitement.

'Funny pussy cat,' said Reuben in a growly tone.

Barbara went over and picked up the huge-eyed miniature feline, bringing him over. I couldn't deny he was very sweet. She held him out towards me. 'Look, you haven't even sniffled yet.'

'I'd better not touch it just in case.'

'Don't be silly, we have to find out if you really have a reaction to him.'

Tom bounced on the sofa. 'Stroke him, Daddy, he's all soft. And he doesn't bite, except he bit Reuben and scratched him.'

'That's because Reuben poked him with an Action Man,' said Barbara thrusting the kitten on to my lap as I sat down. Right away I felt his needle-like claws and heard him mewing.

'He likes you,' said Tom.

'He may well do,' I said, 'but I'll probably pass out in a minute. Have you got 999 on speed dial?'

'Stop joking and just hold him,' said Barbara, her voice betraying exasperation.

The warm, trembling mite snuggled on to my lap. 'What makes you so confident I won't have an asthma attack, then?'

'Ah,' she smiled. 'That's where Mummy has been extra clever and where all my unpaid postie services have paid off.'

'Eh?'

'Not only would Alfie be free because he's one of a batch belonging to a customer that I've helped a few times, but he's also a Siberian long-haired cat.'

'He's certainly hirsute. What's special about Russian cats, then?'

'I'm not entirely sure but Mr Redgarth assured me that they cause far fewer allergic reactions than most cats. It's something to do with their spit.'

'It spits!'

'No, but it licks its fur clean, you buffoon.'

'Sounds very dubious to me.'

Barbara stood with a triumphant smile. 'Well why haven't you sneezed, then? Are your eyes itchy?'

'A bit.' But then I laughed, knowing it wasn't true.

Tom crashed into me with excitement. 'Can we keep him, Daddy? Can we, can we?'

Reuben came up and stroked the little yawning shape. 'Oo, can we?'

Barbara joined the campaign. 'He's not in a cage.'

I was not only outvoted but outcharmed as Alfie flicked his frizzy tail about. 'Well, maybe, if he doesn't make me poorly, and Mummy cleans up the stinkpods.'

The boys jumped and cheered with a great din, frightening our new pet so that he spiked his talons into my thigh. 'Oooowwww!'

Barbara lifted him off but he was hooked into my flesh. His great eyes were the eeriest of green. 'Come on, poppet.'

'Just one thing, though,' I said rubbing the wound once he was free. 'He's clearly too wild for an Alfie; I'm calling him Ulf.'

Helen Guy came up to me at morning break as I sipped my tea during playground duty. She was a bonny farmer's daughter from just outside Shawby and one of the quieter members of Class 3. Her long, corn-blonde hair and strawberry cheeks gave her the appearance of rude health and her broad local accent lent appeal to her character.

'Av jus' remembered it's the trip nex' week, Mr Seed. Where are we off ter?'

'It's to the creamery near Twissham so we can see how they make Swinnerdale cheese.'

'Eck, are we gunna be mekkin' cheese, then?'

I chuckled. 'No, it's not easy to make it in school.'

'Ma gran used ter mek cheese on the farm. We 'ave a press wi' big stones and a right load of old stuff. Shallus ask if ah can bring 'owt in?'

'That would be really kind, Helen, thanks.'

'Eck, ah don't think we'll be able ter get them stones in Land Rover, tho' – they're massive.'

I smiled; she was the only child in the school who said "heck" and I found it charming. 'Well, just bring what you can. Oh, and is your granny still around?'

'Oh aye, she's seventy summat now but still 'elps out on the farm.'

'Do you think she might like to come in and talk to the class about cheese-making? It would be great for our food topic.'

'Eck, I dunno, she's not really one fer the limelight is me gran. I really doubt it.'

She ran off and I made a mental note to remind the class about the visit. The children were enjoying our project on food, especially where it involved practical work but I'd found that it was more than a challenge to organise cooking activities in a small village school that had no proper facilities. There was no hot water in the classroom and the little Baby Belling oven on its trolley was too awkward to lug up the steps into the mobile classroom anyway. I'd organised a group of parent helpers to cook various items from scones to pancakes in the staffroom but this often led to buttery patches on the carpet and lumps of flour on the chairs. The hardest part, however, was having to test samples of the children's produce, knowing that their grime-ridden, badly washed hands had been delving into the mix. Still, I smiled, chewed, swallowed and complimented: it was a part of the job.

A week later the children of Class 3 clambered on to Mr Ripley's elderly coach amid loud arguments over who should have the back seat.

Colin was in the thick of it. 'Oi, Estelle, we baggsied the back – push off!'

She set her face. 'Get lost, we were here first.'

I slipped past a group of bystanders and reached the scene. Dan Alderson was pulling at Vicky Rushworth's sleeve while Trudy and Estelle held her down on the rear seat.

'That will do!' I called, apologising to the driver for the noise and kerfuffle. I sent all of the children involved to other seats and let some of the quiet, restrained individuals have charge of the coveted rear vantage. Colin and Dan went away muttering dark protests, having declared that this was all unfair and that boys always received the raw deal. My two parent helpers Mrs Lawson and Mrs Caygill shook their heads and I guessed that it wouldn't be long until the whole village heard about my class's unruliness.

Thus the trip to the cheese factory started rowdily and from then on things barely improved. The bus journey was only just over twenty miles but after ten minutes Martine complained that she felt sick. I gave her a carrier bag and sent her to the front. Gary then announced that he needed the toilet.

'Can't you hang on until we're there?' I said.

He dug his teeth into his lip and jiggled up and down. 'Ah don't think ah can.'

'Er, what is it you need?' I asked.

'Eh?' he said thrusting a hand crotchwards.

'Is it a number one or number two?'

Howard Sedgwick was monitoring the exchange. 'By t'look of 'im ah'd say it were a number three, Mr Seed.'

We all laughed and, after establishing it was just a wee, the bus drew to a halt, while Gary scuttled behind the roadside wall to cheers and guffaws from the already boisterous passengers. He came back on board with a dim smile, wiping his hands on his jumper and regaling Howard with the details while, once more, I calmed down the rabble.

The Wittonbeck Creamery was a small, family-owned factory which kept up the centuries-old tradition of making pale Swinnerdale Cheese. The owners were related to one of the school's governors and had agreed to allow a one-off visit, breaking their usual embargo on tours despite hygiene concerns. As usual, I was the most enthusiastic about the idea in school and so Joyce had given Class 3 the thumbs up.

Mr Middleton, the foreman, welcomed us into the building and warned the children that they mustn't touch anything unless given permission beforehand. The first thing he did was to take everyone outside and point to the large stainless steel tank into which milk deliveries were made.

I heard Colin Morphet whisper to Ian, 'This is gunna be really boring.'

What had brought this on? The trip had hardly begun and already it was being dismissed. I thought back to my early days at Cragthwaite Primary under the grim leadership of the ultra-traditional and long-standing Howard Raven when the children spent whole days at their desks doing exercises from books. There were no school visits at all then and it had taken the new broom of Joyce Berry to revolutionise the education offered by the establishment and give the dale's youngsters a chance to see and learn about what was around them.

But it seemed now that some of them were taking all this for granted. I watched the class as Mr Middleton explained from where the milk was transported. Most children were looking away, or chattering; Martine was yawning.

As we filed back inside the building, I thought ahead to the summer's residential trip to the Yorkshire coast and the enormous effort of planning, organising, collecting money, supervising and leading that was involved. I couldn't bear the thought that the children wouldn't appreciate such an experience; perhaps the attitudes in evidence here were just a one off.

'The milk must first be pasteurised in this vat,' said Mr Middleton, indicating another large metal container. 'Do you all know what that word means?'

There were a few nods and grumbles and fingers raised.

'Come on, Class Three!' I called, trying to drum up some zest. 'I know all you farm children know this. What about the rest of you? Lawrence, do you know?'

He had been facing the other way, pointing to a calendar on the wall and snickering. He quickly spun round.

'Er, it's a big thing like a barrel.'

'What, pasteurise?'

'I thought you meant vat.' The class squawked while Lawrence reddened. Mr Middleton, who looked like he'd rather be elsewhere, explained the word and marched us on to the next room.

Martine, who had thankfully avoided filling the carrier bag on the bus, sidled up to me. 'When do we get to the shop, Mr Seed?'

I smiled. 'Shop? This is a factory, Martine.'

'But yer said we could buy stuff, like.'

'Yes, they sell cheese at the end, like I explained before, remember?'

Her face crumpled. 'Cheese? Ain't they got any sweets or pencil sharpeners or 'owt?'

'No, Martine.'

She walked back to her partner Vicky and communicated her disgust. 'I 'ate cheese 'n' all,' said her friend.

Mr Middleton pointed to a large, low tank and was about to start talking when he noticed that most of the children had wandered away to peer into various containers.

'Not there!' he bellowed, causing some of them to jump. Colin Morphet laughed and pushed Stephen Gray back towards our guide, knocking the unfortunate boy into some metal shelves with a loud rattle. I gave Colin a suitable glare while Stephen clasped his arm in some pain. Mrs Caygill went over to see if he was all right, as did Anna Reed.

'Right, at this stage of the process something called rennet is added to the milk,' said Mr Middleton, anxious to crack on. 'Does anyone know what rennet is?'

No one responded; once again, my class left a sorry impression.

'Come on, at least have a guess,' I said, thinking that I should have prepared better beforehand.

Vicky put up a hand.

'Is it a type of rock?'

'No, that's granite,' I said, imagining a very hard cheese.

Anna raised her arm.

'Yes?' said Mr Middleton.

'Stephen's wrist is bleeding,' she said. Amid a lot of fuss, a first aid box was located and the now colourless boy was bandaged and guarded by Barry's mum. I overheard Dan threatening to thump Colin for injuring his friend, while Estelle complained that we hadn't seen any cheese yet. Mr Middleton moved everyone on and the class never did find out what rennet was.

After a short break where I reminded everyone not to touch anything including each other, we reached the first part of the factory that they found interesting. Two women in white coats and hats, with gloved hands, stood next to a set of broad shelves containing hundreds of miniature round Swinnerdale cheeses about the size of pork pies. Between them was what looked like an enormous saucepan. One of the ladies smiled as we entered and everyone watched her delicately dip one of the cheeses into the mysterious pale yellow mixture before placing it on a second shelf.

'This is the waxing area,' said Mr Middleton. 'These are the small, two-pound handmade cheeses and we give them a wax coating by hand dipping. Each cheese is half-dipped in melted wax then cooled before the other half is dipped. Any questions about this process?'

'Does it hurt?' asked Martine, without putting up her hand.

The women smiled. 'No, but the wax is quite hot,' said the elder of the two.

Howard raised an arm. 'Have you ever dropped one in?'

The younger of the two ladies looked up. 'Once or twice. We fish 'em out with a long spoon.'

I intervened. 'Does anyone have any questions about the cheese?'

They didn't.

Dan then raised an arm. 'If a rat fell in there would it die?'

I was relieved when we reached the end of the tour and there were no more incidents. I bought one of the small wax-covered cheeses, noticing that the only child to buy one was Helen. 'It's fer me gran,' she said. 'She still likes a bite wi' her apple pie.'

There was a moment for reflection while I stood and waited for the children to return from the toilets and make their way back on to the bus. Personally I'd found the cheese factory really interesting and enjoyed seeing how something was made and yet, strangely, the children had been out of sorts and indifferent. I could only put it down to my own insufficient preparation and excitement in the week before: I knew that a teacher's enthusiasm could generate anticipation and interest like nothing else, but on this occasion I evidently hadn't invested enough time and energy beforehand.

A waving arm interrupted my contemplation.

'Mr Seed, can the boys have the back seat?' It was Lawrence.

'Yes, if what?'

'We're good.'

'Will you be?'

'We'll try.' At least he was honest.

As the last children boarded, I made a resolution that I would never let this happen again with a school trip. I would get Class 3 so well prepared and fervent about the forthcoming residential visit to the Yorkshire coast that it would have to be a success.

When the jittery coach coughed into Cragthwaite it was past home time and several concerned parents were hanging around the school gates. The children streamed off the bus and ran down the path, forgetting that they were supposed to hand in their worksheets and put up their chairs in the classroom. I sighed and waved to the longsuffering driver before apologising to the two parent helpers for such a trying day.

When I turned around I was surprised to see a body there, waiting on the path. It was Helen Guy. She smiled.

'Thank you fer the trip, Mr Seed. It were grand.' She turned and walked away leaving me with a feeling that perhaps there was hope for the human race after all.

Saturday was one of those fresh, bright, breezy April days that brought from Applesett and the Dales around that glorious notion that summer wasn't too far away. The sun blinked out between racing clouds of intense white, illuminating the clumps of daffodils around the village green.

I was in a good mood too, any lingering dejection over the creamery trip having been melted away by Helen Guy's small act of gratitude. I pondered on how such a simple deed could have raised my spirits so much but this was often the way in primary school; so many hours were spent cajoling, reprimanding, hushing and correcting that when some spontaneous kind words or behaviour appeared we teachers would rejoice and convince ourselves that all the effort was worthwhile.

In our cramped front garden at Craven Bottoms, barely six feet across and forty feet long where it wrapped around the front and side of the house behind a boulder wall, things were starting to grow and Barbara was poking at them with a trowel while I kept the boys occupied.

'What do you think this is?' she said pointing to a burgeoning plant.

'A weed. Or it could be a hydrangea,' I replied, enjoying the sun's warmth for the first time that year.

'Don't be silly, hydrangeas are great big woody things, even I know that.'

'Maybe it's a scabious. Or a Triffid.'

'I don't know why I bother asking; you haven't a clue.'

'Why the sudden interest in gardening, anyway?'

'Rosie was showing me her garden and talking about all her plans for it. She said she'd come down here and help us with ours. She knows loads about plants.'

'Actually, that would be good,' I said. 'Most of the houses do have lovely cottage gardens and ours is a bit, well, "lacking in colour" would be generous.'

At that moment the front door opened and Tom appeared, still in his pyjamas.

'Daddy, can we take Ulf outside to play on the grass?'

'Well, maybe if you get dressed.'

Barbara looked up. 'And only if Daddy stays out here to make sure that he doesn't go on to the road.'

'No problem on a lovely day like this.'

'As long as you remember you said you'd also tidy the house and sort lunch; your parents are going to be here in a couple of hours.'

I let the boys stay outside with their little fluffy pet for a few minutes. The timid kitten was unsure what to make of the turf and spent most of its time mewing and sniffing everything around, trying to identify the curious stew of new scents to be found in this daunting environment. We were just about to return inside when Billy Iveson approached with his familiar collie on the way to his daily walk up Buttergill.

'Ay up, lads,' the retired farmer called, cheerful as always.

'Now then, Billy,' I said, as the boys came to the wall.

'Billy!' shouted Tom.

'Biyee!' chorused Reuben.

'Who's that little fella yer got there?' said the crusty-faced Dalesman.

'A cat!' said Tom.

'Byyy, it's a young'un. Just a few days owd, by t'look o' things. Gonna be a good mouser is t'chap?'

'We hope so,' I said, picking up the ball of fluff who was trying to explore through the bushes.

'Grand day, any road,' said Billy as Reuben pulled up a handful of the long grass from the corner of the garden. The toddler leaned on the wall and held it out towards the old man.

I laughed. 'Looks like you've got a present, Billy.'

Graciously the old man accepted the green blades and said thank you. And so began a curious tradition: every day that the boys were outside they would watch out for Billy passing by and each time they would call him over and give him a handful of grass. He never questioned the arrangement and always received this curious gift with a smile and an air of gratitude. It carried on for years and I often wondered if anyone ever noticed him quietly disposing of the grass.

My parents arrived for lunch and were delighted to find the village bathed in spring sunshine. They loved the Dales and right away began to talk about what kind of walk we might do in the afternoon. First, however, my tall, greying father lit the stove – whatever the weather, he could never resist a real fire. My mother, as usual, despaired that he never asked.

After admiring Ulf, everyone sat down to eat, with the highlight of the meal being the small hand-made Swinnerdale cheese which I left whole on the board in the middle. It was truly delicious and everyone was soon chopping at it with a long knife. I noticed that my dad had only tried a small piece.

'Don't you like the cheese, then?' I asked.

He wrinkled his nose a little. 'It has a good flavour but it's just a bit waxy.'

I looked at his plate and noticed the problem. 'That's because you've eaten the wax.'

We all craned forward and saw the evidence for ourselves. Without his glasses, he'd cut a sliver from the outside of the cheese and only nibbled the pale yellow wax coating. Barbara erupted into a long splutter and everyone joined in, the merriment lasting for most of the meal.

In the afternoon, with our teenage babysitter Holly Weatherall installed to look after Reuben and Ulf, the five of us headed up the side of Spout Fell for a walk through the woods and a chance to admire the views across Hubberdale. We followed the track that led over the beck at the bottom of the village via an ancient stone bridge then climbed the hillside. The fields were dotted with buttercups and in the distance lambs explored while their mothers enjoyed the fresh grass which everywhere was sprouting vigorously.

'Look, the first butterfly of the year,' said my father, pointing to a tortoiseshell sailing by on the breeze.

'I can hear a woodpecker, too,' said Barbara and we stopped to listen to the familiar rattle from the woods ahead.

'Can I see it?' said Tom.

'Maybe, if you're quiet,' I said.

'Hurray!' he called, very loudly.

When we reached the mossy woods, the ground was carpeted with broad blades of wild garlic. The ash trees above were still bare but just beyond them delicate leaves were emerging to create the first canopy and cast over the forest floor that soft emerald light. Further on the ground was a riot of violets, anemones, celandines and clumps of soft primroses competing against the emerging stems of bluebells.

'Oh, this is so beautiful,' said my mother.

'Can we see the pecker now?' said Tom.

We chuckled and looked around at the fallen trees. There was birdsong in abundance and the distant sound of a rushing torrent tumbling through the glade. The path reached the edge of the woods and we looked out to admire the view of hazy hills and distant hamlets of tight, squat cottages.

'What's that?' asked Tom as he and I walked along the stony path, leaving the others behind to take some photos. He pointed down at a splattered heap of brown and white droppings among which were little clumps of tiny white bones.

'It must be a bird,' I said. 'But it's funny that they're all in the same place.'

I looked up and there, no more than four feet above my head was a huge tawny owl, regarding us suspiciously. Its very presence made me jump and Tom looked up just in time to see it spread its great brown wings and take off along the edge of the trees.

'Whoah!' I said.

'A owl!' said Tom.

'It sure was.'

We raced back to tell the others and Tom, barely able to produce words and breathe at the same time his excitement was so great, described the 'shooting owl', as he named it.

The path then turned back into the trees and climbed before following the contours along a fairly steep section of hillside. Tom needed the loo so Barbara and I aided him while my parents continued along the path. They had only walked a few paces when there was an explosion of flapping as a pheasant rose in panic from the undergrowth. My mum, who had almost trodden on the hidden bird, screeched in surprise and lurched backwards, losing her footing. She bounced off my father and started to stumble down the hill through the trees in a comical backward dance.

'Where's Granny going?' said Tom, watching the action as we pulled up his trousers.

'I can't stop!' she cried, half-giggling at her predicament, while my father made a dash to try and grab her before she collided with a tree. After a few more staggers, she tripped over a bramble and grabbed a sapling which bent ominously before pinging her up straight.

'Are you all right?' we called, trying not to laugh. I arrived at the same time as my dad and we saw her creased over in a kind of shock but still, somehow, giggling.

'I think I've wet myself,' she said.

On the way back to the house we walked up the village green and, as always, Tom wanted a stopover at the swings. There was a group of five or six boys playing football a few yards away and my father sat on the nearby bench to watch them. As I pushed Tom on the swing I saw my dad stand up and walk on to the grass to pick up something blue he'd spotted. It was a glove. He held it up and called out.

'Does this belong to someone here?'

A skinny boy of about ten trotted over and plucked it from his hand. 'It's mine,' he said bluntly before turning his back on my dad and re-joining the game.

I knew that the evident lack of thanks would irk my father and, sure enough, he was muttering as he walked over to us. 'Kids today . . . not one of them seems to have any manners.'

'Oh, I don't know,' I said, smiling to myself and thinking of Helen Guy. 'There is one I know.'

Chapter Sixteen

Anna

As April neared its end, the trees on the green at Applesett unfurled their new leaves to announce spring proper. The village was busy with people tidying up their gardens, painting window frames and preparing for the tourist season. At home our thoughts had turned to holidays. With our finances still somewhat perilous, we had abandoned hope of a week away anywhere in the summer and had decided instead to negotiate a series of cheap weekends staying with friends around the country. Barbara was on the phone discussing one of these with someone when I arrived home from school one late afternoon.

'Really, are you sure?' she said. 'That's so kind.' I caught fragments of her conversation and wondered who was on the other end of the line. She appeared a few minutes later looking very pleased.

'Good day at work?' she said.

'Not bad; tiring as ever. Who was that on the phone?'

'Ah, exciting news . . .' she said cryptically. 'We're not busy next weekend are we?'

'Erm, I don't think so – I haven't planned anything. Why?'

'Well, Ruth Metcalfe rang earlier and we got talking about holidays and I mentioned that we were doing a few weekends here and there, so she said did we know that Richard and Ellie Suggett have a caravan on their farm.'

'Just remind me who Richard and Ellie are.'

'You know, the funny auctioneer guy from Skeddlebeck.'

'Oh, right, Rick . . .' I cast my mind back to the mischievous, gabbling character who ran the livestock mart.

'Yes, well, Ruth calls him Richard. Anyway, she suggested I give them a call as they don't usually have anyone in the caravan until May and I thought it would be lovely for the boys to spend a couple of days on a farm.'

'But can you imagine Reuben constrained inside a little caravan?'

'No, it's not little – it's one of those big static jobs. It's connected up to mains and water, the lot. What's more, they said we could have it for twenty quid next weekend.'

'Where do they live?'

'It's just outside Arkleton, where the auction is. Apparently it's up the hill behind the village and Ruth says it has amazing views. What's more they've got animals and they said we can help out feeding the lambs and calves.'

I could see she was genuinely excited. 'Sounds like a done deal, then.'

'Well, what do you think?'

'Get it booked.'

'I'm glad you said that because I already have.'

Anna Reed stood at my desk in the classroom patiently waiting for me to mark her number work. As usual it was neat and the answers were all correct. She was a fastidious girl who loved school and one of the hardest workers I had ever taught. She wasn't as clever as the most able children in the class but compensated through her exemplary approach to learning. I passed her the book after ticking everything and smiled.

'Well done, Anna.'

'Oh, can I have a comment, please, Mr Seed?' She was a slim, smartly dressed girl with mousy hair and serious eyes.

'Go on, then,' I said, writing *Good, as always* beneath her work. She skipped away, satisfied, and I knew that she'd go on to the next piece of work without making a fuss or wasting time.

Anna's father was the RAF officer who had invited us to see the Tornado jet, while her mother was a supply teacher, and to me they appeared to be a model family in every way. I hadn't taught Anna's brother Ben because they had only moved to Swinnerdale recently but he often came to events at school and, like his parents, was affable and bright. On parents' evening, all four of them had toured the classroom looking carefully at Anna's work then at the displays I had spent so much time assembling.

'She's doing well still, I gather?' said the sandy, cheerful Mrs Reed.

I nodded. 'Very well. I can hardly fault her work and attitude, and she gets on with just about everyone. A model pupil, in fact.'

Mr Reed rubbed his daughter's hair as she grinned. 'That's smashing, Biccie.'

Must be a pet name I thought, continuing. 'So, er, there's not much more to say, really. Anna just needs to carry on and she'll continue to improve in everything. Do you, er, have any questions?'

'I can see that her academic work is very good,' said Mrs Reed. 'How does she do in the more creative subjects?'

The truth was that she was only average at most. 'Well, she's not as confident in Art or Design and Technology as in, say, English or Maths but she still does her best and some of her ideas are interesting.'

Mr Reed winked at me, while Anna's mum gave a knowing smile. 'Well,' she said, 'she's certainly a fan of yours. Not a day goes by without me hearing, "Mr Seed says this, or Mr Seed says that . . ."'

Anna leaned over and gave her mother a gentle push. 'Hey, don't tell him that, Mum.' She was blushing softly.

I chortled. 'Really? I don't think I've ever had a fan before.'

Mrs Reed nodded. 'Oh yes; you can't do anything wrong as far as this one's concerned. She wasn't that keen on her previous teacher at her last school, were you, pet? But she's very happy now, so we're delighted.'

Mr Reed smiled and gave me a crushing handshake. 'Thank you, we really appreciate it. And if you ever want another visit to the RAF base . . .' He winked again.

'That's very kind. I didn't think you'd want us back after that, er, episode with the Tornado.'

'Oh, no prob at all, really – just give me a buzz.'

Mrs Reed stood up. 'And you'd better give me a few teaching tips too, some time!'

We all chuckled and I sighed, wishing that there were more people like this. Even Ben thanked me and said goodbye.

That had been a few weeks ago and now, with a queue waiting at my desk, I had to snap out of my reverie.

'Byyy, yer looked like you were miles away there, Mr Seed.'

It was Gary. He handed me a smeared piece of paper which was torn along one edge.

'Where's your maths book, Gary?'

'Can't find it. I did look ferrit bu' ah reckon someone's nicked it. It's a rum do.'

'Gary, why would anyone want to steal your book?'

'Ter copy, mebbes?' We both knew that this was highly unlikely. 'Any road, ah'll bray 'em whoever it wa'.'

'Gary, there will be no "braying". If we find your book, I'll deal with it. Anyway, let's see how you've done.'

I scanned the sorry, crumpled page which was full of violent crossings out and indecipherable corrections. Question Two was interesting:

If a can of cola and a toffee bar cost 50p and the toffee bar is 18p, how much is the can of cola? Give your reasons.

Gary's answer was just about readable:

Cola is 30p. I know becos I by one down the shop most days.

At morning break the children were bursting to get outside into the spring sunshine but Anna held back, as she often did.

'Would you like me to clean the board, Mr Seed?'

'That would be very kind,' I said.

She tackled the glossy whiteboard meticulously, ensuring that every mark was eradicated.

'Don't you want to go out and play?' I said, wishing that I was outside.

'I prefer doing jobs. Are there any more? Shall I tidy the maths books?'

'They're fine, Anna. You go out and get some fresh air now.'

She came up to my desk and glanced about before dropping her voice. 'Mr Seed, there's something I need to tell you.'

'Is it important?'

'Yes.'

'Go on, then.'

'Mr Seed, Jason Fisher has got sweets and he sells them in the playground.'

I tried to look disapproving, although it hardly amounted to a major crime considering the problems I'd had with him during the year. 'Oh right, well, I'll sort that out. Thanks.'

Reluctantly she headed for the door.

'Anna.'

'Yes?'

'Why do your parents call you Biccie?'

'Oh, when I was a toddler I raided the biscuit tin but instead of eating the biscuits I was counting them.'

I shook my head and smiled; it didn't surprise me. 'Go on, out you go, Biccie.'

There were five minutes of break left. I thought about investigating Jason's black market bonbon operation but decided that a cup of tea was more urgent. Besides, it would help with his understanding of money in Maths.

The English lesson after break had only been going for a few minutes when there was a knock at the door and Eileen Marsett, the timid school secretary, came into the room looking unusually flustered. A woman followed her: it was Mrs Reed and she was as white as a sheet. I knew right away that something was wrong and hurried over to speak to them while the class stared.

'Get on with your work everyone,' I called before turning to Eileen who leaned into my ear to whisper.

'I'm sorry, Andy, but I'm afraid Anna's brother has had a serious accident on the way to school. He's in hospital now.' She stumbled and I could see tears forming in her eyes. Mrs Reed was shaking.

Eileen gathered herself and continued while I felt my heart rate hasten.

'Mrs Reed wants to take Anna as they've got to go to the hospital now and don't know when they'll be back.'

I reached over to touch Mrs Reed on the arm while she dug her teeth into her lip and mouthed a thank you, then I called Anna over and told her just to leave everything. The class, in silence, gawped as the poor girl stood up wondering what was happening. I could see that her mother was desperate to hug her but simply grasped her hand and turned to the door.

Just outside I spoke to Eileen while mother and daughter hurried away.

'What happened?'

She could barely speak and pushed a lace handkerchief into her eyes. 'Ben was, he was knocked off his bike this morning by a van.'

I tried not to picture the scene. 'Is he at Bilthorpe?'

'He was but they've taken him to Leeds. He has head injuries . . . Oh, Andy, it sounds awful.'

I nearly hugged her but thought about my unsupervised class on the other side of the door. 'I need to go back inside, Eileen – we'll just have to pray. Is there any way to find out how he is?'

'Joyce is going to call the hospital later.' She turned and hurried up the path while I took a deep breath and tried to compose myself before walking through the door.

'What happened?' said Estelle, looking genuinely concerned. 'Is Anna all right?'

'Yes, but her brother's had an accident. I can't tell you any more.'

I drifted back to my desk in a daze and wondered whether I should have told the children anything. In a village like Cragthwaite they would find out soon anyway.

The rest of the morning was strange. The children sensed my shock and behaved accordingly, working more quietly than usual in the sombre atmosphere. When the noon bell finally rang I sent the children out, then rushed into the main building to ask Joyce if there was any news. Like Eileen, she looked haggard.

'The hospital can't give out any details yet,' she said. 'We'll just have to wait.'

'Do you know any more about how it happened?'

'Mrs Reed told me a bit but she could hardly speak and obviously she just wanted to pick up Anna and go. Basically Ben was riding to Ingleburn like he normally does and this van cut across him to take the Beckhouses turning. He wasn't wearing a helmet and I suppose the poor lad must have hit his head on the road. I don't think anything else is broken, mercifully.'

We stood in silence for a moment then Val came into the office with a heavy sigh. 'Bloody horrible.' She knew Ben better than the rest of us, having taught him for a term. 'Such a nice lad, too.'

'They've taken him to Leeds, so it must be really serious,' said Joyce.

'Hmmm,' said Val. 'There's a brain injuries unit in the General Infirmary. At least he'll get the best care.'

'I just hope there isn't too much swelling,' said Joyce. 'I think it's the build-up of fluid that's really dangerous in these cases. It happened with a neighbour of mine years ago.' I made an excuse to go, not wanting to hear any more.

I cannot recall much of that afternoon; it passed in a kind of haze, and I called Doug Burns after school to see if he was going home early or not. Although he taught at Ben's school he knew just the bare minimum about the boy's condition, and said that it had cast a pall over the whole secondary school, not least since one of the sixth-formers had seen him lying in the road.

Back at home, Tom and Reuben were pleased to see me back early but were unable to understand why I didn't want to play. At least they had little Ulf to keep them amused. The kitten was now climbing everything and chasing small objects rolled across the floor, which the boys found highly entertaining.

Barbara was shocked to hear about the accident and could tell from my expression how fearful I was about Ben.

'You feel so helpless in these situations,' I said. 'There's nothing you can do.'

'When the boys are in bed we'll pray for him. I'll call Adam and Ruth and ask them to pray too. At least we can do that.'

Tom and Reuben were safely tucked in by seven-thirty and Barbara and I lit the stove and made a cup of tea before sitting down. There was only one thing on our minds.

'I wonder what the situation is at the hospital,' I said. 'I really want to know.'

'Even if we rang them I don't know that they'd tell us anything. Don't they have a "families only" system these days?'

'That's what Joyce said; I suppose they must be careful with confidentiality.'

Barbara shook her head slowly. 'It must be dreadful for Ben's parents and his sister, though. They must feel helpless even if they do know what's going on.'

'Maybe they've had good news?'

'Maybe . . .' There was a pause. 'I can't imagine what I'd be like if something like this happened to one of our boys.'

We sat for several minutes, contemplating the unthinkable before Barbara reminded me that we were supposed to be praying. We sat with our heads bowed for twenty minutes and did our best, calling out from the heart.

At the end I felt oddly better. 'It feels like we've done something anyway.'

We watched TV for a couple of hours in an absent-minded fashion, unable to do anything else, then sat and chatted again. After some time, I noticed that the stove had gone out and the room was cold. I glanced at my watch and was shocked to see that it was nearly midnight.

'We'd better get to bed,' said Barbara. But neither of us moved.

'I can't,' I said. 'Maybe we need to pray some more.'

'It's very late.'

'Let's try, just for a few minutes.'

We mumbled some prayers then opened our eyes. 'I just can't go to bed not knowing what's going on,' I said.

'You can't call the hospital at this time,' said Barbara.

'There'll be somebody on duty.' I knew that she was right but I somehow felt compelled to do it. I rang Bilthorpe Hospital who gave me the number for Leeds Infirmary. It took some time being passed around and giving my details until I finally heard the voice of a doctor involved with the case.

He sounded tired. 'I'm sorry, who did you say you are?'

'I'm the teacher of Ben's younger sister – she was taken out of my classroom this morning to go to the hospital and, well, I just need to know how he is.'

'I see.' There was a moment's pause. 'I can't tell you much. Well, he's at a critical point. His brain has been swelling but it's slowing. If the pressure doesn't increase much more we're hopeful, but it's touch and go. I can't say any more.'

'Thank you, that's a great help. I know you're doing everything. Erm, are his parents still there?'

'Yes, they're by his bedside.'

'Can you please just do me a kind favour and tell them I called. Say Mr Seed and his wife are praying for Ben.'

'OK, I will, goodbye.'

The journey to the far western edge of Yorkshire took us over an hour but it was with great excitement that we saw two black metal gates along the verdant lane, next to which was a drooping sign proclaiming Birk Bank Farm. I turned the Alfasud on to the rough track and followed it between tight stone walls until a view opened out revealing the folding sweep of hills that made up the western Dales.

'That's beautiful,' said Barbara.

Idle lambs lay in the fields on either side between sprouts of nettles and old baths of weeds, then we saw a cluster of angled barns, thick-set in ancient stone, heavy with crusted slab roofs.

'Are we there?' said Tom, who had quietly sucked his thumb for most of the way.

'We are,' I said, stopping the car outside a long, low farmhouse. A scratchy black and tan cat stretched on the grass and we heard the screech of oystercatchers overhead. We wondered how little Ulf was getting on at Rosie's back in Applesett. Trickles of slurry and piles of straw coloured the cobbled farmyard next door and I hoped that we'd remembered to bring the boys' wellies.

We knocked on the door and were greeted by the raven-haired Ellie Suggett with a smile as broad as it was genuine.

'Hello Seeds, welcome to Birk Bank!'

We were ushered inside the snug farmhouse kitchen and I settled next to the Aga with a half-awake Reuben in my arms. Two little children emerged to check us out: Sarah aged three and Nathan, a muddy-faced toddler of two.

'Richard's just out tending to the cows,' said our host, handing us fat mugs of tea. We talked about the journey and once again we reiterated how kind it was of these people we barely knew to let us stay on their farm for a pittance. A few minutes later we viewed the spacious caravan and the boys began to run round excitedly exploring.

When we emerged, the tall curly haired figure of Rick Suggett emerged from a shed, bucket in hand.

'Oh, it's you,' he said in mock disappointment, looking at me. 'And this must be Barbara. I've heard a lot about you . . . Some of it was good.'

We all laughed while Ellie shook her head. I had warned my wife that this man was cheeky and rude but funny too, and the confirmation had arrived swiftly.

'Come on inside,' he said, 'and we'll find you some jobs to do.' He turned towards our boys who regarded him with a mixture of fascination and suspicion. 'You must be Thomas, and this big strong one must be Reuben.' He held out his palm to shake hands with Tom then at the last second withdrew it, waggling his fingers against his nose and sticking a tongue out. Tom giggled while Reuben hid behind Barbara.

An hour later we were sitting in front of a monster steak pie and bowls of steaming vegetables at the big kitchen table.

'How's that young lad who had the accident near Ingleburn?' asked Ellie.

It took me by surprise. 'Oh, Ben Reed? I didn't know you knew anything about him.'

'Adam phoned that night and asked us to pray. They took him to Leeds, I gather.'

'Yes, he had nasty head injuries but he's stabilised now. It was a horrible night for the family because he was in real danger at one point.' I glanced at the four children, not wanting to scare them by saying any more.

'So, do they think he's going to be OK?' said Rick.

'Remarkably, yes. He's conscious and talking now but very fragile.'

Ellie handed me a giant plate of food. 'What a relief.'

None of us said another word for a moment; the wonderful smell of the meal was simply overwhelming. As we ate I pondered on how strange it was to feel instantly so at home with our hosts, people who lived so far away and yet, somehow, felt close at the same time. I was really looking forward to the weekend.

After a while conversation turned to what we might like to do on the farm during the next couple of days.

'It boils down to how much muck you can manage, basically,' said Rick.

'Ooh lots,' said Barbara. 'I love animals.'

'Reet, we'll set yer to work, lass,' said Rick.

The following morning we rose early, eager to make the most of our short stay. Barbara was already out helping with the livestock and the boys were playing happily inside under Ellie's gaze while I went to explore the farm, starting with a sturdy stone shed. I'd always loved old agricultural buildings possibly because they reminded me of blissful childhood days playing in a barn across the road from where I grew up in Cheshire.

The gloomy interior was a tangle of buckets, brooms, shovels, ropes and hooks. Black cobwebs hung everywhere. Suddenly a rush of wings and chiming squawks drew my eyes up: a swallow had darted in, circling madly. It fretted with my presence then swooped towards another door and was gone.

As my eyes adjusted to the half-light, a chocolate-hued calf with delicate eyes clambered up from the straw, its nose dripping. In the next pen five mottled lambs pressed together in a corner. Their ears flicked and their tails shook as they regarded me inquisitively. I stepped out into the yard past bags of dairy feed. Ginger chickens fussed about and barrows, bikes and old tractor parts were piled up next to a pile of steamy muck, hot with yellow flies.

I headed back up the daffodil-lined lane to enjoy once more the scintillating vista beyond the farm with the low sun, milky in the crisp air. A footpath took me into a field by a strutting cockerel and from here the view opened up further, revealing great hump-backed hills with three towering peaks beyond, dark and heavy on the horizon.

I saw Barbara walk into a larger shed and returned, curious to see what she was doing. Inside the dusty barn she was brushing the flank of a mucky ginger cow and evidently enjoying herself.

'I didn't know cows needed grooming,' I said.

'It helps to get the old winter coat off – look, you can see the new coat underneath.'

'How come you know so much about it?' I said, unable to notice much difference.

'I love this sort of thing; I used to help run the Farm Club at my school, remember. And Ellie told me what to do . . .'

'So what else have you got planned?'

She pointed to a pen a bit further on. 'The orphan lambs there need feeding. I'm going to get the boys to help with that. Can you go and make sure they're dressed?'

I went back inside the house and cajoled our sons into putting on some clothes. They were happy playing in their pyjamas with

Nathan's impressive collection of farm toys but the promise of feeding real lambs did the trick.

'What do they eat?' said Tom.

'Milk.'

'Just milk? Don't they have cornflakes?'

'Tom, you're turning into a proper joker, you are.' I tickled him until he squealed and Reuben demanded a go.

With little wellies on they followed me to the stone shed where the five hungry orphan lambs pressed forward, eager for sustenance. One nibbled at my knee through the iron bars. Ellie and Barbara walked in carrying two feeding bottles.

'Right, boys,' said Ellie. 'These lambs are very hungry, so you need to sit on the bale of straw there in the pen and just hold out the bottle with the teat out like that and they'll come and feed. I'll do the others in the pen next door on the feeder.'

She passed Barbara the bottles then lifted three of the excited lambs into the next pen. I picked up the distrustful Reuben and passed him over on to the straw.

'Are they friendly?' asked Tom, who had never been the bravest soul.

I was tempted to say something wicked but replied, 'They're gentle as lambs, of course.'

They weren't. As soon as Barbara gave the boys a bottle each, the two hungry creatures lurched forward and rammed their heads on to the rubber nipples, pulling and sucking furiously. Tom's eyes were wide and he held the bottle at arm's length, almost letting go, while Reuben simply wailed, causing Barbara to take over as I rescued him. I tried not to laugh at my elder son, meanwhile, who looked more like he was in a cage with two lions than a couple of baby sheep.

'Can I stop now?' he said in a wobbly voice, turning his head away as the lamb, its tail flapping madly as it thrust its waggling bottom out, sucked even harder.

'Go on, then,' said Barbara with disbelief, taking the second bottle.

Ellie was kind. 'Well, it's not for everyone.'

Reuben quickly stopped sniffling when he realised that the hay bales in the corner were perfect for climbing up and diving off, and soon enough everyone was happy.

The rest of the holiday weekend passed too swiftly. We climbed hills and paddled in streams, had ice cream in Skeddlebeck, ate the finest scones in the land and played football, of sorts, with the raucous Rick. The kind April sun stayed out for us, illuminating banks of delicate flowers in the verges but all too soon it was time to go home and on Sunday evening we reluctantly climbed in the Alfa and headed east.

'What lovely people,' said Barbara. 'Did you have a good time, boys?'

'Yesssss,' they chorused.

'Can we come here next week?' asked Tom, quite innocently.

I smiled. 'Maybe not next week, but we'll come and see them in the summer.'

As we motored along the high pass between some of Yorkshire's highest summits on the way back, I reflected on the past few days.

'Quite a week. Maybe Anna Reed will be back in class tomorrow. I wonder how Ben is doing in hospital?'

'At least Anna will be able to keep you up to speed when she's back.'

* * *

Anna did return to Cragthwaite Primary the following day and she was able to report that her brother was still making progress and hoped to be out of hospital in another week. I didn't ask her too many questions, knowing what a traumatic episode this had been in the family's life. She returned to being a model pupil in Class 3 and continued to be my number one fan.

I didn't see Mr or Mrs Reed again for over two months and it was towards the end of the term, in the heat of a July Sports Day that Anna's mother walked on to the school field accompanied by a frail-looking Ben. He wasn't back at school yet but was clearly well enough to be out and about, and their very presence at the event brought me great cheer. At the end of the races, while everything was being put away she came over for a word, leaving Ben by the fence. I smiled and waved at him seeing that he was looking this way. He lifted a hand back, shyly.

'Hello, Mr Seed.' She smiled warmly.

'Good to see you again, Mrs Reed.' Anna came and joined us.

'I'm so sorry that I haven't been in to see you – I've been meaning to for weeks but, you know, Ben still needs a fair bit of looking after.'

'How is he doing? It's good to see him here.'

'Really well: the doctors are delighted with his progress and we're hopeful that come September he'll be back at school.'

'That's wonderful news. There's been no, er, lasting damage?'

'It doesn't appear so; his mental processes seem to be all right. He has a few headaches now and again, and he's lost a little confidence but, well, under the circumstances I think we can be very grateful it's only that.'

'It must be a huge relief for you.'

She nodded and looked me in the eye. 'I just wanted to say to you, about the night of the accident, when he was in Leeds . . .' She hesitated for a moment and I could see her eyes become glassy. 'We were so, so scared . . .'

I could see that the presence of her daughter was making this difficult so, noticing that there was still sports equipment to be put away, I asked Anna to carry a basket of skipping ropes inside.

Mrs Reed fiddled with a tissue. 'They warned us that night that his life was in the balance.' She gulped, barely able to speak.

I felt tears well up in my own eyes. 'I simply can't imagine it.'

'I just wanted to tell you, that your phone call at midnight . . . that came at the most frightening time . . . It, well, it just meant so much to us to know that you and your wife were praying. We're not believers ourselves but, honestly, at that moment we were pleading with God.'

I didn't quite know what to say. 'I, well, just felt I needed to call. I'm glad it helped.'

'It really did. Bless you.' She turned to look at her pale son, standing alone by the fence. 'I'd better go.'

I said goodbye and pretended to blow my nose, hoping that no one was watching. It was a day I would remember for a long time.

Chapter Seventeen

Tim

The noise was very strange, almost like the waves on a rocky shore dragging small pebbles into the surf. It was a repeated crunchy, pulling sound and it was right outside the side of our house.

'Can you see what it is?' said Barbara as I peeped through the living room curtains.

'Not really, it's too dark but I'm sure it's Wanda and Ralph.'

The mention of our temporary neighbours' names usually brought a shiver and this evening was no different. They owned the small cottage attached to the back of Craven Bottoms and had spent five years converting it into a *Country Life* second home with expensive furnishing and meticulous renovation. They only visited the village twice a year in general but, whenever they did, our minds without hesitation went back to our first disastrous meeting with them when our own kitchen was being rebuilt and a young workman had ruined their posh new bathroom in spectacular fashion.

Since then, no matter how hard we tried, we just couldn't seem to get on good terms with the Holts. They were self-made wealthy business people who, despite being so close, inhabited another planet from us, seeing the world completely differently. We'd heard car doors closing a few minutes previously and thought it might be them arriving for the weekend since it was a Friday night but then we heard strident voices from the path to their cottage followed by the peculiar sound.

'I'm going to peek through the dining room window,' said Barbara. 'It's dark in there so I might be able to see.'

She returned a minute later, her face betraying an amused bewilderment.

'Well?' I said.

'It's definitely Wanda and Ralph.'

'What's the noise then?'

'They're raking the gravel.'

'Eh?'

'Come and see.'

I followed my now giggling wife back to the unlit dining room where we crept in slowly before craning around the side of its wonky old bay window. There was Wanda Holt in the dark, rake in hand, levelling out the small stones of the path up to her garden. Her jerky stomping movements suggested that she wasn't in the best of moods.

'What is going on?' I said. 'It's nearly half past nine.'

'But why would you rake a path in the daylight even?'

We both started sniggering then retreated, telling each other to 'shhh'.

The following morning a hazy sun drew us outside, promising another captivating spring day in the Dales. Once back from her postal round and rested, Barbara went to work on her garden which, with Rosie's help, was already vastly improved and showing signs of colour among the bushy greens. The boys played in their sandpit and, it being a Saturday, I just enjoyed pootling about doing odd jobs and contemplating a stroll later on.

I wandered over to the Holts' path which bordered the edge of our tiny lawn at the side of the house.

'Well, that midnight raking paid off,' I said. 'It's beautifully even now.'

'Quiet!' hissed Barbara. 'They could come out at any moment.'

I glanced down at their huge black BMW parked on the verge outside and wondered how much it cost.

'Look at my mud pie, Daddy,' called Tom. 'It's sand really but I'm pretending it's mud.'

'Poo pie!' called Reuben, finding his own remark ludicrously funny.

Barbara stood up and rubbed her back. 'Please try and keep the sand in the sandpit, boys. Mummy's putting in a big effort to make the garden nice.'

'Do you want some poo pie, Mummy?' was Tom's reply.

A moment later the door of the cottage opened and Wanda Holt emerged. She didn't see us at first but looked at her watch and cried back into the house.

'Come on, Ralph, or we're going to be late!'

'Morning, Wanda,' said Barbara as she turned to face us.

'Oh, hello.' As usual, there was no joy in her greeting.

'Hi,' I added, trying to appear jovial.

She strode towards us as Ralph appeared and locked the door. She was an immaculately dressed woman in her fifties with tight auburn hair and lots of jewellery. Her husband was bulky, greying but also smartly attired with a sports jacket and tan loafers. He nodded towards us but I sensed there was trouble to come.

I was right.

'Could I have a word, please,' said Wanda, not waiting for a response. 'I know that you have two young sons and that boys will be boys, but please will you make it clear to them that this path is *not* part of your property and they should *not* play on it.'

I was bemused but Barbara looked almost hurt. 'Well, what exactly have they done, Wanda?' she asked calmly.

'They clearly regard the path as just part of their playground and they move the gravel all over the place. It looks a mess, doesn't it, Ralph?'

'Wanda spent ten minutes raking it level last night,' he said, somewhat sheepishly I felt.

I stepped over towards the path. 'They do go on the path occasionally, I'll admit – they like playing with their cars and toy trucks on it.'

'I know,' snapped Wanda. 'I found two of them while I was raking.'

'To be fair though, Wanda,' said Barbara. 'It's very hard for a three-year-old and a nearly two-year-old to stay off it when it's completely open to our garden.'

She raised an eyebrow. 'If it were my children there wouldn't be a problem. Anyway, we phoned John Weatherall this morning and he's coming round in a few days to put up a wire fence. Come on, Ralph.'

With that they disappeared through the gate, climbed into their sedan and rumbled off.

'You can give them some poo pie, boys,' said Barbara.

That afternoon we returned from a visit to the waterfall to find John Weatherall on the forbidden gravel, marking out distances with a tape measure. To our relief, the BMW wasn't there. The wiry builder, still in his dusty work clothes, gave his brow a wipe.

'Ay up, grand day.'

'Hi John,' I said. 'I hear you're going to be putting up a security fence to keep these two horrors out.'

'Yep, eight foot wi' razor wire top and two machine gun towers.'

Barbara laughed. 'It wouldn't surprise me . . .'

John stood up and had a stretch while the boys edged forward to look into his big, ancient canvas toolbag. 'Byyy, you don't need ter tell me, I know all about the job. Kids playing on gravel – what a crime.'

'So what kind of fence is it going to be?'

'Well that's up to them but don't worry, I'll mek sure it doesn't ruin your estate. Garden's looking canny, anyroad.'

Barbara gave a broad smile while Tom studied the battered, metre-long yellow spirit level poking out of John's bag. He tapped me on the leg. 'Daddy, look at the size of that fish fart.'

John let out a hearty bellow of a laugh, making Reuben jump. 'Well, 'ave been a builder twenty-six years and 'ave never heard it called that.'

I smiled. 'It's what our friend Doug calls his spirit level.'

'How are they gettin' on? I don't see much o' 'em round the village.'

'Well, the house is nearly finished now. I suppose that's kept them busy,' I said.

He nodded. 'Aye, it needed a bit o' work that place.'

'Would you like a brew, John?' asked Barbara.

He looked at his watch. 'No ta, best be off. I normally finish be now on a Sat'day. Oh, by the way, the Holts have asked me to replace some of the flags on their roof so we're goin' to be clambering around up there next week – don't be alarmed if you hear footsteps above yer bedroom ceilin'. And, yer might want ter keep the lads out of the garden just in case. Well, 'ave never dropped a 'ammer off a roof but Bri does it about three times a week.'

I laughed, knowing Bri Shawby from the darts team, but Barbara let out a sigh. 'I wish we could afford you to fix our roof, John. It still leaks in three or four places.' It was true, our bedroom wallpaper had begun to peel off in several spots and the small study where I worked was damp.

John gave his head a slow shake of disbelief. 'Well, the crazy thing is we repaired their roof four years since – it doesn't leak – Wanda just dun't like that some o' the stone slates don't match. They cost a bloody fortune them things 'n'all . . . Anyways, must be off fer some bait.' He picked up his toolbag and trudged down the path, his hefty boots leaving big craters in the gravel.

At school the summer term was now well underway and on Monday lunchtime the small staffroom was full, with most of the teachers trying to do a little marking while munching their sandwiches. I was reading through a pile of my class's stories about exploring an island and wondering why children found writing so hard. I'd decided that it was because they didn't do enough reading, when I turned up a singular yarn.

Its author was Tim Musgrave, a quiet, brawny, dark-haired boy who gave every indication that he was eternally destined for the role of straggler. He was no trouble in class: he kept his head down and did his best but, alas, his head was mainly empty and his best was far below what any teacher would hope for. I surveyed his writing with an unwelcome air of resignation.

The iyland

Me and Dan went to the iyland it was big. We fownd a cayv then we saw a rivver then we climed a hill then we ayt some frute then a wulf chasd us. We hid in the cayv it was dark and we was scard then we made a fire and we sor golld in the cayv we was ritch. I wok up it was all a dreem.

I didn't know where to start with the marking. Earlier in the morning he'd completed a whole page of multiplication on the basis that 7 x 8 was 54, leaving the page without a tick in sight. What's more, I knew from experience that it was a waste of time to try and focus on more than one aspect of writing when talking through it with him. But which one to choose?

Hilda leaned over. 'Looks like you've got one of my lot's there. Whose is it?'

'Tim Musgrave.'

She raised her eyebrows knowingly. 'Ah yes, poor Tim. Nice lad but he won't be bothering the Nobel Committee any time soon.'

Emma, her baggy purple trousers and lime green top brightening everyone's day, looked up. 'Oh, what a job I had getting that mite to learn his sounds.'

'He's not a mite anymore,' I said, 'but it doesn't seem he's improved a right lot.'

'Well, just get the poor sod sorted before he reaches Class Four,' said Val, not for the first time. 'Actually, I recall his brother Jack from years ago. He was a plodder too.'

'*Yorkshire born, Yorkshire bred, strong in t'arm and thick in t'head,* must have come from somewhere,' mused Hilda.

I put down my pen and pondered for a moment. 'But *is* it possible for a lad like Tim to become cleverer? I don't mean just improve a bit, I mean, well, to change and . . .'

'. . . Get a brain,' offered Val.

'Good question,' said Sue, who was on her knees in the corner trimming a stack of Reception paintings. 'I've often wondered that myself.'

'More to the point, can bright kids turn stupid because I've three or four who are doing their best to find out,' said Hilda.

'Oh, Hilda,' said Sue sitting up and stretching her back, 'for once we were having a serious conversation.'

She squashed up her mouth. 'Sorry I spake . . .'

'I think it's possible for kids to improve a lot,' said Val, disregarding Hilda. 'Sometimes they get off to a bad start or there's family troubles or they're just late developers.'

'Sounds a bit like me,' I said. 'Last time I was at my mum's I found a postcard I wrote home when I was about ten. Everything about it was shocking. I didn't really learn to write until I was thirteen or fourteen.'

'But I bet you weren't like Tim when you were eight,' said Emma. 'I mean, I just can't imagine someone like him, say, becoming a teacher when he's older. I want to believe it's possible but I can't.'

'Well, if he does,' said Hilda, 'just don't send yer kids to that school.'

We all laughed; she simply couldn't help herself.

The following afternoon I carried a boxful of small, leafy plants into the classroom and arranged the pots on a table at the front as the starting point for our new class project on herbs. There was parsley, basil, marjoram, chives, mint, dill, lovage, sage, lemon balm, thyme, oregano and coriander, all grown by Rosie Burns from seed. She had given Barbara a crate full of pots for the garden a couple of weeks before and this had inspired the project; I thought it would be a welcome change to do something outdoor-based.

'Ooh, what's this?' asked Helen, leaning over the plants as the children filed into the room following the one o'clock bell. 'Are we gunna be gardenin'?'

'Sort of,' I said, smiling at her enthusiasm.

Martine leaned over the pots for a sniff. 'Er, them stink!'

After the register I stood up and picked out the chives from the box, holding the pot so everyone could see. 'Who knows what this is?'

'A plant!' Cue laughter; inevitably it was Howard.

'Grass?'

'Rushes?'

'Spring onions?'

I acknowledged Cathy's effort. 'That's the closest.'

'Leeks?' said Dan. 'Me granddad grows massive uns o' them. He puts 'em in an old tub and feeds 'em cr—, er, muck, from Sunters'.'

'Well, leeks is close but it's actually a herb, like all these plants,' I said.

Estelle was straining with her arm in the air. I pointed to her. 'Chives! My mum has a herb garden and I've grown chives before. They have lovely purple flowers.'

'That's right, well done, Estelle. And I'm delighted that your mum has a herb garden because that's exactly what we're going to make.'

There was a buzz of excitement from the children which continued as I showed them photos of herbs and herb gardens from various books I'd collected. I described what herbs are and what they are used for before explaining that everyone, in pairs, would be responsible for growing one type of herb from seed for the garden.

'Any questions?' I said.

Martine was first. 'Why don't we jus' use them uns?' she said, pointing to the pots.

'Well, these are going to be back-ups in case anything goes wrong, but the main reason is that I want you all to have a go at growing herbs from seed, so that you learn how it's done.'

'Where's the garden gunna be?' asked Fraser Garth.

'Good question. Well, there's a sheltered spot by the side of the school next to the PE shed.'

'But that's all grass,' said Howard. 'Don't we need a flower bed, like?'

'Fair point. The flower beds at the front are all full of roses and bushes, though. New plants won't do well competing with them. No, we're going to dig up a patch of grass to make a new plot.'

There was a general gasp of disbelief before Tim raised his hand. 'Mr Seed, can I do some diggin'? I love diggin' – I 'elp me mam wi' garden all t'time.'

'Yes, everyone can do some digging,' I said, which produced cheers. The gasp hadn't surprised me, though. The last time there had been an attempt to grow some vegetables outside, the County groundsman had made a huge fuss that the grass cutting was now more difficult, and the resulting fearsome row with Miss Croker had stayed long in the children's memory. Bearing this in mind, I'd consulted Joyce about the herb garden.

'Oh, just do it,' she said. 'I'll say it was my decision. I'll make him a cup of tea and offer to give his superiors a glowing report.'

Twenty minutes later there was mayhem in the classroom. The tables, having been covered with newspaper, were now layered with compost. Despite my clear demonstration of how to sow the seeds, the children argued, shouted and ignored all the usual conventions. Trudy dropped her tiny seeds on the floor and couldn't find them.

Ian had attempted to water his with the tap which had washed the entire contents of the tray into the sink. Vicky had sneezed while scattering her seeds and the unlabelled trays on Barry's table had been covered over then mixed up so no one knew which was which. Lawrence was digging through one of them with a ruler trying to find what he'd sown.

'Right, stop,' I cried. They carried on.

'STOP!' They froze. I reminded them to label their trays then take them outside for watering. It appeared unlikely from the chaos that anything would grow but we had to try.

'Shalla bring some pots from 'ome, Mr Seed?' said Tim, whose face was more alert than I'd ever seen it before. 'Me mam's got loads to spare, and we'll need 'em for prickin' out.'

'That would be great, thanks, Tim – and well done for using the right words.'

Outside Martine and Jason were fighting over the watering can.

'Give it to me, please,' I said. 'Who knows how to use it properly?' All twenty-four hands went up. I chose Tim. He smiled and stepped forward.

'Fust, yer mus' mek sure that t'rose is on tight cos otherwise you'll wash everythin' away like Ian did in t'sink.' Everyone laughed. He pulled off the rose and looked inside. 'Yer should also jus' swill out t'rose fust to shift any blockages.'

He picked up the can and carefully poured water backwards through the rose before tapping it on the ground and screwing it on tight. Everyone, including me, was impressed.

'Jus' test it next, ter mek sure flow is okay.' He tipped a bit of water on to the grass. 'It's not bad but we should really 'ave a finer spray fer waterin' seed trays. Shall I do ours now, Mr Seed?'

'Yes, go ahead, Tim.'

He placed his tray away from the others, pressed down the compost then lifted the watering can well above it and gave it a light covering. 'Gotta mek sure that the compost's wetted evenly, like.'

It was an excellent demonstration and I patted Tim on the back, knowing I couldn't have done any better. Martine and Jason resumed their fight for the second go when I turned back but at least they now knew what to do. Eventually, all the watered seed trays were put in polythene bags in the classroom and the rest of the afternoon was spent removing sufficient compost from the desks and floor to avoid Pat Rudd's wrath.

The following day I set the class to designing the layout for the small herb garden. Some of them got a bit carried away with the inclusion of brick paths, benches and a gazebo, but they greatly enjoyed the activity, not least Tim, who came up to me with a detailed, comprehensive drawing.

'Ave jus' bin wonderin', Mr Seed,' he said.

'Yes, Tim?'

'That plot yer've chosen next to the shed. It faces west by ma reckonin' but me mam says herbs like to be warm so mebbes we should 'ave a south-facin' plot?'

'Good point, Tim,' I said, humbled that I hadn't even thought of this. 'I'll ask Miss Croker about it later.'

'Herbs!' said Val when I told her my plans. 'You're in Swinnerdale now, not the Med. You'll be lucky if half of them grow and the rest survive the winter.'

'Mrs Wood has a herb garden in Cragthwaite.'

'It's probably in a heated greenhouse.'

'Oh come on, Val, it's not that cold here.'

'Well, I suppose if you can find a spot with decent soil that's south-facing and out of the wind then you might stand a chance, but don't blame me if all the bloody kids end up disappointed. I wouldn't count on making pot-pourri just yet . . .'

I wandered to the back of the school at lunchtime and scanned for a likely spot. The sun was shining here all right but a cool breeze buffeted off the hills and I suspected that Val was right. Perhaps the project had been a mistake? But there was no turning back now.

'Look, Mr Seed!' Tim Musgrave bustled into the room with a large box full of neatly stacked square plastic plant pots. 'I told you we 'ave lots.' It was eight-forty on the following Monday morning and my mind had been on other things.

'Wow, erm, that's fantastic, Tim. There must be over a hundred here.'

'Me mam says yer can keep them anyroad. I also 'ad an idea, Mr Seed. If we pot all the herb seedlin's we can sell all the spare ones to parents. That's what we do at 'ome with us spare beddin' plants at side of t'road.' His eyes were bright.

I put down my pen. 'You know what, Tim, that's an excellent idea. We could use the money to buy more compost and spend the rest on the herb garden.'

'Aye,' he said, beaming broadly. He had really come alive with this topic and I was seeing a completely new side to him. 'Ave yer decided on a plot yet, Mr Seed?'

I told him where I thought it might be best located, just on the south side of our classroom. 'Miss Croker says it might be too windy, though.'

He ran outside to look then hurried back in. 'Well, we could put up summat like a trellis to protect the herbs. And a polythene cloche would be good 'n' all.'

I smiled. 'Tim, you know so much about gardening.'

He shrugged. 'Aye, well, I enjoy it. Ah might be a gard'ner when ahm older, like.'

He scuttled to the back of the room to where the seed trays were. 'Might be a spot o' growth be now.' He tapped the plastic bags over the trays and peered. 'We've got summat!'

I went over for a look and, sure enough, the first few green shoots of basil were pushing through the compost.

Just then, Fraser came in and peered at the tiny seedlings too, before calling out, 'Yesss!' and running outside to tell his friends the news.

'Well, at least we'll have something for the garden,' I said.

'I'll ask at 'ome if we 'ave anything to mek a cloche with,' said Tim.

'OK, that would be great but you'll have to excuse me, Tim. I need to set everything up for Maths first lesson.'

His face dropped. 'Fractions again is it?'

I nodded then watched him walk away, resigned to another morning of hopeless battling against numbers and words.

A fortnight later, by some curious miracle, all of the class's seed trays had germinated and there were small green shoots pushing up from each one. Some had fared better than others but every pair of children had at least four plants to work with. Tim and I had discussed the next stage of the process and I had suggested that he demonstrate the delicate operation of pricking out the seedlings into the pots.

He gave a modest shrug. 'Reckon ah could do it but ah don't know if they'll listen to me.'

'I think they will.'

The compost was ready and each pot was labelled in advance with a small sticker. Once again, there was great excitement in the room when the tables were pushed together so that everyone could gather round to see Tim's exposition.

'Sit down if you have a chair and stand where you can see if you don't,' I said. 'Colin, come and sit next to me.' He hadn't noticed me watch him flick a lump of compost at Lawrence. 'Now, over to Tim.'

'Right,' said the eager nine-year-old. 'First thing is to fill all yer pots wi' compost to the top. No need ter press it down.' He did this swiftly then placed them in a large seed tray. 'Next we'll tek 'em outside to water 'em.'

I followed the children outside, enjoying my back seat while Tim arranged them in a circle, having placed his tray on the ground. Once more he went through his watering can checks. 'Ave brought a fine rose this week,' he said. 'And a spare can so we can crack on wi' job.' The class watched in silence as he watered the pots.

'See how the level o' the compost has gone down now it's wet. The pots want to be just over three-quarters full, really.'

Tim tapped the tray then took us all back inside. I settled the class while he picked up a teaspoon.

'Fust, mek a hole in the compost in each pot like this.' He pressed in with the spoon handle and turned the pot to make an even depression in each one. The class looked impressed.

'Right, next job is probably the 'ardest and most important part o' the operation,' he said, sliding a tray of parsley seedlings towards him. 'Yer 'ave ter 'andle young plants very tenderly or they'll die.'

The class craned in as he unravelled the mystery with a gentle authority.

'Fust, allus pick up the seedlin's by the leaves.' With delicacy he held a leaf between two fingers then, using the handle of the teaspoon, prised up the soil underneath. 'Yer dig in like this, and gently push up under the roots, until she's loose. Then yer lift 'er out, so.' With great care he lifted up the seedling, showing the full length of its roots which amazed some of the children.

'It's like me granny's hair,' said Helen.

Tim continued. 'Then yer carefully dangle the roots into the hole in the compost like this, and press the soil in around gently.'

The first one was done and the little plant stood up proudly in its black pot. The class spontaneously applauded and I joined in; it was a wonderful moment.

May had become my favourite month in the dale, with its verdant freshness painting the meadows and fellsides while growing lambs scurried around in happy gangs bleating on the wind. The children of Cragthwaite Primary School were larking about on the field, picking daisies and chasing balls. A game of something approximating cricket was in progress and I was sipping my tea, glad to be outside on playground duty now that the sun had properly warmed the valley.

Four weeks after starting the herb project the plants were now in the ground and growing steadily under the careful eye of Tim Musgrave, who even now was checking for weeds. Only the basil had been kept indoors after Tim's mum advised that it was too sensitive to survive in the Yorkshire hills. Joyce had talked the PTA into buying us some concrete flags to create a chequerboard arrangement to make access easier for the children, who enthusiastically watered their herbs each day. They also kept a colourful record of their work in special Herb Project folders.

I wandered over to see Tim who, with his father's help one

weekend, had not only erected a trellis that the parents had also funded but made some small cloches for the more delicate plants while they were being established.

'It's looking good, Tim.'

'Not bad. Even Miss Croker said so yesterday.'

'Wow, that is a compliment.'

He stood up and wiped the trowel he was using. 'Are we doing some of us project folders this afternoon, Mr Seed?'

'Maybe for half an hour if we finish everything else. How many pages have you done now?'

'Forty-two.' He couldn't help smiling.

I pictured the fat sugar-paper file, stuffed with stuck-in seed packets, diagrams, photos, drawings, designs, cut-out magazine articles and two pages of scrawled, illegible writing about the uses of herbs. By the end of the term, the file would be even larger and, despite its almost indecipherable written content, Tim would have a prize for it. But he didn't care too much about that; for the first time in his school career he was happy, spending every available moment tending the most magnificent herb garden arrayed with bushy greens: curled parsley, tall elegant dill, cool grey sage, and clusters of swaying chives about to unfurl their beautiful flowers.

At home our own tiny lawned garden was now hemmed in by an ugly green wire fence, completely out of keeping with the village's stone walls. Our boys would never push their toy dumper trucks through the gravel again. Above our heads the noisy John Weatherall and his crew of craggy builders had been scuttling over the roof of Wanda and Ralph's cottage for days, heaving giant inch-thick, three-foot square slabs of local stone up a scaffolding tower, each one requiring three men and a lot of swearing.

'They're taking a long time,' I said to Barbara one day as I returned home from work to find Bri Shawby and the broad frame of Dave Whiterow holding on to the chimney while they fiddled with some lead flashing.

'They've spent most of the day on our roof, too, by the sound of it,' she said.

John himself then appeared on the ridge having climbed over from the other side. He saw me and saluted. 'Get kettle on, lad – we're parched.'

'I have two sugars please,' called Bri, in between bashing the lead with a mallet.

'That's it, no tea, just two sugars,' quipped the ever-jesting Dave.

'Are you coming down, then?' I called.

John wiped his face. 'Aye, we're about done now. Before you do the brew, just step across in front o' the chapel and tell us 'ow it looks.'

'What, next door's roof?' said Barbara, as confused as I was.

'Aye, well, yours 'n' all – the job overlaps tha knows.'

We duly went through the gate and a few yards down the road to where we could actually see one side of the roof which covered the two houses. It looked remarkably different: lighter and dustier and neater.

'But our roof looks much better, too,' murmured Barbara. 'All of it.'

I couldn't help but agree. 'No wonder he spent so long up there,' I said. 'The daft berk. How are we going to pay for that? I told him we've got no money.'

'So did I,' said Barbara who was already walking up the green to look at the other side of the roof. I followed her. It was the same story; there was no denying what we could see with our own eyes – John had fixed our roof.

He climbed down the ladder attached to the scaffolding, laughing as he saw our furrowed faces. 'No more leaks for a while now,' he said, looking disturbingly pleased. 'She's all patched up.'

I held out my hands. 'But John, we told you we just can't afford this.'

Once again he let out a quiet laugh which started to rile Barbara. 'We really don't have the money, honestly.'

'Yer don't need it – so no more chunterin'.'

'You can't afford to do this for free, John,' I said.

'Dead right I can't. That's why next door are footin' the bill.'

There was a moment's silence. John looked up at Bri and Dave who were now starting to disassemble the scaffold tower. 'Was a stinker of a job was the Holts' roof wan't it, lads? All sorts o' complications . . .'

'A proper bugger,' said Dave.

'Mare,' said Bri.

Before we could say anything he walked away. 'Fret not; we used the spare slabs that were taken off next door. Will cost you a damn good cup of tea, though.'

Chapter Eighteen

Pamela

Cragthwaite Primary School had been, for over a century, a very traditional institution of education. First came the cramped stone Victorian building, tucked away behind the church, with its narrow, pointed windows and cold paved yard encased in high walls. Hilda and Val had both taught there before the new school was built in the 1970s and occasionally they reminisced about its two small draughty rooms crowded with wooden desks with inkwells.

'Byyy, it was learn or else in those days,' Hilda used to say. 'Canings, reciting the Bible, dunce's caps . . . and that was just for the teachers.' She slapped her knee and snorted at the joke we'd heard several times before.

'You didn't have dunce's caps, Mrs Percival, come on!' called Joyce who for once had joined us in the staffroom.

'There was plenty of whacking by the Beak, though – that bit's true,' said Val, recalling Joyce's stern predecessor.

'Oh, I remember those days as a young teacher,' said Joyce. 'The school I was at in Knaresborough used the slipper. I hated it.'

'How often did you have it?' chuckled Hilda.

Joyce smiled at the joke. 'I probably deserved it, actually,' she said. 'I reckon I was a bit too big for my boots in those days.'

'Well, you've done a fabulous job at this school,' said Emma, whose hair took up most of the room. 'It's a much happier place now than when I started.'

'Thank you, my dear, you're very sweet,' she said. 'I do love it here – it's so traditional and old-fashioned and yet so friendly as well.'

I thought about that statement a few days later as half-term approached and my mind was taken up with the problem of what to do about Pamela Sykes.

Pamela had arrived during the previous summer, her family having moved north from Kent when her father took a job working at the National Park office in Skirbridge. She found it hard to fit in at first, having been in a large school in a town before. Her accent was strange and foreign to the Yorkshire children, too, and many in the class found her manner a little odd.

Pamela's appearance set her apart also: she was tall with very dark hair, which was unusual in the Dales, and she looked far older than most of her peers, almost like a young teenager at times. But that was not the only way in which Pamela was different, for Pamela liked boys, and liked them rather too much.

As the 1980s drew towards a close, little had really changed at Cragthwaite in one regard since the first school was founded. The girls and boys played separately; the boys in the main stuck to football or chasing games, and the girls skipping and clapping rhymes, and all was well with this ancient arrangement until Pamela arrived.

She had kept to herself during the autumn and spring terms, tentatively making friends with Trudy and getting by with her schoolwork without ever appearing too bothered how she was doing. Her parents laughed off my concerns that she was a bit of a loner.

'She's always been like that, has Pammy,' they said. They didn't even seem to mind that her work was only average. They had fallen in love with the Dales and were simply relieved that their daughter was coping with the culture shock. 'If she wants to come to school at all that's good enough for me,' said her mother, which surprised me considerably.

I didn't raise the issue of boys on parents evening because at that point it hadn't really become evident. It was when the summer term began and the children were allowed out on to the school field that the rumours began to spread that Pamela was keen on boys, and one boy in particular: Stephen.

The playground reports that Pamela fancied Stephen had come as a bit of a shock to the innocent pupils of Class 3, not least to Stephen himself. He was a quiet boy who kept himself to himself but he was undeniably good-looking and the rapidly circulated story that Pamela was 'going out with him' created a sensation at the school, especially when she didn't deny it. The tale was mainly spread by the class busybody Martine and it soon reached the staffroom.

'What's all this about Pamela and Stephen?' said Val one morning. 'My class keep yapping that they're going out.'

I laughed. 'That's all my lot are saying too – half of them don't know what it means.'

'So it's just tittle-tattle, is it?'

'Well, Pamela's not your typical nine-year-old, thinks she's more mature, and she's just openly taken a fancy to Stephen Gray, that's all. I don't think it's mutual so they can't exactly be madly in love.'

'Well, anyway. I've banned my lot from talking about it – these things always end up with someone getting upset and it's very disruptive. Might be a good idea to have a word with yours.'

I agreed and after break, while the class were filing inside I had a quiet chat outside the classroom with Pamela. Her appearance was almost sulky, a flap of black hair falling across her eyes as she half looked at me.

'Pamela, I'm sure you've noticed that lots of people are, well, talking about you. I'm sorry this is happening and I'm going to have a word with the class about it. It might be a good idea if you made it clear that you're not, er, going out with Stephen, though. I think you're a bit young for this kind of thing.'

'But I really like him. It's not wrong to like boys, is it? We should get along with girls *and* boys my mum says.'

'Yes, but we don't want to encourage rumours and people saying silly things, do we?'

She shrugged. 'I don't care what they say.'

I was a little bamboozled by this and also aware that the class were unsupervised. Wondering what else I should say, we hurried back to the room. At least from what the boys told me at lunchtime Stephen wasn't reciprocating the lust. I decided against speaking to him but instead told the class that I didn't want to hear any more tales of this kind. The amount of sideways eye-flicking among the girls was stupendous.

All went quiet for a few days and we were able to concentrate on work. The success of the herb garden had inspired Joyce to get thinking about using the school grounds in more imaginative ways and she addressed this point at the next staff meeting.

'As you know I've just been to a series of heads' meetings about science and how we might become better resourced to teach it. The cluster of Swinnerdale primaries has been given a budget and we're going to buy some more expensive items to share among the schools.'

'Who chooses these?' said Val, as blunt as ever.

'Well, I was just coming to that. Every school can suggest items then at the next cluster meeting the heads will vote on the ones we think will be most useful.'

'So when do you want some suggestions?' I asked.

'As soon as possible. Look them up in the catalogues and give me a written list with a price please.'

'Well I can tell you now I'd like a skeleton to teach about the body,' said Val.

'No problem,' muttered Hilda. 'Emma's got a couple of those in her closet.'

Joyce moved the meeting along swiftly. 'The other proposal made was that each school should have a portion of the budget and spend it on developing a wildlife area in the grounds.'

'Ooh, that sounds fun,' said Emma. 'We could plant trees and have bird boxes and stuff.'

'A place for wildflowers would be good,' added Val. 'Then we could attract butterflies and moths to study insects. We might even be able to film them with the video camera.'

'And what about a pond?' I said. 'We could get frogs and fish, then.'

Everyone seemed highly enthusiastic about the idea except for Hilda. 'It all sounds wonderful but what we'll end up with is a load of thistles and litter. I remember Ingleburn tried to make one of these nature areas a few years back and it just became an eyesore.'

But our senior teacher was outvoted and we all agreed that we should use the money to fence off a section of the grounds at the top of the field.

'I'm sure the PTA will help out with trees and the cost of the fence,' said Joyce.

That had been some weeks ago and now, as the summer term was underway, everyone at the school was excited to see this new facility take shape, although for the time being it just resembled the corner of a neglected meadow with straggly grass.

While it was being established, the wildlife area was out of bounds but the children were fascinated by it, not least as it offered a refuge from the prying eyes and irritating bellow of Mrs Hyde the grumpy dinner lady who patrolled the playing areas during the lunch break. Until they were caught, children played hide and seek in there and made dens in the bushes. In fact, it was so full of children at one point that any wildlife in there would have been flattened or scared off for certain.

Joyce therefore decreed that everyone was to stay away from the top of the field unless there with a teacher for schoolwork but this only succeeded in adding to the allure and mystique of the place as the term wore on.

'Mr Seed, Pamela's still after Stephen yer know,' said Martine one afternoon at the end of school. 'She's been temptin' 'im wi' Jelly Tots.'

'Martine, you were told not to talk about it and, anyway, I thought all this was over.'

She held out her hands. 'I know, Mr Seed, I aren't tryin' ter talk about it, it's jus' that, well, I can't deny what 'ave seen wi' me own eyes, canna?'

'Well, I suppose not. But are you sure this is happening?'

'Cross me 'art: ask Cathy or Trudy or Vicky or Estelle.'

'Right, well, I'd better have a word with them tomorrow . . .' She turned to go. 'And Martine?' She turned to look at me. 'Try not to talk about it, please.' She knew and I knew that I may as well ask the sun not to rise.

* * *

The following day was blissfully warm from the start and I intended to make the most of it, changing my plans before school to incorporate a long session of outdoor games. I thought we'd start with some throwing and catching then running activities, finishing with a game of rounders. In my busyness to get the equipment and activities organised, I quite forgot to have a word with the two young lovers in my class and was only reminded when I overheard Barry through an open window at playtime saying that he'd seen Pamela trying to lure Stephen into the long grass with sweets, possibly a sherbet fountain.

Martine had confirmed that the class vamp had not been slow to appreciate the possibilities offered by the new wildlife reserve but I couldn't believe that she'd have the nerve to defy the head-teacher's ban. I made a mental note to call her in for another word after I'd picked up a coffee and got changed for PE.

The staffroom was hot and airless so I opened the windows and put the kettle on. I could see Val out at the front of the school with Hilda and Sue: it was simply too glorious a day to be inside. I was just stirring my cup when the staffroom door, slightly ajar to let a breeze through, crashed open. There was Martine, barely breathing, her face crimson, her eyes wide.

'Mr Seed, quick: Pamela's kissed Stephen in the nature area!'

I never did get that cup of coffee.

'What does everyone do round here?' said Rosie as she stood in our kitchen sipping a cup of tea while the last moments of Reuben's birthday party raged in the living room supervised by the wonderful Holly.

'Well, they, er, get on with life, really,' I said.

'You mean the locals do – well they've got their farms and their B&Bs and things but what about other incomers?'

'Well, work and kids, if you're like us,' said Barbara who had been glad to escape the cacophony of screeching toddlers for five minutes. 'And enjoying the fabulous countryside, of course.'

Rosie put down her cup. 'Yes, I love the hills and the views but there are only so many walks you can go on. I mean what do people do culture-wise? It's miles to a theatre or cinema and there's not much in the way of live music.'

'There's the folk group in Hauxton,' I said.

'What, that bearded codger with his penny whistle?'

'That's a bit harsh,' said Barbara, trying not to laugh. 'They have visiting acts – that Irish group were good when we went.'

'Well, Doug walked out when we were there; he said he'd rather listen to a camel giving birth.'

Rosie then asked me about school and I couldn't help relaying the story of Pamela, leading up to the infamous embrace.

'What happened to her afterwards?' asked Barbara as she pushed some sticky sweets into party bags.

'Oh, Joyce called her parents in and Pamela agreed to leave him alone; especially as the poor boy was taken by surprise at the time. It's all blown over now.'

'Well, what a to-do,' said Rosie. 'I never kissed a boy until I was nineteen and even then I think I had to pay him.'

As Barbara giggled, I headed for the living room thinking that we had left Holly long enough. There were just five children at the little party and all were hot and sweaty, having hared around playing games most of the time. They were sitting quietly now as Holly read them a story with Reuben held on her lap, his cheeks burning red. He didn't even notice that I had come into the room. I smiled at Holly then went to answer the doorbell.

Ruth Metcalfe stood outside with five-year-old Robert. 'Has it been good? I hope David behaved himself,' she said.

'He's been fine,' I said, preferring not to mention the food fight or the tug of war over Pass the Parcel that he'd been part of. 'How's Adam? I've not seen him for a while.'

He lifted her eyebrows a little. 'Oh, he's been better. Lambin' wasn't so good this time round.'

I didn't know what to say. Life appeared to be a constant struggle for hill farmers. 'Is there anything we can do to help?'

'Not unless you've sixty Swaledale lambs going spare, but thanks for the offer.'

'At least the weather's better now.'

'Well, that's something. If we had any grass it would be growing, that's for sure.'

She wandered into the living room while I went to tell Barbara that she was here. When I got there, Rosie was sitting on a stool in the kitchen, her mouth agape.

'What do you mean, you've never taken your children to the seaside?'

'I've told you, I don't like beaches, well, not British ones anyway. Sand, sewage and candyfloss is not my idea of a good time,' said Barbara.

'But kids love it, especially when the sun's out like this. You can't deprive your boys of building sandcastles.'

A resolute expression passed over Rosie's face and then she said, 'Look, I'll take them. Have them ready with a couple of spare pairs of clothes at nine o'clock next Sunday morning.'

'Really? Are you serious?' said Barbara.

'Yeah, I love the Yorkshire coast: Whitby, Robin Hood's Bay, Ravenscar . . . And I can't stand back and let your boys grow up deprived.'

I gave a thumbs up, thinking of the joy of a day by ourselves, then told Barbara that Ruth Metcalfe had arrived. As she moved towards the door, Ulf, who was perched on one of the kitchen shelves, saw a gap and decided to spring forward. The kitten leapt and landed on Rosie's lap digging in its thorny claws for grip. Rosie let out a screech and threw her tea across the floor in shock. Poor Ulf fled down the hall in terror and Barbara and I tried not to laugh while Rosie rubbed the wounds in her thigh.

'That thing's wild,' she cried.

'Sorry, Rosie,' I said, mulling that she might want to re-evaluate her definition of 'wild' after taking Tom and Reuben to the seaside.

The following Sunday, Barbara and I found ourselves in the strange position of being at home without children. Doug had opted to stay at home and continue with his DIY and we had planned to climb Spout Fell then investigate some of the tea shops in Brackendale, the other side of the great hill.

'Just remind me why we're going up a mountain and not just straight to the café for cake,' said Barbara as she pulled on her walking boots.

'Well, first because we can't do it with the boys, second because it's good exercise and third because the weather's still quite good and we'll get a fantastic view.'

'Hmmpphh, well, it'd better be as good as you say.'

It was. Once across the little bridge over the beck by the waterfall, we climbed the stone steps and strode out on to sloping fields dotted with lace-white pignut and glowing buttercups. Up near the trees the May blossom was thick on the bushes like snow and everything around was a heavy green.

'Isn't this great, to be able to walk at our own pace,' said Barbara.

'And not have to trick children into continuing without moans.'

We'd become masters at chivvying Tom and Reuben on walks near the village:

Who can get to the gate first?

You'll never get through that stile on your own.

First one to pick up a leaf is the champion.

You'll never beat Daddy to the end of the field.

But now, instead, we could enjoy swerving butterflies, the delicate spiked leaves of ashes only just opening, the scented breeze so gentle compared with winter's roar and, best of all, each other's company.

'It's very kind of Rosie to do this,' said Barbara.

'I wonder if she fancies it every week.'

'You know, I think it's partly just so she can get away from the village – they haven't settled, have they?'

'It doesn't surprise me; they're just, well, town people, I suppose.'

'Rosie loves the garden and Doug's happy renovating the house but when that's done . . .'

'I won't be surprised if they leave, you know.'

As we pondered this, the first lower ridge of Spout Hill's flank was reached and the view began to open out. Mist hung in the distant valleys marking out the folds of the land in a silver relief. We stopped for a moment, finding ourselves panting heavily as we traversed a zigzag path up the steep scree-lined slope that led up to the final line of trees.

'I need a rest. Or oxygen,' gasped Barbara, hanging on to my arm. 'Are you *sure* this is doing us good?'

'We'll get the best view of the village in a minute,' I said.

'As long as we can have a proper rest I don't care. We should have brought Sherpas.'

After five more exhausting minutes we reached the high, ragged wall that separated the last of the improved fields from the wild open moorland above. We slumped down at the base of the five hardy sycamores that battled the wind here for most of the year and regained our breath.

The village 700 feet below was laid out for us like a quaint model. It sat, enclosed by thick trees, resting on the flat sloping ridge that divided Hubberdale from Buttergill, with squat stone cottages straggling along the edge of the long green.

'We live there,' said Barbara, grinning stupidly before gulping down some water. 'I still can't believe it.'

'It's special, isn't it?'

On the green I could make out the maypole by the slate-topped school. Also prominent were the square-built chapel, the white-faced pub and the spire-like stone cross near the smithy. Little people moved about slowly and toys cars glided along the road in silence.

Beyond the village, looking up broad Swinnerdale, flat-topped Bleabrough swelled up behind the crest of the far hills in a curious light.

'Do you really want to go right to the top?' asked Barbara.

'Yes, because then we get an even better view. We've come this far so we may as well finish it.'

Reluctantly she agreed and we pushed open the rusted metal gate in the wall and entered the bleak, boggy roughness of the upper reaches of the fell. A path wound its way through the clumpy ground but I skipped off it to the left.

'Come this way and I'll show you something really odd I discovered.'

'Oo-err,' said Barbara. 'It had better be good if it means we have to go even further.'

'It's only two hundred yards or so.'

She looked doubtful again but followed behind me along a narrow sheep track skirting the ridge. We climbed over a hillock and there it was, a peculiar white dome of rock poking out through the grass about seven feet high and fifteen across.

'*Is that it?*' she said.

'Well, yes, but you haven't seen its secret yet.'

'Eh? You mean I need to get close to experience the full disappointment?'

I gave her a playful push. 'Oh stop it, you cynic.'

We walked up to the strange lump and when she arrived the mystery of this curiosity became apparent.

'It's made of fossils!' she called. 'Wow!'

It was true, the whole bulging outcrop was composed of tightly packed fossilised creatures: shells and belemnites and ammonites and more.

'It's amazing, isn't it?'

Barbara knelt down and ran her hand over the surface. 'I've never seen anything like it – it's just solid, well, fossils. And so white!'

I laughed, telling her how I'd discovered it by accident as it wasn't on a footpath and we agreed that it was well worth the diversion.

Approaching the top of the hill twenty minutes later, the breeze freshened and we put back on the jumpers that earlier had been stripped as we'd sweated. The view here was truly magnificent. The steep hidden valley of Buttergill was now in view, its winding spurs melting into distant grey hazes. A curlew played behind us, sailing past on the wind with its great bent bill, calling a warning to guard its ground-borne nest.

We trudged the last few yards over the springy, sodden ground to the summit of the great fell marked by a wobbly cairn. The wind, almost entirely absent in the village far below, tugged at our clothes and hair, reminding us that we were nearly two thousand feet up.

'We did it!' cried Barbara, surveying the mists of the flat Vale of York to the east, sloping away to meet the pale grey sky. 'I'd forgotten just how, well, high this hill is!'

'You glad you did it, then?'

She gave me a warm hug. 'Of course I am. It's wonderful. Can we see the tea shops from here?'

As we walked down, a familiar thought crossed my mind, one which was there every time I climbed one of the fells of the Dales: how small everything was really, including the troubles which weighed down our daily lives.

Chapter Nineteen

Jo

Joanne Spence liked to be called Jo and you wouldn't argue with her. She was a strapping farmer's daughter from the isolated hamlet of Clint Rigg above Cragthwaite, ruddy-faced and, like all of her ilk, rewardingly practical and down to earth. Jo liked to be busy with things, including her work, and she had little regard for anyone who wasted time in one way or the other. Many times I had heard her favourite expression, 'Oh stop faffin' and get on.'

She came up to me one day in the classroom after the morning bell rang. 'Mr Seed, can I be a monitor? I was talking to me mum about her school days last night and she says she were scissors monitor in the class fer two years.'

'Well, I don't really have monitors, Jo. You can help to give out the books and things like that, if you like. I appreciate how helpful you are, though.'

'Yes but me mum had a badge with an M on it.'

I smiled, remembering a similar convention at my own primary school in the sixties and how the limit of my achievements was to be responsible for drawing the hall curtains if the sun was too bright.

'Well, I'm glad you're keen, Jo, so I'll discuss it with Mrs Berry and see what she says, all right?'

She appeared reasonably happy with this and quickly turned around to head outside, unaware that Barry Caygill was standing behind her waiting to ask me something. As she stepped forward he tried to move out of the way but was too slow and her arm caught him in the chest.

'Oh, sorry,' she said as Barry stumbled backwards sending two chairs flying before landing on his bottom with a hefty bump.

'Are you OK, Barry?' I asked as the apologetic Jo stepped forward and lifted him off the ground with ease.

'Yeah,' he squeaked, partly in embarrassment that a girl had sent him flying. 'I came to ask if I can bring me motorbike to school.'

'You haven't really got a motorbike, have you?'

'Yeah, it's a junior trials bike. I ride it round Sunters' field and I can enter a competition when I'm good enough, me dad says.'

'Well, it would be interesting to look at – maybe you could give us a talk?'

'I don't wanna talk, I just wan ter bring it cos Lawrence doesn't believe I 'ave one. Can I come to school on it?'

'What do you think, Barry?'

'No.'

'Correct.'

Val was pinning a display of potato prints to the corridor wall as I passed.

'Is that straight?' she said. 'I've been doing this thirty-two bloody years and I still can't put a picture up level.'

'Left hand down a bit,' I said.

'Like that?'

'No, too much.'

'There?'

'Spot on. Er, Val, do you have classroom monitors?'

'I used to, back in the seventies, but they've gone out of fashion now. Hilda still has them, of course. She has about fifty of 'em: sink monitors, floor monitors, crayon monitors . . .'

'What does a floor monitor do?'

'Monitor the floor for paperclips and dead bodies I suppose . . . you'll have to ask her. Is this straight?'

'Left hand down a bit.'

The staffroom door opened and Hilda walked out, coffee in hand. Val and I exchanged glances as she came over.

'Nice pictures, Valerie. You want the right hand down a bit on that one, though.'

'Andy was just asking me about monitors,' said Val, giving her arms a rest.

Hilda waggled her glasses. 'Waddya want to know, boy?'

'Erm, well, I was just thinking about them. What's the most useful one to have?'

She stared upwards. 'Now, there's a question. I can't do without my door monitors, and milk monitors, and every teacher needs a board monitor and book monitors . . .'

'What about scissor monitors?'

'Oh yes, vital. And pencil sharpening monitors.'

For once she was being serious.

Val looked towards me. 'You do realise that a monitor is a large carnivorous lizard, Hilda?'

'Mock not my monitors, Valerie. They keep me sane.' Hilda turned and disappeared into her room, giving me and Val a chance to snigger.

'Who's in charge of them, I want to know,' I said. 'Does she have a monitor monitor?'

Joyce came round the corner and stopped. 'What are you two smirking at?'

'Oh, just Hilda and her monitor fixation,' said Val. 'Andy's thinking of buying into the concept. He's going to have a gob monitor for Martine Clarkson.'

Joyce shook her head in bewilderment as we cackled again. 'Andy, can you spare a moment for a quick word in my office?'

My mood rapidly changed; Joyce stepped back. 'Nice display – not quite straight, though.'

I followed the head to her claret-coloured office and sat in the low armchair opposite her desk. She put a hand on my arm as she passed to pick up a file. 'Nothing to worry about, love; I just have a suggestion.'

I noticed the file was labelled INSET. 'What's it about?'

'Before I get on to that I'd better tell you that I've had a complaint about Jason Fisher. Apparently he's been pinching My Little Ponies off the infant girls at playtime and hiding them high up in the leylandii.'

'That's a pity because he's been quite a lot better recently. I'll have a word.'

'Thanks, Andy; now, my suggestion.' She flexed her long painted fingers and interlocked them. 'Well, there was a cluster heads' meeting last week and we have a slight problem. County gives each group of schools a budget to run their own in-service training programme but we've never used ours.'

'Why's that, then?'

'It's very simple – no one has the time to organise anything. All the other heads teach as well as do the admin and I'm just too busy with a thousand and one other things. Basically, we need someone with ideas who isn't a headteacher.'

'Perhaps young and male and, er, me by any chance?'

'It's just a suggestion, Andy. There are advantages: one, you get to organise courses and events that you'll or we'll find useful; two, you decide where they are held; three, you have a bit of money to spend; but lastly, and perhaps most importantly for you – it'll be very handy to have on your CV.'

'Oh, right. I don't really have a CV,' I said, not entirely sure what one was.

'Listen, you've been here nearly five years now. I'd hate to lose you but you need to be thinking about promotion soon and this is just the kind of experience that could give you the edge over the competition.'

'Do you think I could do it?'

'Of course I do. You're just the kind of keen, energetic ideas person that these very, well, traditional schools need.' She gave a telling wink.

Whatever challenges the post would bring – and I suspected they would be legion – I liked the sound of improving my future career, and so the following day, the other local heads having agreed on the proposal, I found myself in the singular role of Upper Swinnerdale Primary Cluster INSET Co-ordinator.

'I can't believe it,' I said to Val in the staffroom. 'I'm a flippin' monitor.'

On the first Saturday of half-term I'd decided to go with Tom back to the tiny hillside village where we'd first lived in Swinnerdale over four years ago to watch a Civil War re-enactment group relive the Siege of Castle Heywood. I was sure that he would enjoy the spectacle of uniforms and flags, just as I was sure it would all be too much for Reuben. The event didn't appeal to

Barbara either and she arranged instead to sample the delights of afternoon tea in Iris Falconer's grand house across the green with our younger son.

Castle Heywood was bustling with visitors and looked very different from the tiny, one-horse village we recalled from our early days in the dale. There were cars parked all along the dusty intersecting roads which separated the two rows of stone cottages, and people milled about, mostly heading for the great fortress which was decked out with pennants and from which we could hear shouting and horses' hooves.

'We lived here before you were born, Tommy,' I said.

'What, in the castle?'

'Not quite,' I laughed.

Tom held my hand and skipped along with great excitement as we approached the castle, its huge square walls rearing up over the village and casting heavy shadows. He jumped as we heard musket fire and I tried to explain that there would be soldiers but not real ones and there was nothing to be afraid of.

'Bang bang,' he said, imagining a pistol, and I wondered if Barbara would approve if I bought him a little plastic sword from Ingleburn. As we neared the entrance I found a mound of grass and picked Tom up so we could see over the bushes at the side of the road. On the slopes below the south-west tower there was a surprising amount of activity with forty or fifty men dressed as Parliamentarians gathered round two small black cannon. A cluster of visitors wearing brighter colours and holding cameras stood behind a rope to one side. I was just about to warn Tom that there might be a big bang when a blast of smoke shot out of one of the heavy guns and a moment later we heard the boom, like a small crack of thunder. Tom jolted again and covered his ears, unsure whether to be terrified or not.

'It's not real, Tommy, just pretend,' I said. 'No one's hurt.'

A second later there was a blood-curdling squeal from one of the turrets above us and lots of people shouting and screaming in a disturbingly realistic re-enactment of a multiple maiming by cannonball. I half-expected to see a severed Royalist leg tumble down from the battlements as we moved away to try and find a less violent scene to observe. At least Tom wasn't crying, although I did wonder how many nightmares he'd have that evening.

Things were thankfully quieter round the back of the castle and we enjoyed looking at some carts piled high with sacks, wooden bowls, pewter plates, tankards and other realistic seventeenth-century supplies. I let go of Tom's hand to give him more freedom to explore but then quickly grabbed it again when the five or six other visitors near us abruptly turned round and pointed.

'It's all right, Tom, they're just actors,' I said again as we watched a knot of eight roundhead soldiers skulk around the corner of the castle, their commander urging them to keep quiet. They were dressed in leather tunics and baggy britches, each man wearing the familiar shiny helmet and carrying an enormous sixteen-foot pike with a metal tip. They were an impressive sight and Tom stared as they crept forward in their mission to spring some kind of surprise rear-guard attack, no doubt.

'What are they going to do, Daddy?' he whispered.

'I don't know, we'll have to see.'

'What are those big sticks for?'

'Poking people.'

'I hope they don't poke us.'

'Shhh now, just watch.'

The moment was tense and our little group stood silent, just a few yards away, as the grubby-looking men edged around the wall.

We wondered what would happen as the tension built. Without warning a small door of the castle further along the wall opened a fraction. The commander reacted instantly.

'Get down!' he hissed.

The soldiers obeyed immediately, each dropping on to one knee and crouching. We held our breath for an instant, then every watcher burst into laughter at the sight of this cluster of desperate men trying to lie low with eight giant shiny-tipped pikes still sticking up and waggling like a pole-vaulters' convention.

'Eee, you could spot them from Harrogate!' hooted a bald man next to me and we guffawed all the more as one of the pikes swayed and hit the road with a mighty crack.

'Back, men!' called the leader, anxious to try and redeem the enactment. Only Tom didn't wipe an eye as they shuffled round the corner in retreat, their great spears wagging. He still just gawped, trying to make sense of it all.

That evening I relayed the tale to Barbara with glee.

'It was like Civil War Dad's Army: priceless . . .'

'Oh, I wish I'd seen it,' she said. 'I thought it was going to be really boring.'

'Did, er, Tom say anything to you about the day?'

'Just what you heard at tea time. He did mention the big noisy cannon again when I tucked him in for bed.'

'Oh, right; he'll certainly remember the day anyway.'

I left it there and silently prayed that our eldest son wouldn't wake up with horrific night visions of mangled bodies and invading armies.

Back at school, some weeks after my meeting with Joyce, I had organised two events for local teachers. The first came out of my growing concern that children were not reading enough and was called the New Book Group. It met once a month at a different school each time and was led by a librarian from Ingleburn who brought along a stack of new children's books for us to borrow and share with our classes. The only proviso was that each teacher attending had to report back on the previous month's books, saying how the children had liked them. We then exchanged the previous books so that, as time went on, each school was able to borrow a real variety of exciting new reading material. It soon became popular with the small group of teachers that attended and gave me some reassurance that I'd made a sound start in my new role.

The other event that I organised was not so successful. It had begun at a staff meeting at Cragthwaite when I'd explained to the others what my new responsibility was.

'Basically I can organise local INSET events here in Swinnerdale. So, the question is, what sort of sessions are you interested in?'

There was a resounding silence.

Unsurprisingly, Hilda was the first to break it. 'I finished my teacher training in 1949 – why would I need any more?'

Nobody replied so I tried to coax them along. 'Well, I think it would be helpful to have a PE session: it's always good to have new ideas for lessons.'

'If you think I'm going to be prancing around in a leotard you've another think coming, young man,' said Hilda.

Joyce shared some of the frustration I was feeling. 'Oh come on, Hilda – Andy doesn't mean that you'd have to do a practical workshop. It could just be sharing ideas or someone giving a talk.'

'Or perhaps a demo lesson,' I added. 'I'm sure that Jeff Osbourn would be happy to come and do one of those and we could just watch.'

'Who's Jeff Osbourn?' asked Emma.

'The Senior PE Adviser at County,' said Val, who had been uncharacteristically quiet.

'Oh, that chubby fella,' said Emma.

'Any other ideas, then?' I said, my pen poised.

'Put down science,' said Joyce. 'It would be good to get someone to come in and tell us how to get the best out of the wildlife area.'

'We need to get some wildlife in there first,' mumbled Val. 'The kids have scared it all away.'

'I fancy batik,' said Emma, suddenly sounding interested.

'Who is he, some Turkish pop star?' said Hilda, enjoying her own remark.

'It's this fabulous eastern technique for making designs on fabric. You paint hot wax on it then use dye to make colours and patterns.'

'Hot wax and dye . . . sounds perfect for five-year-olds,' laughed Hilda.

Emma wasn't perturbed. 'Maybe for Val's class it would be good? I've got this amazing batik skirt that a friend bought me from Java and, well, you can at least see if anyone else is interested.'

'What about you, Val?' asked Joyce.

'Well, tedious as it may sound, I think we should be addressing the demands of this flamin' new curriculum. I want someone to come over and tell me how I'm supposed to fit seven hours' teaching in a five-hour day.'

Joyce exhaled and tried to smile, looking at me. It hadn't been the most fruitful meeting but at least we had a few ideas.

Two days afterwards Joyce called me back into her office.

'Right, well I presented our INSET suggestions at the heads' meeting and the one they liked best was the PE demo lesson. They thought some of the other subjects would be a bit heavy going for an after-school session – teachers are tired and it takes a while to travel from the top of the dale. So just organise the PE one for now.'

'No batik then?'

'No batik; I think finger painting is radical enough for them out in the hills.'

I called County Hall right away and asked to speak to Jeff Osbourn. He wasn't in but phoned me back the following day and said that he'd be delighted to come to Swinnerdale and do a demonstration session with children.

'You're the young man who did the triple jump on my course at Shreeve Hall a couple of years ago, aren't you?'

I was flattered, thinking back to a little moment of glory under the eye of an athletics coach who had been brought in for the day. 'That's right; I'm impressed that you've remembered me.'

'Oh yes, you did the county proud that day.'

'Thanks, er, anyway, are you happy to work with my class of lower juniors? I think it would be good to show the teachers some ideas for using the large apparatus in the hall – I seem to be the only one who gets it out.'

'I'd be delighted to, Andrew.'

We fixed up a provisional date which Joyce then confirmed with the other schools and the event was arranged for a Wednesday after school at Cragthwaite. It soon became apparent that I had overlooked something, however: the small matter of having to organise twenty-four children to stay on after school, and so a flurry of letter writing and phone calls followed. With various other commitments and problems, only nineteen children could make it, but on the day there was at least some excitement.

'Who's coming to watch us again, Mr Seed?' asked the beefy Jo during some afternoon work with atlases.

'Teachers from other schools in Swinnerdale.'

'Why do they want to see *us* lot do PE?'

'Well, so they can get some ideas for their own PE lessons.'

'Can't they think of their own ideas?'

'Yes, but they've heard that Class Three here are the best at PE for miles.'

'Don't be daft, Mr Seed.' And with that she went back to her atlas.

I wandered across to the other side of the room, where Jason Fisher was chattering to Ian Tattershall. I'd recently talked to Jason about the My Little Pony episode and he had at least appeared contrite, although in class his concentration was often wayward.

'Have you finished your map work then, boys?'

'Nearly,' lied Jason.

I looked at his page. He was supposed to have traced South America and marked all of the countries and their capital cities. So far we had Chile and about half an inch of Peru. Ian had done North America.

'You only have fifteen minutes to finish this and do it well,' I said, pointing Ian to the correct map. 'If it's not done then you might have to complete it after school instead of the PE.' They sprang into action.

When the bell rang I sent the children with Sue Bramley to get changed for PE, hoping that they all had their kit, then went to see if Jeff Osbourn had arrived. He was in the hall talking to Joyce and sipping tea, an upright, portly figure with grey, heavily Brylcreemed hair. As always he was flawlessly turned out in his old-school tracksuit and blindingly white plimsolls. I quickly set out some chairs around the sides of the hall for the visiting teachers, then checked that we had all the equipment needed for the session. I noticed that someone had tidied the PE store.

'Right,' he said, 'I'm going to need wooden bats and balls, mats for some stretching exercises and then, of course, the large apparatus.' I'd forgotten quite how sergeant-major-like he was. He scanned the climbing frames folded against the walls and pulled at one of the ropes attached to the ceiling.

'Well, I'll leave you to it,' said Joyce walking away. 'I need to organise coffee for our visitors.'

Outside the hall I heard the babble of children and went to calm them down as they lined up. Martine was peering through the small window in the door.

'Is that old bloke takin' us fer PE?' she whispered very loudly to Vicky. I reprimanded her then demanded that they line up quietly.

Jo put up a hand. 'Can me and Estelle put out some benches fer us to sit on?'

'That's a good idea. Go in and put two in front of this wall, girls.'

I peered in as Jo picked up her end of a long wooden bench with ease while Estelle struggled with the other end. She really was a strong girl.

Five minutes later Jeff had the class doing some warm-up exercises while the first teachers arrived. I saw familiar faces from Applesett then Ingleburn, followed by West Doddthorpe, and finally the upper-dale staff from Chapelgarth and Kettleby. All of them went straight to the tea trolley. It was now late and we should have started but one school was missing: the tiny Ingleburn RC. I could see that Jeff was anxious to get going so I stood up to welcome everyone and say that we'd better make a start when the hall door bumped open and the shrivelled figure of Sister Mary Brendan bustled in, muttering away, completely unaware that she was interrupting me. We all waited and the children sat fidgeting as she rattled the coffee cups and selected a biscuit.

The lesson began fifteen minutes late but Jeff, to his credit, knew that it wasn't our fault and he rapidly had the children warming up purposefully with bats and balls. My class's bat skills reflected the full range of ability and soon there were tennis balls flying everywhere, including one deliberately hit against the ceiling by Jason. With proper authority Jeff barked at them all to stop and get ready for the next activity and, very impressively, they did so right away. Jo and Howard did a good job of getting out the mats; I just wished that Gary's black toenails weren't so prominent or that his shorts weren't on inside out.

The children worked hard at their stretching exercises, having been somewhat alarmed by the power of Jeff's command earlier. I wondered whether Val was one of his protégés in that department. The visiting teachers were not exactly enthralled by the demonstration, however: several stifled yawns, two were marking books and Sister Mary Brendan had her head back and was sound asleep. I just prayed that she didn't start snoring.

The next part of the lesson did arouse more interest, though, as the children set out the large apparatus and the county PE adviser had Class 3 doing some impressive sequences of balances and movements from one piece of equipment to the next. He picked out individuals for praise and asked the best gymnasts to demonstrate for others. The children were really enjoying it, although I overheard a teacher from Chapelgarth mutter to her colleague, 'This would be useful if we had a flamin' hall.'

Next Jeff moved some of the mats into the spaces and asked the children to move around the hall without touching the floor. This they found great fun and only Jason spoiled it by hogging the ropes and waggling his legs, pretending to be Tarzan while Jeff had his back to him.

'Right, stop and sit down, children!' Once again I was impressed with the way they obeyed instantly. 'Well, the bat and ball skills earlier need a bit more practice. The stretches were quite good but I am pleased to say that your apparatus work has been very good, so well done.' Several of the class sat up and grinned broadly.

Jeff continued. 'So . . . even though it's late, because you have done well, we're going to finish with a little treat and play a game.' There was a low cheer from the children; some of the teachers looked at their watches and one, bag in hand, surreptitiously slipped out through the door. Sister Mary Brendan continued her slumber. At least Val and Emma were doing Cragthwaite proud, making notes and evidently enjoying the session.

The game was very simple: Jeff chose two chasers and told them they had to tag the other children to get them out. No one was allowed to touch the floor and anyone out must sit on a bench. 'It's called Pirates,' he said. 'Who wants to be a chaser?' Every child put up a straining hand. He selected Jason, to my surprise, and Jo.

It was mayhem. There were children leaping, rushing and diving everywhere. Some were screaming, while others performed suicidal jumps to try and escape the rabid pursuers. Several bruised themselves bumping against the metal bars of the apparatus and when Susan tripped and was trampled underfoot in the mad rush to escape Jason's lurches, Jeff called the game to a halt and ordered that they calm down or it would have to cease.

The slower individuals were soon out and the game developed

into an absorbing cat and mouse chase, with the more nimble children taking up high or open vantage points to escape their would-be captors. Jo suggested to Jason that they work together to trap some of the quicker ones but he completely ignored her and it soon became apparent that he was only interested in getting out the girls. Not only that but he was sneakily giving hard prods instead of touches whenever Jeff wasn't watching.

'Oi!' cried Estelle as he shoved his palm on to her shoulder. 'That's nasty.'

I considered intervening but didn't want to compromise Jeff's authority: it was his session and I could see that he was aware that we had run over time and simply wanted it to finish quickly.

A few moments later there was only the cat-like Ian, who the pair couldn't get near, and the athletic Cathy left. Jo looked over at Mr Osbourn and we could all see that he was glancing at his watch and considering calling it a day, declaring the two of them winners. But then Cathy, now exhausted, made a mistake and stopped on a mat in the corner. Jason, his eyes blazing with the chase, saw his chance, knowing that if he could swing over on the rope she would be trapped. Jo was nearer and right by the ropes but didn't make a move towards her friend. Instead, she foresaw Jason's plan and glanced once more towards Jeff who was reaching for his whistle.

The moment was exquisite in its justice. Jason pounded forward to gain momentum and leapt at the nearest rope, knowing that he needed to swing across to the cowering Cathy in one movement. He was in mid-swing, sailing through the air when Jo stepped out and, with a brawny forearm, reached for the next rope the other side of Jason's arc. With an audible thump the boy ceased his progress and dropped to the ground like a bag of coal. The whistle blew.

Only one person missed the enjoyment of the spectacle: as the audience clapped and the children put the apparatus away, a small, wrinkled nun bent her head forward, clacked her tongue a few times and opened her eyes. To my amazement she simply stood up, put her teacup on the trolley and walked out.

When everything was put away, I lined my class up to get changed. Jo cast me an anxious glance. She knew she had been seen but her expression told that it was worth it; I couldn't disagree. As she walked past I made a mental note to award her a new if secret role: Jason monitor.

Chapter Twenty

Colin

The old bus trundled out of Swinnerdale and headed east towards the dark hills of the North York Moors. The phlegmatic Mr Ripley sat at the wheel, unconcerned about the line of cars behind us, their frustrated drivers veering out in the vain hope of a clear stretch of road. It was the first week of June and Class 3 were setting off on their first ever residential trip: three nights on the Yorkshire coast.

'Hello Harry.'

'Yes Harry?'

'Tell Harry.'

The same words were repeated over and over in turn with fierce concentration by a small group of selected boys and me. It was a game that Val had passed on for whiling away the time on long coach journeys and in particular keeping quiet those who found it hard to sit still and stay out of bother. I was playing it with Jason, Gary, Dan and Colin, and their dogged, competitive natures stirred up a desperation to win. Any kind of mistake and a dot would be felt-penned on the offender's nose, causing him to be referred to as 'One Spot' from then on. It was three lives and you're out.

Colin had been invited to join this group on account of his propensity to be a pain when it came to school trips. He was a small, freckly boy of crafty disposition who loved nothing more than to boast. Wherever we went he had always been before or he knew a better place and so our destination was pronounced boring. Whatever carefully planned, exciting activities were in wait, Colin had already done them, and more. He was tiresome at best on these occasions, while at school could show a surprising resourcefulness and often used to produce nuggets of knowledge in class or unexpected solutions to knotty problems.

'Hello Harry,' I said to Dan for the twenty-sixth time.

''Ello 'arry,' he said, producing a 'Haaaa!' and pointing fingers from Colin and Jason.

'You were supposed to say, "Yes Harry", you dur,' crowed Jason. I gave him a disapproving look then produced the blue felt pen and penned a wobbly dot on Dan's nose while he tried to protest.

''Ello 'arry,' he said to Gary.

'Yes One Spot?'

'Tell Harry.'

Emma peered down the aisle from the front of the bus and smiled seeing Dan's predicament. Back in the autumn term she'd suggested in the staffroom that she'd like to go on a residential visit in the summer, never having done one before as an infant teacher.

'You can take my place any day,' Val had said. 'I've done twenty-odd trips with juniors and the buggers have kept me up to the early hours once too often. I've got to take my class later in the summer anyway so you can go with Andy's.'

'I thought you said twenty trips with odd juniors for a minute,' laughed Hilda.

'Oh, plenty of them were odd, don't worry,' grumbled Val.

Emma gave a little clap. 'Well, it'll all be new to me so I don't mind. I'm quite excited now – I've never been to Northumberland.'

'Oh,' I said, 'sorry, it's not going to be Northumberland: Joyce and I discussed it a while back and she thinks it's too expensive now.'

'Aye, we don't want a repeat of that awful bloody business with that poor lass, what was she called?'

'Martha,' I said, thinking back to a few years ago when an unfortunate girl had been left behind after her mother refused to pay, despite offers of a subsidy.

'Oh, so where are you going with your class, Andy?' said Emma.

'Joyce has asked around amongst the other heads and someone's recommended a youth hostel near Whitby.'

'Ooh, so it's still the seaside, then? Whoopy-do!' Emma gave a little squeak which caused Hilda to roll her eyes.

The Hello Harry game was long over and after nearly three hours on the road the bus had gone quiet, with every child staring blankly out of the window.

'Is that the sea?' said Estelle, pointing to a grey smudge on the horizon. I confirmed it was and a low cheer arose along the seats. Mr Ripley, who hadn't said a word the whole journey, turned off the main road and we began to lumber down a twisting country lane. The countryside was markedly different to the Dales: there were hedges for a start and fields of ripening corn, something unknown around Cragthwaite. We passed red-roofed farms and then turned off again down a narrow track with briars almost scratching the windows of the little coach.

'Not far now,' I said as the murmur of excitement spread. Five minutes later the bus tilted forward and we plunged down a precipitous slope with high-banked sides and woods all around. The children craned into the aisle to try and see forward through the gloom.

'Where are we stayin' again, Mr Seed?' said Martine, who was wearing pink shorts with a purple top.

'Skerry Hole Youth Hostel.'

''Ave you bin before?'

'No,' I said.

'What if it's 'orrible?'

Before I could answer the bus slowed from a crawl to a stop and a cluster of sombre stone buildings came into view. Just behind them were some forbidding cliffs and beyond these rocks was the grey rolling North Sea. Once more a little cheer went out and the children stood up and started grabbing their belongings.

The youth hostel was a converted water mill built deep in a gulley cut by a fast-flowing stream coming off the moors into the sea. It sat alone in this tight wooded cleft between cliffs 300-feet high. The children, once off the bus, took no notice of the buildings and had eyes only for the beach in front of it and the towering cliffs to either side.

'Can we go on the beach now?' said Lawrence. 'I'm desperate to do some skimming.'

'Am desperate ter do some swimmin',' said Howard.

I reminded them that we needed to unload first and store our bags in the hostel. As usual it took ten minutes to pick up all the detritus left on the coach.

Val's vast experience of school residential visits had been invaluable to me in the planning of this trip and I had acquired several important tips from her. The first of these was to go on a long walk right away. If this didn't happen then the children's excitement would keep them up all night and lead to tired, fractious bodies the following day.

'Exhaustion is the buzzword,' she'd said. 'It's them or you.'

With this in mind we simply dumped our luggage in the hostel's storeroom, quickly confirmed our arrival, ensured each child had a packed lunch then set out on the clifftop walk to Robin Hood's Bay. I gave the usual stern warnings about staying in pairs and not wandering off.

'These cliffs are *very* dangerous,' I said. 'And high. Do NOT go near the edge. In fact, in places they are crumbling away so stick to the footpath and you might make it.'

Some of them half-giggled with nerves; others, Colin among them, laughed off the caution as if it were for babies.

'Can we go now?' said the impatient Lawrence.

'Yep, you lead the way,' I said. He and Stephen strode forward up the lane beside the beck, excited to be in front. I put out an arm to hold back the others who surged forward to follow.

'Eh?' said Estelle.

'Just wait a moment,' I murmured.

When the two boys were fifty yards up the lane heading the wrong way I led the remaining children over a small wooden bridge across the beck to the side and towards the cliff path. Several of the class laughed and waved at Lawrence and Stephen, who turned and rushed back, mortified that they were now last.

The path rose up abruptly to ascend the great sandstone cliff in a series of zig-zags. After just a few moments everyone was puffing. The path became steeper then turned into a giant muddy staircase of steps created with heavy wooden boards.

'Me legs are killin' already,' said the hefty Beverley Butterfield.

'I've lost Martine!' called Vicky.

I halted and looked back. 'You can't have done – we've only been going two minutes.'

'She's stopped for a rest,' called Trudy from the back. It was true: Martine had only climbed about forty steps but was already out of breath. There were at least 200 more to go. I shook my head and smiled as Emma caught my eye.

'You'll have to slow down, Mr Seed,' she said in between pants. 'I'm not used to this.' I could see that from the yellow jump suit and sandals she was wearing.

With five or six stops and a barrowload of moaning, we reached the top of the cliff and emerged through the trees to be greeted by the most spectacular view far out to sea and along the great rugged coast. Immediately the class forgot their exhaustion.

'Look, a ship!'

'Wow, yer can see *miles*.'

'Is that Whitby?'

'Those people look tiny!'

'How far are we from the edge?'

'Heeeeyyyy. Can we 'ave us sarnies now?'

Only one voice dissented. It was Colin's. 'It's not all that high. I've been on higher cliffs in Scotland.'

We ignored him and I ordered everyone back into pairs for the trek along the narrow cliff-top path. The children enjoyed the feeling of adventure as the fresh sea breeze pushed at our faces and noisy gulls wheeled overhead. We saw cormorants sitting on the black rocks hundreds of feet below and ahead the red roofs of Robin Hood's Bay tumbling towards the sea in their own tight valley. After making most of the distance we found a broad area of tufted grass and I let the now-famished children attack their packed lunches.

'I thought we were goin' to walk along the beach,' muttered Colin.

I tried to remain patient. 'We're going to do that on the way back. Remember, I explained at school.'

'What if the tide comes in?'

'The tide's coming in now and it'll be going out when we return, Colin.'

'These rolls are gruesome; I hate egg.'

At least everyone else was having a good time. I sat next to Marcus Hyams, a quiet boy and one of the younger members of the class. He returned my thumbs up while tucking into a rare wholemeal roll. Seeing that he and the other gentler souls were happy, I looked over to ensure that Pamela and Stephen were well apart. They were. The affair was, it seemed, at an end. The walk, meanwhile, had given everyone a roaring appetite and the children busily stuffed their faces while the gulls soared a little closer hoping for scraps.

Martine's lunch box contained four sausage rolls and two packets of crisps. She opened one of the bags and tipped her head back, pouring the contents down her throat in two goes. I wanted to look away but was strangely transfixed. She put the empty bag down and the wind promptly blew it away and over the cliff.

'Whoops,' she said, amid laughter.

I warned about litter, then dealt with a grave accusation from Lawrence that Gary had a can.

'I thought we weren't allowed fizzy drinks,' he said.

'You aren't.'

'But he's got one.'

'What do you suggest I do?' I said.

He thought for a moment. 'Throw him off the cliff?' That's what I liked about Lawrence: at times he did see the absurdity of life.

The next person to approach me was Cathy, holding out a plastic container.

'I can't get my drink open, Mr Seed. It's one of those stupid straw ones.'

The design was very curious: a corrugated plastic beaker with a rubbery film over the top. The drink inside looked like an e-number cocktail and the tight plastic top was bulletproof; I couldn't shift it at all.

'I think you're supposed to pierce it with the straw,' I said. 'Have you got it?'

Estelle came over and handed me the straw which was already well buckled. 'We tried that,' she said. I tried too, but the plastic refused to be beaten. With five or six children and Emma now enjoying the spectacle of me wrestling with a small drink, my frustration reached a crescendo and I went for brute force, bringing the point of the straw down with a hard jab from height. The straw broke the seal but the resulting pressure of the stab sent a long squirt of sticky juice over the top of my trousers. I stood up instinctively with the result that the whole class saw the long wet patch.

The laughter was so long and loud that the gulls peeled away.

'Mr Seed, you should have gone at the hostel, really!' splurted Emma, unable to resist.

Robin Hood's Bay is a magical place although it can be overrun with visitors at weekends and holidays, yet on this midweek June day it almost felt like we had the place to ourselves. We clustered around Bay Foot where the fishing village's slipway meets the water and watched the foamy waves bash against the sea wall and roll up into the dank tunnel where the beck emerges.

'Is this where the smugglers used to hide?' asked Anna, craning over the railings to try and look into the mouth of the tunnel.

'Well, that's just a legend,' I said. 'But there really were smugglers in the town.' She looked at me wide-eyed not noticing an extra-big wave slap against the wall. Its spray shot forward and gave Anna a cold shower, much to everyone's amusement.

I moved the children away from the water and quietened them down. 'Now, Miss Torrington and I need a cup of tea and you are going to have a special treat.' If they weren't listening before they were now. 'Remember at school that I told you that this village is very old and has lots of narrow little alleyways and places to explore. Well, we are going to allow you to go around the old part of the town in groups of four to find all the places on this list.' There was a hubbub of excitement. 'Listen! If we think anyone can't be trusted then they will have to stay here with us.' That seemed to do the trick. I outlined the rules about staying in the old part of the village, off the roads and not attempting to go near the water under any circumstances. 'You have to find ten houses with Robin Hood connections, the new sea wall, the Institute, two churches, and the fossil cobbles.'

'What are the cossil fobbles, I mean fossil cobbles?' asked Trudy.

'Fossils set into the ground. Any more questions?'

'Can we go in the shops?' It was Colin.

'Colin, once again, I explained this in school. The answer is not today but we will come here on the last day, providing you all follow the rules.'

I checked that all the groups had a watch, then warned them to be back in forty minutes. I added that in twenty minutes I would walk around the town checking up on them while Miss Torrington stayed by the bay, ensuring that no one fell in the sea. They went off, clipboards in hand, in great exhilaration while Emma and I popped into the nearby café.

We took our tea and sat outside the pub at the seafront so that the bay was within view.

'Did we put a sensible one in each group?' I asked.

'Well don't ask me,' said Emma. 'They're your kids. Anyway, they all look like models of restraint and respectability compared with my dribbling five-year-olds.'

'Have you recovered from the cliff walk yet?'

'Only just – you should have warned me it was virtually an Alp – you know how unfit I am. Thank goodness for Martine cos I would still be there now if I hadn't have rested with her.'

'It'll have done you good.'

'Done me good? I've strained my inner being doing that.'

We enjoyed five minutes of tranquillity then Emma suddenly stood up.

I looked around. 'What is it? Have you seen someone?'

She shook her head. 'I've got to move: the smell of fish and chips is driving me mad.'

A few minutes later I set off to check up on the groups, ducking off one of the village's two narrow roads up some dark steps and into one of the numerous ancient narrow alleys that so characterised this exquisite place. I soon heard the babble of children's voices and peered around a corner to see Susan, Barry and Ian jotting down the name of a house.

'There's another one – Friar Tuck's,' said Barry.

'How d'you spell that?' asked Ian.

'It's written by the door, you div.'

At least they were working. I wondered where their fourth member was then I spotted Anna, further up the passage. She was crouching down and running a finger over a large curled ammonite among the cobbles. There was something delightful about seeing a child in wonder like this. I quietly snuck out the school camera and grabbed a shot without her seeing.

Turning back to look for other groups, I passed narrow, tumbling Georgian cottages along the colourful snickets: Bow Villa, Little John House, Sherwood Cottage, Arrowside. Suddenly I almost crashed into Gary Blacow who was hurtling down some steps followed by the rest of his quartet.

'Whoah, sorry, Mr Seed!'

'Gary, why are you running? What if I'd been a little old lady carrying a dozen eggs?'

He thought about a smart answer for a moment. 'Sorry.'

I looked up at Cathy, Fraser and Estelle hoping for more sense. 'So, what is the big hurry?'

'I don't know; we were just following Gary.'

I should have guessed there would be no sense: children just like dashing about. I checked their work and was pleased to see that they had found everything except the sea wall.

'You've got five minutes, but *walk*,' I said.

They moved on, giggling, then disappeared around a corner leaving the echo of suspiciously rapid footsteps.

I found another group staring longingly into a sweet shop window, then one more who looked completely lost. Further on, up the steepest section of the hillside I heard more familiar voices. Once again, I stopped around a corner to eavesdrop. Vicky, Jo and Tim were listening to Colin.

'I go off on me own all t'time when ahm on 'oliday.'

'I would never dare do that,' said Vicky.

'It doesn't bother me.'

'It's nearly 'alf past, we'd better 'ead back,' said Tim. Good old Tim.

'Ahm bored anyway,' said Colin.

I stepped out making Vicky jump.

'Finished your work everyone?' I said, peering at Tim's list. 'What's this one?' He'd written *Made merry on log.*

Jo glanced over. 'I think it's Maid Marian Lodge.'

They followed me back down to the seafront and I was amazed to find the other five groups already waiting there with Emma. There was quite a lot of noise and several children were pointing at a patch of sand which had emerged among the rocks now that the tide was retreating.

Martine jiggled up to me. 'Mr Seed, thank God yer 'ere – am bustin' fer the lav.'

'Sorry,' said Emma. 'I don't know where they are.'

While half the class disappeared to the toilets, I stepped out on to the shore to see if the sea was far enough out for us to walk back to the hostel along the beach. When I returned there was a kerfuffle and I saw a teddy fly through the air.

'Oi, give it back!' screeched Trudy at Lawrence who caught the small bear then launched it as high as he could. The wind caught it and it sailed over to the jumble of small fishing boats which had been laid up outside the white pub. To cruel cheers from some of the boys the teddy landed on the high cabin of a wooden coble and stayed there.

'Whoops, I didn't mean to do that,' said Lawrence.

I let Emma berate him then reassured Trudy I'd get it back, even though she was meant to have left it at the hostel. With everyone watching I managed to clamber up on to the boat and use a pole to rescue the beleaguered soft toy, raising cheers from the girls. The squawking gulls overhead seemed to join in the celebration.

Returning to the mob, I put on an authoritative voice. 'Right, no more messing around or we won't go back along the beach and you'll miss a chance to see the caves and to look for fossils.'

They calmed quickly. 'Good, now back into your twos so we can count you.' The children rearranged themselves into a line quickly and I went along checking numbers, relieved that order had been restored. To my great annoyance, however, there were unrestrained sniggers behind me.

I turned, exasperated. 'What now?'

The whole class was pointing at me and making noises. Even Emma couldn't help joining in. 'Sorry,' she said, 'but you won't believe this. You'd better take off your jacket.'

The explanation for everyone's amusement became apparent immediately. A gull had left a white streak down my back. I closed my eyes and sighed at the double injustice as Class 3 hooted and took photos. Only one thought occupied my head as we stepped on to the beach: *Why, oh why, couldn't it have done one on Colin instead?*

The walk back along the beach was mercifully less eventful and the children enjoyed hunting for fossils at the base of the sea-battered cliffs. We let them explore caves and skim stones in the sea. They found dead crabs, mystical shells and salt-bleached jetsam and drew comical faces in the sand. It was because of moments of freedom like this that I loved taking children away on trips, and for some it was the first time they had been to the coast.

'Beats my usual Tuesday afternoon,' said Emma, the wind blowing her long hair into huge shapes. 'This is way better than "Polly Put the Kettle on".'

'And easier than going back up that cliff.'

We arrived back at the hostel an hour before the evening meal which gave time to sort out belongings and have a quick tour of the building led by Mr Kirk, the sharp-eyed warden.

'There's a group in from a secondary school in Pontefract,' he said, 'but otherwise you've got the place to yourselves.'

The buildings were a warren of rooms on several levels but everything had simplicity and character. The girls went off to see their dorms with Emma while Mr Kirk took the boys through a large bedroom with several beds to a smaller side room with fourteen bunks squashed together.

'You'll just about fit in here,' he said. 'Sorry you can't have the big room but the older lads are in there.'

'How old are they?' asked Lawrence.

'Oh, fifteen or sixteen, I think. A lot bigger than you, anyway,' smiled the warden before addressing me. 'They're on a field trip until later, by the way, so the dining hall is all yours this evening.'

After a hearty meal in the long, cellar-like vaulted refectory with the children surprisingly quiet, we gathered them together in the lounge and went through the work they'd done on Robin Hood's Bay. We discussed how it was once purely a fishing settlement but now relied on tourism, and pondered on the mysterious origins of its name.

'Perhaps Robin 'ood took 'is 'olidays there,' speculated Howard, with tongue in cheek.

'Why is there a big sea wall at the far side of the village?' I asked. The answers were varied and interesting.

'For the view?'

'To give the locals summat ter do?'

'To stop fossil hunters digging all the cliffs away?'

Colin waved his hand. 'I know.'

'Yes, Colin?'

'It's because some o' the houses have fallen into the sea. It's ter stop it happenin' again.'

'Very good,' I said, pleased to be able to encourage him for once. 'How did you know that?'

'I've told you, I've been there before wi' me mum and dad. That's why I found it boring.'

I ignored the last part and tried to return to geography. 'Yes, the cliffs all along this coast are crumbling away as the sea crashes against them at high tide and during storms. Does anyone know what we call that?'

'A bit of a bummer,' whispered someone at the back a bit too loudly.

'It begins with "e",' I said trying to drown out the titters.

A hand went up. Unfortunately it was Martine's. 'An emergency?'

'No, it's not an emergency,'

'It would be if yer house fell in t'sea!' At least she cheered us all up.

Dan had a guess. 'Earthfall?'

'That's a good try, Dan, but it begins E-R.'

'Er . . .' said everyone, much as they had been doing before.

There were no guesses.

'E-R-O,' I said.

I could see Martine's hand rise again and Emma's eyes go wide. I couldn't risk it. 'It's erosion,' I said.

'Awww, I were gunna say that,' said Colin.

'I weren't,' mumbled Martine.

I drew the coastal geography session to an end and told the children to put on their wellies so that we could go rock pooling. This brought forth a mighty cheer.

When they were ready and lined up, I warned them about the

dangers of the deadly slippery sea lettuce when they were clambering over rocks.

'Is that real?' said Gary, looking very doubtful.

'Yes, it's bright green, you can't miss it.'

Emma leaned over. 'I thought you were making it up, too.'

Once outside we gave the children a final warning about not straying too far and the dangers of being cut off by the tide, then let them loose for their final 'wearing out' session before bed. As predicted, they dashed about from one pool to the next comparing finds and hoping to see a giant squid, electric eel or, at the very least, a prize lobster.

I sat on a rock to rest but Emma was very concerned that the children put every find back where they found it: she was an early environmentalist even if she knew next to nothing about the environment. At least Lisa Bowe was keen to help her.

'Look everyone, quick!' shouted Helen. All the children within earshot dashed over, eager to see what must have been an octopus or a gold doubloon buried in the sand.

'What is it?' cried Estelle, first on the scene.

Helen pointed down gravely. 'I think ah've found some sea lettuce.'

I laughed at the moans of disappointment, then dealt with Jason, who was creeping towards the sea for a sly paddle – something which had been expressly forbidden on account of the dangerous currents – then Pamela, who had managed to fill her wellies with seawater, then Barry, who had skinned his knee, and finally Susan, who wouldn't say what was wrong at first until it became apparent she was homesick. I called Emma over to comfort her before waving those who had strayed too far to come back, especially now that the sun was on the horizon and dusk was lengthening the cliffs' vast shadows.

Back inside the hostel we discussed rockpool finds and tried to identify everything using the books and charts that were provided. To finish the evening, I quietened the mood with a story: none other than the start of the unsurpassed *Treasure Island*.

At half-past nine we sent the children to get washed and ready for bed, and girded ourselves for a long night of patrolling, as was the rule. I was grateful that the secondary school group still weren't back as I settled the Cragthwaite boys into their bunks, then made the usual threats about the consequences of whispering, rude noises, jumping on beds, ghost stories, midnight feasts and getting up to explore. Actually, I thought there was very little chance of the last one as our room opened out on to the main dorm and my boys would be way too scared of the big lads in there.

I left the bedroom with lights out to check how things were with Emma and the girls. She yawned long and hard as I saw her walking between the two rooms they had been assigned.

'They just won't shut up,' she said. 'If I get one lot quiet then the others kick off. It doesn't help that I'm knackered myself.'

I sympathised, trying not to sound too boastful that the boys were very quiet. 'Actually, I think I'll go to bed myself,' I said. 'My bed's in the same room so it'll be easier to keep an eye on things.'

When I returned the lights were on and a massive pillow fight was underway.

The excuses were numerous.

'He started it.'

'It weren't on the banned list.'

'It's creepy in 'ere – we had to lighten t'mood.'

'My pillow slipped off the top bunk.'

'Howard keeps farting.'

'This bed creaks so I can't sleep.'

'It's too dark with the lights off.'

Colin mocked the last one. 'Oh, what a baby. I'm not scared of the dark or a few creaks. Stop being wimps.'

I told him and all of them off, yet again, and said that I'd now be staying in the room, which brought a few muffled protests but relief for others. Fifteen minutes later the lights were off and I was lying in a profoundly uncomfortable bed, still giving warnings about silly noises and snickering.

At just after eleven the comedy groans, bogus burps and fake rat scratchings finally ceased and the tireder of the boys were now asleep. I myself was beginning to drift off when there was a heavy bump, followed by the sound of deep voices then a great din as the main dorm door crashed open and twenty or so raucous fifteen-year-olds galumphed into the echoing room next to us, shouting and singing.

'What's that?' came a sleepy voice from nearby, followed by others. It soon became apparent that every one of the Cragthwaite boys was now awake again. I wondered whether to go in and say something but then a fierce teacher's voice came through demanding quiet and reminding his fifth years that there were other guests in the hostel. The lads calmed down considerably but they didn't stop talking and their voices sounded through the door, with several swearing, as did hefty bumps and bangs as they collapsed on their beds and threw down their bags and shoes.

'Where's Bradshaw?' said the teacher, sounding exasperated.

'He's in the bog, sir, I think,' came a cocky voice.

'Prob'ly pukin' again,' called another, to much laughter.

'Voices down; how many times do I have to tell you!'

My hopes that they would settle quickly weren't high. 'I know it's hard boys,' I said, 'but try and get to sleep. If they carry on being noisy, I'll go and have a word.'

It was the last thing I wanted to do.

The next few moments I shall almost certainly never forget, nor the boys who were with me that night.

Once more the far dormitory door bumped open, this time to cheers and cries of 'Braddy!' and 'What a headcase!'

'Quiet!' growled the teacher. 'Bradshaw, hurry up and get in bed. We're going to sort out you and Potts in the morning.'

The voice replying was unmistakably slurred. 'Not scared of you, Smithy.'

'Right, I am not having this. Come out of the room with me now!' The fury in the teacher's voice was real.

'Get lost, I'm gunna bed.'

'You're coming with me.'

At this point there was the unmistakable sound of grappling followed by swearing and a great thump as something crashed a bed against the wall. The teacher bawled and the boy shouted back as they wrestled. My heart was pounding and I could feel the fear of the young boys in our room. I leapt out of bed, grabbed a dressing gown and opened the door.

The scene was even uglier than I'd imagined. The teacher, a bald, brawny man of about forty was leaning over a writhing youth who was spitting out threats, pinning him to the floor with his knee while the watching boys stared in disbelief.

'Keep flamin' still!' snarled the enraged teacher.

'Get off me yer bastard!' yelled the skinny teenager who I could now see had blood seeping from his arm and mouth. Both were panting heavily.

The teacher twisted his head towards me. 'I'm really sorry about this – two of them snuck off to the pub.'

'I'll get the warden,' I said, dashing across the room.

I was back a minute later to find the teacher still sitting on the drunken boy while another lad passed some tissues over to soak up some blood.

'I made it clear no alcohol!' the sweating man barked.

As the warden rushed in behind me, I looked up and saw several small pale faces peering through the doorway of our room at the frightening scene before them, their eyes round with shock. I hurried over and ushered them back inside. They bombarded me with questions, while I counted them.

'Where's Colin?' I said.

'He's in the toilet,' replied Howard. 'Too scared to come out.'

At least this was one experience he hadn't already had somewhere else.

Chapter Twenty-One

Beverley

Predictably, there was only one topic of conversation at breakfast. The girls, who had no notion of the previous night's drama, were desperate to know the details and, for once, didn't sit apart from the boys but mingled while they munched their cereal, drawing out the grim details of the altercation with questions.

'Did you see them fight?'

'How big were they?'

'Did Mr Seed join in?'

'What did you all do?'

'Did Colin really poo himself?'

The chief interrogators were Estelle, who loved being in charge and so hated to think that something exciting had happened without her knowledge, and a big, bold girl called Beverley Butterfield. She had garnered a reputation throughout the school as something of a drama queen. She could be loud and brash, rather like her father, who was Cragthwaite's resident builder, but I found her chirpy outlook appealing. Although she was as large as Jo, Beverley's bulk was wobbly rather than muscular but she was not self-conscious in any way.

She bounded over to me. 'Are we allowed more toast, Mr Seed?'

At least it wasn't another question about fights. 'How many slices have you had?'

'Just three.'

'*Just* three, Beverley? Isn't three enough?'

'I usually have four at home. Oh, *go on*, Mr Seed.'

I chuckled. 'One more, then.'

She took two, looked to see if I'd noticed then reluctantly passed one to Martine.

As the children were clearing away the dishes, something some of them had evidently never done in their lives, Mr Kirk, the warden, strode into the room and spoke to me in a low voice.

'I really must apologise for last night. I've been doing this job for eighteen years and I have never seen anything like that.'

'It was rather shocking.'

'Anyway, they're going straight home this morning and the school's been banned from YHA hostels. Erm, how are your young lads?'

'Well, I think they're OK; it took some of them a while to get to sleep but at least it stopped them messing around.'

He shook his head and said sorry again. 'Well, if there's anything I can do to help for the rest of your stay, you know . . .'

He walked away trying to look cheerful for the children. I thought back to the intense drama of the episode and wondered what the boys would say when they got home.

Our morning was taken up with a second cliff walk, this time south towards the great jutting point of Rookby Head. As we stepped out of the door ominous dark clouds brooded overhead, giving the sea a callous sheen. The children had been reminded multiple times to bring waterproofs and it appeared that they would soon be tested.

'Isn't it a bit windy for a walk on the cliffs, Mr Seed?' said Estelle.

'It's blowing inland so, no; good try, though.'

I lined the class up in pairs ready to tackle the dreaded 300-foot climb once again. 'Miss Torrington, would you like to lead this time and I'll stay at the back?'

'Love to,' she said half-mockingly, her face still grey after a dreadful night's sleep. At least she was wearing something more suitable than the yellow jump suit this morning.

The line of youngsters began their ascent of the path up the cliff, knowing this time what to expect. With Emma maintaining a snail's pace at the front, the children weren't so strung out and the unfit individuals suffered less. I still needed to coax Maxine and Beverley along, though.

'They should build a lift,' said Beverley.

'Can we go somewhere flat fer the rest o' the trip, Mr Seed?' gasped the wheezing Martine. 'I shunta had that extra Weetabix.'

'Just keep going and think of the view from the top, girls,' I said.

'But we've already seen it,' said Beverley. 'Eee, ahm paggered.'

There was an unruly scrap to sit on two benches at the top with the boys indignant, saying that the girls should have climbed the steps quicker.

Emma was trying to reason with the boys as I arrived, but Jo simply yanked Barry and Colin off one of them before Beverley found an ingenious way to remove Jason: she simply went over and sat on him.

'Oi, gerroff! Shift your fat ar—'

'Well, move then,' said the grinning girl. Emma and I were laughing too much to intervene.

'We need to go anyway or we'll be too late to get to Whitby this afternoon,' I said. The pairs reluctantly re-formed and we followed the windswept path, looking down on the rocky shore far below and spotting dark ships on the horizon. After just a few minutes, the first drops of rain fell.

'We'd better go back, hadn't we?' said Trudy.

'Oh come on, it's only a few spots,' I said.

The spots became more frequent as we went on and soon a steady shower was falling, dampening the children and their mood. Hoods went up and hats went on, with the farmers' children noticeably better prepared and uncomplaining. Some of the others began to mutter, however, and after twenty minutes with the rain now falling harder, the first sounds of mutiny were sounded.

'Snot fair.'

'Me mam paid fer this, why should us get wet?'

'It's down my neck.'

'I think we should turn round now.'

Emma up ahead looked more miserable than any of them. She was wearing the cheapest type of cagoule and it was now stuck to her clothes, merely transferring water into her hair and body. Her mascara was suffering and her jeans had turned very dark and heavy-looking.

'It's not much further,' I fibbed.

'Well, where are we going?' asked Estelle.

'To Rookby Point, I told you that earlier.'

'But what's there?'

'You get a fantastic view across the bay.'

'So, nothing really. And we won't be able to see the view anyway with this rain.'

I couldn't argue. The protests continued.

'What were we going to do when we were there?' asked Beverley.

'Draw the view,' I said.

'Well, we can't do that if it's raining, either.'

We turned around and headed back.

The afternoon brightened up in time for our visit to Whitby. A local coach picked us up with the children full of admiration for its newness and luxury. Our theme for the visit was Captain Cook and we trailed between the whale-bone arch, statue, harbour and museum, where about a third of the class showed interest in the world's greatest navigator while the others just rushed from one glass case to another, looking properly at nothing in the time-honoured fashion.

Walking through the steep fishing port I saw a sign advertising *The Dracula Experience*. Beverley saw it, too.

'Ooh, can we go there, Mr Seed? I love scary things.'

'I'm sorry, Beverley, it's just a bit too scary.'

'Why are you smiling, then?'

It was a good question but I was thinking back two years to when I'd visited the attraction with a previous class and been almost deafened by the screams of a girl who was given an unexpected shock. 'Oh, I'm just remembering something,' I said absent-mindedly, which caused Beverley to look at me and at the same time lean over and whisper deviously into a friend's ear in that way that nine-year-old girls do.

Back at Skerry Hole in the early evening our 'wearing out' session was rounders on the beach, the only problem being that there wasn't much sand around the youth hostel, only rocks, seaweed and pebbles. Consequently, we had to clamber for about 500 yards over greasy sea lettuce, barnacle-encrusted black boulders, slimy bladderwrack and dark smelly pools before we found a suitably broad stretch of sand.

'Can I pick teams?' cried Dan, running up to me.

'No, I'll sort out the teams,' I said, detesting as I did the ritual humiliation that the old playtime system entailed.

I lined up the girls then the boys to face me. Everyone was desperate to be on Ian's team as they always won and I saw Jason hurriedly switching places to be next but one from him on the basis that I usually pointed saying, 'One, two, one, two . . .' to make two teams.

'Keep still!' I called, then went down the line saying, 'One, one, two, two, one, one, two two . . .' to groans from certain quarters.

'We 'aven't any posts,' said Howard, who'd been carrying the bat and ball.

'No problem, we'll just use jumpers.'

With a jagged stone I carved some rough pitch markings into the crusty sand and announced that the Ones would bat first. The Twos wailed briefly and then, with Estelle and Lawrence bossing everyone, wandered into fielding positions. The unsporty sought each other out for chatting purposes deep along the shore and the batters lined up with the ferocious Ian wielding the club first. As always, those waiting for a turn by the side stood only two feet away.

'What do you think will happen if you stand there?' I called to Gary who was next in line.

'Er, we'll get clobbered by Ian?'

'Correct. And how hard does he hit it?'

'Very?'

'Right again. So what should you do?'

'Move back?'

I nodded at his genius and the line shuffled along about five inches with much complaining about toes being squashed.

'Er, what shall I do, Mr Seed?' called Emma.

'Watch the batters please and send anyone who doesn't move far enough back to the end of the line.'

Gary swiftly turned round and bawled at everyone to move back. When they didn't, he pushed the queue causing them to topple into the damp sand like dominoes. The Twos howled with glee.

When the game finally began, Ian cracked the first ball predictably into the sea to huge cheers from his team-mates. Lawrence stormed after it, then realised he'd need to take off his shoes and socks first. Ian could have run eight rounders while this was occurring and asked politely if such a rule were allowed.

Lawrence gamely fished the floating tennis ball from the waves, moaning about the temperature of the water, and hurled it back, dripping. Gary stepped up next, swinging the bat, to face Estelle's bowling. I could see from his eyes that he intended to target the spiky rocks to his left. Estelle launched a quick ball and Gary met it with a sharp splat, sending a sting of salt water and sand into his eyes.

'Euurrgghh!' he cried, putting a hand to his face and staggering blindly towards where he hoped first base would be. 'The ball was wet! Snot fair!'

Children have little sympathy on these occasions and his wails and protests were met with merriment and a cry of, 'Out!'

I considered reinstating him as he lurched about rubbing his eyes but the gloomy skies suggested that the game might not last long and the protests would be much more violent if not everyone had a turn to bat.

The game continued: Tim needed the toilet and had to go in a cave; Helen trod on a jellyfish; Jason made a great catch; Vicky found a starfish while fielding; and Ian hit the ball in the sea again.

There was simply no way that the Twos would ever get the class's star sportsman out so I was just announcing a time-limiter of three bats each when Beverley clumped forward with her hand up.

'Mr Seed, can I bowl now? Estelle's had a really long go.'

I assented and she picked up the soggy ball which the waiting batter, Stephen, demanded should be dried in order that he avoid Gary's earlier fate. When she bowled he missed the ball altogether and made a desperate dash to first base. The ball was misfielded and Stephen then ran on.

'Yer forgot to drop the bat!' called Ian who was next in line. Stephen, in the middle of a death-or-glory dash to third hurled the bat down as he ran and it rolled into a small puddle in the sand. Jason screamed at his team to get the ball to fourth and another score was just averted.

'Oh no, get back!' called Beverley as she turned to see who she was bowling to next. Jason ordered Lawrence to stand in the sea as Ian picked up the dripping bat and eyed up whether it was possible to reach the cliffs. Lawrence refused and I told Beverley to get on with the game. Ian, knowing this was his last hit, was going for a really big one: he stood, legs wide and half bent, arm tensed, the bat drawn right back. In the distance, Jason scampered even further away in his desperation to make a catch or prevent a rounder. It was a vain hope.

Beverley launched the ball and the whole class stood in silent horror as our school trip suffered its second gruesome incident in two days. Ian sprang at the ball, uncoiling his body with a venomous swipe. As always, the bat connected perfectly, firing the ball away with a blur like a tracer bullet. But, alas, the bat was sandy and wet and as it arced around its momentum tore it out of Ian's hand. We all watched and grimaced instantaneously as it flew like a wooden torpedo across the beach and into the face of Beverley Butterfield. The sound was sickening and she collapsed on to the sand amid gasps, not least from Emma, who held her hands to her mouth as I ran across.

The bat had hit her on the nose and she lay half-conscious, her face a bloodied mess, which almost brought my heart to a temporary halt.

'Get the first aid bag quick!' I called and Cathy rushed over with it, tears in her eyes as Emma came across and let out an involuntary squeal which frightened the other children even more.

'Everyone keep back!' I cried and Emma quickly ushered the staring crowd away while I applied a tissue to poor Beverley's face and fought to remember my first aid training. Remarkably she opened her eyes and tried to sit up. Her nose was slightly bent and the blood appeared to be coming from her nostrils rather than a facial wound. I wasn't sure whether this was a good sign or not but one thing was certain: she was way too woozy to walk and we needed to get her back to the hostel pronto. I would have to carry her.

'Can you hear me, Beverley?' I said.

She coughed and gurgled. 'Yes; my face aches.'

'Don't worry, you'll be fine. I'm going to carry you to the hostel and we'll fetch a doctor, okay?'

She closed her eyes and nodded. I gave thanks that she was cognisant then knelt down to pick her up.

'Do you need a hand, Andy?' said Emma, whose face was paler than the casualty's.

'I'll manage,' I said, straining. 'You'd better stay here and take them for a walk down the beach – it's too early for them to go back.'

She nodded as I straightened up, my back registering Beverley's disconcerting bulk. I set off tottering over the sand, pleased to see that Beverley was able to hold a tissue to her nose and keep her head forward.

'Thank you, Mr Seed,' she mumbled.

'Any time,' I said, silently chuckling at my own remark.

Then we came to the rocks. The first few were all right – the barnacle-coated black ones – but just beyond these were the lumpy grey boulders covered with the lethal sea lettuce. In between them were rock pools and piles of slippery brown bladderwrack. I picked my way between the hard obstacles considering how difficult this was without having to convey a large wounded schoolgirl with a mangled nose.

'Is it far?' she croaked.

'No, soon be there,' I said, unable even to see the hostel yet, hidden as it was between the giant cliffs. I almost stumbled; she wisely held on to my collar. I took a wide path to avoid a patch of slimy green sea lettuce and the buildings of Skerry Hole came into view, frustratingly tiny in the distance. *Why wasn't it one of the smaller kids?*

My arms were almost finished when I finally made it on to the pebbles in front of the cove. 'Can you stand up a moment, Beverley?' I said, mightily relieved when she nodded. Gingerly I put her feet down and steadied her. She wobbled a little but stood upright, reaching up to feel under her nose.

'I think the bleeding's stopped,' she said.

'That's good,' I croaked, smiling while stretching to recuperate my spine and get some blood back into my arms. After a minute, I lifted her again and lurched over the pebbles and up the concrete slipway to the hostel. The weary Mr Kirk nearly choked on his coffee when he saw me bump through the door carrying a bloodied figure. We put her in an armchair and I rapidly explained what happened.

'Can you call a doctor?' I said.

'They won't come out at this time.'

'Not even for an injured child?'

'If it's serious they expect you to call an ambulance, otherwise I'll have to drive her into Baytown.'

I was astonished but we climbed into the warden's van and set off for the surgery in Robin Hood's Bay where an elderly doctor pronounced that Beverley's nose appeared to be just badly bruised and swollen rather than broken. He gently ran three fingers along it, causing her to jolt.

'I think she'll be fine – she's a big strong lass.'

I looked at him. 'But will her nose, er, take long to, er, heal?' He appeared to understand that the real question was would her nose look all right, and he gave a reassuring nod. 'Oh aye, at her age she'll soon be right as rain.'

This cheered Beverley immensely and with some painkillers in hand we rumbled back to the hostel with my mind now rushing between Emma and how she was managing the class on her own, and whether we should call Mrs Butterfield immediately or leave it to the morning when perhaps Beverley would sound less dazed.

In the event, I rang Joyce first who advised me to call Beverley's mum right away. Mrs Butterfield's response was so typical of the no-nonsense Dales parents of the day.

'Oh, she'll be reet, Mr Seed. Who's not 'ad a bang on the 'ooter in their time?'

'So you don't think it's necessary to come and pick her up?'

'Drive all t'way ovver there? Nay lad, as I say, a good night's sleep and she'll be reet.'

Remarkably, that's what happened. Beverley slept long and deep and felt much better the following day. Her nose was a spectacular red with a green and yellow lump but she laughed along with the others during the final day and barely made a fuss. Skerry Hole was a school trip that would not slip easily from the memory.

Barbara greatly enjoyed my retelling of the various episodes of the visit and soon everyone in the village had heard what had happened on my watch. After a few days the comments died away and with them the grey clouds which had settled over Yorkshire for more than a week. The sun burst through and lifted our spirits and by the second weekend in June the weather was hot, causing Tom to ask if we could have a picnic. For once we were able to agree with one of his ideas; the only question was where to go.

'What about Skirbridge Falls?' said Barbara. 'It's lovely there and there's lots of shade.'

'It'll be packed out on a weekend like this. I know; remember Adam told us about those wildflower meadows in Wherndale? Why don't we go there? The flowers should be out around now.'

'Ooh yes, that sounds perfect.'

We swiftly packed food and blankets before jumping into the rusty Alfa and heading north into the steep, beautiful valley above Swinnerdale. The view was magnificent as we topped the soaring brow of the moors and Tom enjoyed spotting tractors out haytiming as I edged the car down the precipitous one in three track to join the single road up Wherndale to the unspoiled stone village of Craywell.

Reuben was packed into our new backpack toddler carrier and

we wandered through the tight cottages jumbled together between stone-roofed sheds looking for the footpath sign. We passed the delightful Institute building with its proud red door, crossed a quaint little square, then saw the wooden arrow, inviting us into the flat-bottomed hay meadows beyond.

'Wow,' said Barbara. 'What a place.'

It was glorious: in front of us was a twisting valley with rising fells either side topped with precipitous limestone scars, resplendent in the sun. An inviting flagged path lay before us, trailing through seven meadows radiant with a million buttercups. Tom scuttled forward to explore the path and Reuben wriggled and demanded to be let out of his carrier.

'I've got to get a photo of this,' I said. 'I've never seen anything like it.'

The boys bustled through the little stile gate at the far side of the first field and Barbara went after them while I grabbed the gear. The flowers increased in richness as we went on, each meadow speckled with colour from red clover, white pignut, purple cranes-bill, yellow buttercups, pink betony and myriad types of grass. The flowers danced in a light breeze while beyond big ash trees lining the river swayed.

I finally caught up with Barbara. The boys were sitting among the flowers twiddling stalks of grass. I took another picture, hopeful of capturing the moment forever.

'I think we should come here every year at this time,' said Barbara. 'I can't believe there's no one else around.'

We reached the last meadow which edged the rushing River Whern and Tom spotted a long wooden bridge on high pillars across it. Despite protests, we insisted on holding Reuben to cross it. The river here came sweeping round a wide stony bend past piles of boulders, its water a rich umber. Further down it dropped and danced over a series of ledges and just ahead we saw a low grassy bank next to a broad beach of small pebbles at the water's edge. It was shallow here and safe: the perfect spot for a picnic.

After eating, Barbara lay back and closed her eyes while I oversaw the boys' attempt to empty every stone into the river. They were having a wonderful time.

'What do you want to do next?' I said when we returned to the blanket for drinks.

'Just stay here all day,' said Barbara. 'It's bliss – I love the sound of the water.'

'Adam said there was a good circular walk so perhaps we could do that and go back a different way.'

'Okay, did you bring the map?'

'Whoops.'

'Well how will we know where to go?'

I looked across and saw two people following a footpath a quarter of a mile away across the river. 'Ah, look, that must be the other path back to Craywell.'

She sat up. 'All right but where do we cross the river again?'

'There must be another bridge up ahead, or maybe stepping stones.'

Tom perked up. 'Ooh, can we go over the stepping stones, Mummy?'

'Well, we don't know if there are any. And who's going to carry Reuben?'

'He's walked all this way, I'm sure he'll go a bit further.'

She looked at me doubtfully. 'Well, all right then.'

We packed everything away and told the boys we were going to explore more of the valley. Tom cheered but as soon as we started to walk along the river bank Reuben wailed and reached up for a carry.

'Hmmpphh,' I said, as Barbara lifted him into the carrier, smiling in an annoyingly superior way.

At first the path was level and gentle but soon it began to climb and turned into a stony track. The heat made the going difficult and Tom began to slow down while I started to sweat with our son's full toddler load on my shoulders.

'I can't see a bridge,' said Barbara. 'Perhaps we should turn back now.'

'What about the stepping stones?' said Tom.

'Look, there are some old mine workings ahead!' I said, trying to make them sound like Disneyland. Tom showed some interest, asking if we could go down a mineshaft but Reuben just wriggled and threw off his hat, wailing that he needed a drink.

'I could do with a tea shop, too,' said Barbara. 'This is all a bit wild.'

At the abandoned lead mine the path branched off and the sign pointed to Busk, one mile on.

'Ah yes, that's the village on the road,' I said, recalling the map in the car.

'Another mile!' wailed Barbara. 'Does it have a café?'

'Bound to, all the villages here do.'

'Well, there was one back in Craywell,' she conceded, 'but how will Tom manage all that way and all the way back?'

'I'm sure he can do another mile,' I said, doubting whether I could with chubby Reuben straining my back, 'and if necessary I'll leave you there, walk back and get the car.'

It wasn't the first time that this had happened and it seemed to placate my thirsty wife, who started to make us all hungry by talking about scones and cream.

The route did indeed carry on for a mile but what the signpost did not say was that the mile was all uphill over an increasingly rocky path. Barbara had to carry Tom at one point, which meant I ended up with the picnic bag as well as Reuben, who was now asleep and nearly crippling me as the sun caused my t-shirt to stick to my body.

How did this happen? I said to myself. *I'm carrying another child over rocks.*

Then, after thirty agonising minutes, we passed through the welcome shade of some trees, followed a bend and saw the tell-tale black silage bags of a farm and beyond it a cluster of houses: the village!

'It's a very *small* village,' said Barbara. Indeed it was: about six houses in actual fact. 'Where's the tea shop?'

'Well, I didn't say there was definitely a tea shop.' She gave me one of the blackest looks in the annals of history.

We found a bench in a shaded spot by a little beck and Barbara lifted the rosy Reuben off my back to my intense relief. I felt incredibly light, although my back was dripping with perspiration. She stifled the boys' moans with the remainder of the picnic, while I took a swig of water and headed back along the path to face the two miles to the car.

'Be quick!' she demanded.

I disappeared, then returned two minutes later. 'Forgot the car keys.'

It was one of those days.

At half past four, I motored slowly into the minuscule hamlet of Busk and picked up my family. They were bored, hot and hungry. But I was smiling.

'What are you so happy about?' said my wife, with no attempt to disguise any grumpiness.

'You wait . . .' I said cryptically.

'Oh no, not another of your schemes; this one was bad enough.'

'No, this one is really good, I promise.'

'Does it involve a really big tea shop? Because if it doesn't, I'm not interested.'

'It does!'

Her countenance finally lifted and I asked the boys if they were hungry.

'Yes,' said a weary Tom. 'Very.'

Reuben was direct, as ever. 'Want ice creeeeaaaammmm.'

At ten to five we stepped inside a long, low stone building, once a large village house and now the Cottershaw Tea Rooms.

'I passed this place in the car coming to pick you up,' I said, 'and I remembered that Iris told us about it last year – she said it was not to be missed.'

Barbara's face lit up. 'Oh yes: the Yorkshire High Tea.'

I gave my name at the little desk and we were escorted to a seating area by a bustling woman in tweed.

'It'll be ready in five minutes, sir,' she said.

I looked at Barbara and grinned like an oaf.

'You ordered Yorkshire High Tea!'

'I did.'

She leaned over and smothered me with kisses. 'Clever boy, you're forgiven.'

'Where's ice cream?' grumbled Reuben.

Those were five of the longest minutes of my life, as the boys strained forward to get hold of the food we could see and smell in the distance, while Barbara and I almost drowned in saliva.

Then it happened: the tweedy lady returned and said, 'This way,' and we were led into paradise. It was a sight that beggared belief – a round table four foot across was completely covered with home-made delights: roast chicken sandwiches, scones, bacon flans, teacakes, warm crusty bread, boiled eggs, slices of ham, game pie, salad, curd tarts, apple pie, fruit loaf, cream, jam, chocolate cake and so many other things. At the centre was a giant pot of tea and a pile of china plates and cutlery next to it. Everything, in fact, except ice cream.

Twenty-five years on I'm still recovering from that feast. We all ate too much and even Reuben stopped complaining when we told him he could choose anything he liked. I stuffed my face until my body begged me to stop but I didn't feel guilty afterwards; not after the fortnight I'd had.

Chapter Twenty-Two

Lisa

The week after Skerry Hole was hectic. First thing on Monday morning the children of Class 3 dashed around the back of their sagging old temporary classroom to see how the herb garden was faring. Tim was there, weeding on his hands and knees, as he had been doing since eight o'clock. The herbs were flourishing in the warm weather and the garden was beginning to fill out with healthy foliage in a swirl of greens. Reluctantly the children returned to the classroom where they cast their minds back to our coastal visit.

As the week went on, the class produced some memorable writing, recounting the day at Robin Hood's Bay, the cliff walks, the beach adventures and the various mishaps. To her and my enormous relief, Beverley's nose gradually returned to its previous shape, size and colour as the swelling subsided. Her imposing dimensions assisted the discouragement of unkind remarks from Class 4 but she did become understandably tired of having to explain to people in Cragthwaite what had happened.

At the midweek staff meeting the agenda inevitably led with the subject of school trips.

'Well, first of all,' said Joyce, 'I think Andy needs to be congratulated on how well he dealt with the various crises during the visit.'

'Hear, hear,' said Val.

'Can we hear a bit more about them?' said Hilda. 'Purely for professional reasons so we can learn,' she added with a hopeless attempt at deadpan.

Emma gave her head a little shake. 'I've already told you about the rounders bat episode, twice. Andy was heroic the way he carried that, er, large girl over those rocks with blood everywhere. I couldn't have done it.'

'Yes but what about the fight?' said Hilda. 'You weren't there then – we need it from the horse's mouth. No offence, Andy, although I've heard you eat a lot of oats.'

Joyce cleared her throat. 'Can I remind you this is a staff meeting, please? The important thing is that Beverley is all right and, despite the incidents, the children had a memorable time and learned a lot.'

'Yes, like when to duck,' whispered Hilda to herself.

'Right, item two,' said Joyce, 'school photographs.'

'Oh joy, another day of disruption,' mumbled Val.

Joyce flicked through a pile of papers and surprised us by producing a photo of a large hawk. 'I've had a phone call from this company who do bird of prey demonstrations. They've recently branched out into school photos – basically they bring a big eagle, or whatever it is, and take pictures of the children with the bird perched on their arm.' She found another picture of a nervous-looking boy holding up a giant owl on a gloved hand. We all craned forward for a closer view.

'Well, it's certainly different,' said Val, her brow raised.

'Do we get money off if it eats a child?' said Hilda.

Joyce carried on as usual. 'It actually costs not much more than the usual photographers.'

'I think it's a great idea,' I said.

Emma looked doubtful. 'My little ones will never be able to lift an eagle. Some of them'll be terrified anyway.'

Val scanned some written details. 'They don't actually use an eagle. It says here it's a Harris hawk which is quite docile and fairly small and light.'

Joyce looked up. 'What do we think?'

It was a yes vote.

On the day of the photographs, I was in the classroom explaining about the hawk when a ticklish cough which had been developing for a few days decided to flourish.

'You must be quiet near the bird (cough) and keep still while (cough) you are (cough) wai—(cough) —ting.'

Martine's hand went up. 'Worrif it pecks us?'

'(Cough) It (cough) won't.'

Her hand stayed up. 'Won't it spike us arm wi' them big claws?'

'Talons (cough).'

'Eh?'

'(Cough) You wear a (cough) thick (cough) leather glove (cough).'

Martine's questions opened a barrage of other enquiries.

Estelle was first. 'What if it flies off?'

'I think (cough) they are (cough, cough) tied to— (cough, cough, cough)'

I never did finish that sentence. The tickle in my throat reached crisis point and my face turned purple as, unable to breathe, I went into a spasm of coughing that rendered me immobile. The children gawped with fascination as I fought for air, flecks of spittle firing out of my open mouth as my eyes glassed over and I considered what kind of a death this would be remembered as. Just as I neared collapse, a grimy plastic pot from the paint cupboard was pushed in front of my face. In among some remnants of powder paint, glue and dust there was some oily water. I gulped it down, sucked some oxygen into my lungs and edged back from the brink, turning to see my saviour. It was Lisa Bowe.

Lisa was one of those quiet, unassuming pupils that teachers adore. She was sensible, artistic, friendly, attentive, capable and kind. I looked through blurry eyes at her gently smiling face as she reached to take the cup. She had long crinkly brown hair and dimpled cheeks.

'Thank you (cough), Lisa.'

'Would you like some more, Mr Seed?'

'Yes (cough), please.'

I returned to face the class, wiping my eyes, to see some of them apparently disappointed that I hadn't expired; no doubt it would have made yet another great story to share at home that evening. Others did look a little concerned but most were just faintly amused. Lisa made no fuss and sat down.

An hour later the whole class was lined up outside on the edge of the field watching a man, a woman and a fierce-looking brown hawk. A tripod was set up opposite a chair and Gary Blacow, first in line, was invited to be seated. He walked forward with a swagger, grinning back to his compatriots who egged him on, while I tried to record the scene with the school's cumbersome video camera.

'Go, Gaz!'

Gary was asked to sit down while the woman went behind her camera and the man, hawk on arm, stepped forward and gave Gary an enormous suede glove. The bird was about the size of a pheasant, mottled brown with a great hooked beak and yellow face. Gary held out his arm and once the man had done something that none of us could see, the stern hawk hopped on to his glove. In a moment, Gary's bravado melted away and he leaned back, looking slightly uncomfortable with the dark predator so close. The class laughed and the woman tried to coax him to smile.

'It's massive and really scary,' said Gary as he skulked back to the line and Dan went over to the chair, putting on the glove. 'Flippin' heavy too.'

It was fascinating to watch the reactions of each child from my class as they took turns to sit next to the imperious bird of prey. Anna was as pale as a tissue and almost shaking, while Howard risked poking a finger towards it, which the man suggested was inadvisable. Tim was calm and gave a broad, genuine smile, and Jo showed no fear at all. Ian looked all right until the hawk decided to open its great wings which caused him to yelp and nearly spring off the chair.

'Don't worry, she's just stretching,' said the man.

'They do that before they attack,' called Howard. I found it very hard to keep a straight face, not least when Ian's smile for the camera became a tight-faced grimace of dread. Trudy, a lover of animals, wanted to stay with the bird all the time, while Barry, to everyone's surprise, just flat refused to put on the glove and hold it at all. Instead the man provided a perch for the hawk in the background while Barry briefly leered at the camera then shot back to the security of the line.

'Is it me next?' said Lisa, jiggling with excitement. 'I can't wait.'

She was the only person who bent her arm to bring the hawk closer and her smile for the picture was gleeful and full.

'You enjoyed that,' I remarked as she reluctantly returned.

'I've always loved birds of prey,' she said. 'Can I take my own photo of the hawk, do you think? And can we do some drawings or paintings in the class?'

Her enthusiasm was infectious and I agreed that it would be a great idea to create a hawk gallery, since we had all been so close to one of nature's great hunters. When the last child had been photographed, the man gave the children a brief talk and a chance to ask questions. As always on these occasions, the class had some peculiar queries.

'Can you buy 'em in a pet shop?'

'Is it faster than a car?'

'Could it kill yer if it wanted ter?'

'How much are they?'

'Who would win in a fight between a Harris hawk and a snake?'

I was glad I wasn't supplying the answers.

The following day I set aside the whole afternoon for art. I put out all the paints and several large sheets of good-quality paper along with as many pictures as I could find of birds of prey. I asked Joyce for the photo of the Harris hawk that she'd been sent in the company's mailshot and I gave this to Lisa because I knew that she was desperate to paint the very bird that we'd met.

'Oh, thanks, Mr Seed!' she said. 'Is it all right for me to do a big painting of it?'

I nodded knowing that her artwork was exceptional and that she wouldn't waste time or paper. The rest of the class set to work with pastels, charcoal, pencil, pen and ink, water colours and collage, and for nearly two hours there was that scarce and glorious classroom atmosphere that all teachers revere where every child is immersed, oblivious to the usual natter and shuffle of the junior schoolroom. I simply toured the tables quietly, offering encouragement, advice and admiration. It was a moment to treasure and I sighed in the knowledge that no headteacher, governor, education adviser or inspector would see it; where o where was Mrs Sykes?

As three o'clock approached some children finished and with finger on lips I set them to washing up paint pots or quietly finishing other work so as not to break the concentration of the majority still working. Some were never going to finish, some had 'gone wrong' and others had produced something that they were proud of.

Stephen came up to me with a small, delicate ink drawing of a kestrel. Although blotchy, it captured the essence of the bird with flair.

'Do you like it, Mr Seed?'

'Stephen, it's excellent. You've put care into every detail, well done.'

'But have you seen Lisa's hawk?' he said.

'Not since she was sketching the shape at the start of the afternoon. Is it good?'

His face betrayed a wonder. 'You've *got* to see it.'

I looked across to her table of four and noticed that the other three had all but stopped work and were simply gazing at Lisa's picture as she worked with total absorption, rapidly mixing colours and lightly dabbing her painting. I went over as a rising whisper traversed the room. Word was out and for the first time chairs were scraped as children stood or stepped across towards Lisa and craned to catch a glimpse of something special.

The moment I saw her painting I almost cried. Using only the cheap, messy powder paints that were the staple of every primary school at that time, a girl of just nine had created something so exquisite and striking that it took the breath away. There was the Harris hawk of the previous day, large and stirring and as fierce as it was meant to be. The other paintings in the room were tentative and soft and flat but here was something in vibrant texture with fiery colour and sharp line.

For a moment I didn't know what to say so I joined in with the chorus of the other children who were now gathering around the table, their admiration and awe spontaneous.

'Wow,' we said. There was nothing else to say. 'Wow.'

Lisa looked up, wary of her arm being knocked but also to acknowledge the acclaim that was all around. My eyes were glazed again, not in a coughing fit this time, but in an emotional swell that I had never known simply looking at a child's work.

'Shall I get Mrs Berry to see it?' said someone.

'Yes,' I answered without turning around.

I looked at Lisa to try and express my delight but I could tell that she knew from my face how I felt. My mind snapped back fifteen years to when I was just a little older than her, at primary school myself, and I had completed a painting of two miners emerging from a pit in a steel cage. Their smudged faces were there before me and I knew that I had done something special. My teacher at the time was young, enthusiastic and a lover of art. I could still picture the flouncy early seventies pink dress that she wore as she came over and looked at my picture, then turned and simply hugged me loudly in front of the whole class.

In Cragthwaite men didn't hug so I held off, knowing that Joyce would do that for me. But Lisa knew how I felt: she saw it in my eyes.

Barbara came in and flopped on the settee, still wearing her Royal Mail uniform. It was another baking hot Saturday in June and she looked exhausted.

'Can you get me some painkillers and a cold drink – I've a stinking headache.'

'You poor thing,' I said, heading off to the kitchen. When I returned, she was fending off Reuben, who wanted a cuddle: a sure sign that she wasn't well.

'Come on, boys,' I said, lifting him away. 'Let's go and play outside and leave Mummy in peace.'

Once they were installed in the sandpit I popped back in to see how she was doing. She was half asleep.

'I think I'm just really tired,' she said. 'I didn't sleep well last night and it was just so hot walking round today.'

'Would you like me to take the boys out somewhere this afternoon?' I said. 'Then you can have some proper peace.'

'Ooh, that would be *really* kind.' Her eyes were still shut as she spoke.

Half an hour later the car was stuffed with drinks, hats, sun cream, nappy bags, toys and two excited boys as I motored along the quiet Hubberdale road.

'Where are we going, Daddy?' asked Tom.

'You've already asked me that,' I said. 'Capplesett Rocks.'

'What that?' said the sweaty Reuben.

'It's a place with lots of big rocks you can climb on. They're all strange shapes.'

'Have you been before?' asked Tom.

'A few years ago when I was a student. It's really good.'

'What's a student?'

Tom was well into the wanting-to-know-everything-about-everything phase and after ten minutes I was worn out and managed to fob him off by saying that I needed to concentrate on the road, which was a bit naughty since we had only passed a tractor and two bikes in the last eight miles.

I was genuinely excited about taking my sons to Capplesett Rocks, however; they are one of the real treasures of the Dales – huge dark boulders carved into weird bulbous shapes by wind and water with many resting precariously on small natural plinths. In between were wild ferny glades, wonderful for hide-and-seek, and there was even a café with a panoramic view up Ashendale. The only problem was that it wasn't easy to reach from our side of the Dales and the boys soon became hot and bored in the little airless car. After about forty minutes, Reuben fell asleep but Tom returned to interrogation mode.

'Why are they called Capplesett Rocks?'

'What will we do when we get there?'

'Can we have ice creams?'

'Did they have TV when you were a student?'

Finally, after going the wrong way three times, I saw the National Trust oak leaf sign pointing to the entrance and we rumbled into the dry, stony car park which was almost full. It had taken an hour and twenty minutes.

'We're here!' I cried, waking Reuben, whose glowing pink face and ominous grizzle suggested that he wasn't going to be in the best of moods.

Outside the temperature was extraordinary for the Dales, touching thirty degrees and Tom almost wilted when he stepped down from the Alfa. I reached inside to pick up Reuben from his car seat; his body was like a human casserole, dripping perspiration. He grouched and wriggled as I tried to apply sun cream and a floppy hat.

'Need drink,' he whined.

'Can we go on the rocks now?' asked Tom. I had a feeling that this trip was going to be problematic.

I shoved everything into a bag and we headed off into the undergrowth, where straggly birch trees gave some relief from the sun. Reuben walked about fifteen yards then wailed for a carry. I couldn't face another day like we'd had at the wildflower meadows.

'Look!' called Tom. 'What's that?'

It was a rock, rising up from the ferns: a big, smooth, wide mound of Yorkshire sandstone and on it was a little girl laughing and having fun. The effect on my boys was instant: Tom hurried towards it and Reuben almost dived out of my arms. Within thirty seconds they were up on the rock, exploring and crying out at all the other wonders that could be spied from this vantage point.

'There's some massive rocks over there!' yelled Tom.

'Let's go!' cried Reuben who adored climbing.

For half an hour the boys were in paradise as we ventured deep into Capplesett's delights. Each rock they found was bigger and more thrilling than the last; some had holes and arches, some were as high as a house, some were impossible to climb but they tried anyway. I smiled thinking how Barbara would be fretting at this point, convinced that they would fall off or slip or crack their heads but little boys are not, in general, great risk takers, and they were content to clamber over the lower, safer formations and simply admire the perilous ones where fearless teenagers leapt from boulder to boulder.

Another drink and a brief rest kept them going then our exploration took us to the hill at the centre of the reserve and within sight of the café. The boys saw people coming out holding lollipops and that was it.

'Ice cream!'

We queued in the heat for fifteen minutes and my hopes that the boys would settle for a cheap lolly disappeared when the man in front of us turned around with two huge creamy white cornets topped with raspberry sauce.

'Want that!' said Reuben who had been oddly quiet for a couple of minutes.

'Me too!' said Tom, and I asked for three.

The ice creams were already dripping as I handed them to my sons with grim warnings to hold on to them tight. Their hands, although wiped, were disturbingly dark. I headed for the nearest shade but both boys were hardly moving, their full attention fixed on the tops of their giant cornets which the sun was rapidly turning to liquid.

'Come on, or they'll melt,' I said.

Tom trotted forward but Reuben was barely ambling and what is more, to my disquiet, his chubby legs were suspiciously far apart. Between them, the back of his shorts dangled low and heavy. The sense of foreboding was accompanied by a pungent, unmistakable pong. I looked at him and he glared back in full denial: he had filled his nappy.

Despite loud protests I took his hand and half-dragged him away from the poor, sniffing tea drinkers at the picnic tables who looked at their shoes as we passed, and over to the nearest shaded patch of grass between two low rocks.

'Has Reuben done a poo?' said Tom. He had asked a lot of inane questions during the day but this took the biscuit.

'Yes, and you're going to have to hold his ice cream while I change it.'

At the realisation of this my younger son let out a scream of such force that a woman walking nearby came over to see if a murder was in progress. When she saw the brown stains at the top of Reuben's legs she swiftly retreated. With some difficulty I wrestled the cornet out of his hand and passed it to Tom. It was as though I'd removed a limb. He kicked and flailed as I lay him back and I quickly realised that Tom couldn't hold my ice cream, too: I was going to have to change his nappy with one hand in mid-tantrum. It was never going to work and so I took one last tragic lick then tossed my expensive cone into the bushes. Tom's eyes nearly exploded. Reuben continued to wriggle furiously.

'Keep still!' I yelled as I opened the changing bag and prayed that there were at least 200 wipes and a litre of water in there. An unfortunate boy peered around the rock to see what all the noise was about just as I opened the nappy to reveal something so ghastly that it should never be spoken about. The poor lad reeled back, groaning as if sprayed by CS gas.

Tom also retreated, holding Reuben's ice cream at a perilous angle while the drips from his own flowed down his arm and off his elbow. Reuben continued to writhe as I did my best to extract the mess but it was up his back and deep within every fold. I seriously thought about dipping him in the nearby stream except I would have poisoned all the toddlers playing there.

He strained towards Tom, his mouth open in emotional agony. 'Ice cream!'

Never was the resemblance to 'I scream' more apt.

After using the entire contents of the changing bag, I fitted a new nappy and let him at the sad remnant of his cornet. It was a soggy grey cone filled with warm pink liquid but at least he had it back. Tom, meanwhile, was performing a panicky dance as a wasp investigated his sugar-coated face. After swatting it away, I rapidly deposited the noxious parcel and to this day pity the individual who had to empty that bin.

After more drinks and futile hand-wiping the boys scrambled up on the nearest rock and were away with their raucous climbing and jumping once again. They lasted another forty minutes before they ran out of steam. The boys ambled back to the car, black with dust and bits of leaf sticking to the ice-cream trails on their arms and legs.

We arrived back home at seven o'clock to find Barbara lying in the garden on a recliner looking relaxed and well, if a little surprised at our late arrival.

She smiled. 'Hasn't it been beautiful; what did you get up to, boys?'

It was not the question to ask.

Chapter Twenty-Three

Fraser

I looked at the half-empty classroom and checked my watch. It said five past nine.

'Where is everyone?'

'The Yorkshire Show,' said Lawrence, his mouth betraying mild frustration.

'Oh, right . . .'

I should have remembered: it was a Tuesday morning in early July and the same thing had happened every year I'd been at Cragthwaite. All the farming children and quite a few others simply took the day off to travel down to Harrogate for the Great Yorkshire Show, the vast gathering of all things agricultural, rural and Yorkshire.

'Wish I was there, snot fair,' grumped Jason, echoing the refrain which seemed to have been his theme for most of the year.

'Nothing is fair – I wish I was there, too,' I said, pulling open the register. Actually, even if there had been the opportunity to go, I wouldn't have had time because this was the most dreaded and busiest part of the primary school year, beating even Christmas, and it was all down to one thing: the writing of reports.

In many ways I enjoyed writing reports. The good ones were always a pleasure, of course, and there would be several of these this year I told myself; and even the occasional 'bad'un' could at least provide an opportunity to exercise a little wit or make an honest remark that might just cause a child to realise that they needed to knuckle down. Then there was always fun to be had imagining the things one would *love* to write but would never dare to:

If Ian's English was as good as his football he'd have at least three Nobel Prizes; alas, it isn't.

Another successful year for Susan: she came top in bossiness and fussing for the fourth year running and thoroughly deserved her Being a Madam *award.*

Pamela surprised us this year by what she achieved in the nature area.

Martine is unique. It's just as well.

But there were some reports where light-heartedness was out of the question and during my few years of teaching I'd discovered, the hard way, that some parents were impossible to please or, alternatively, possessed a curiously skewed estimation of their offspring's capability. Then there was Jason Fisher. What on earth could I write about him? How honest could I be, knowing that his father would erupt at any criticism he regarded as unfair? Jason had most certainly improved over the year but, truth be told, he was still no saint.

That lunchtime, aware that I was already behind schedule with reports, I stayed in the classroom, told the children not to disturb me, wolfed my sandwiches and sat down with several sheets of blank paper and a line guide. As always, I went for an easy one first: Fraser Garth.

I didn't need lists of marks or pages of written work or exercise books to look at, nor test results nor reading ages. I knew every child in my class well: who was good at what, how much they'd improved, what they were capable of, their attitudes, willingness to make an effort and their potential. I'd spent at least ten months with them, watching, listening, talking, reading their work and seeing the understanding – or lack of it – on their faces as I explained what the world was about.

Fraser Garth was a lovely lad. He wasn't the brightest in the class, nor even the hardest working but he had a glint in his eye and a generous spirit that rewarded everyone who got to know him. Writing his report would be a doddle.

The following weekend was taken over by Tom's fourth birthday which was on the Sunday. I spent Saturday scribbling more reports, then tidying the house in preparation for his party the following afternoon, while Barbara went potty in the kitchen.

'This is hopeless!' I heard her call, clattering tins in a cupboard.

I went through to see what the trouble was. 'Erm, everything all right?'

She stood up amid piles of baking trays and containers. 'No, it's not – I can't get anywhere.'

'With what?'

She looked down the hall to check that the boys weren't listening, then shut the kitchen door.

'Tom wants a snake cake for his birthday.'

'What's a snake cake?'

'Well what do you think? A cake in the shape of snake.'

'Ah . . . what about using some empty food cans for baking tins and then joining the pieces together?'

'I can think of about fifty reasons why that won't work.'

I made three more impractical suggestions before she pushed up her glasses, ran a hand through her brown hair and stopped me.

'I've got it. Of course! I'll make a flat circular cake, then cut part of it away so it leaves a spiral, then ice it with patterns and, *voilà*, we'll have a coiled python.'

'You are a genius,' I said, giving her a kiss before a wail from Reuben sent me down the hall to discover that, following a 'teddy war', the living room was now messier than when I'd started tidying.

After lunch on Sunday, our babysitter Holly came to the door, soon followed by Iris, to help with the party. I had done my best to prepare the house for the ten rowdy little boys and girls who would shortly be descending and Holly was now installed to read Reuben and Tom calm stories before the storm. I went to the dining room where Barbara was organising the party tea with Iris. My poor wife was still recovering from a long, fiddly struggle to make Tom's cake look like a snake the previous evening, having eventually flopped into bed after midnight.

'Anything I can do?' I said.

'Is everything uncluttered, vacuumed, toddler-proofed?' asked Barbara, rubbing an eye.

'Yep.'

'What about Ulf?'

Our rapidly growing, half-wild kitten would be a complete menace at a children's party. 'I've moved his litter tray and things upstairs into the boys' room.'

'OK, we're just about sorted, then. Well, why don't you go and do some more reports until the kids arrive?'

I looked outside at the sun falling on Spout Fell's green slopes.

'Actually, I think I'll go for a quick bike ride. But don't worry, I'll be back half an hour before the action starts.'

June's heat wave outside had subsided and, although sunny, the day was cool with a fresh breeze blowing off the hills. I took my favourite route up Buttergill, this time following the wilder western track which branched off the road through the steep valley. Within a few moments, the dust and clutter of the house were forgotten, along with the brain-ache of report writing. I was sailing along to the sound of swallows and lambs and the breeze cutting through the pines above. The road, as always, was empty and I smiled at the deer warning sign wondering who it was for. I'd heard there were deer here sometimes but had never seen one.

Below me a little blue tractor chugged across a precipitous field towards a crumbling barn before my concentration switched as the road fell abruptly and I flew down a hill and into a water splash where a spring dribbled down to the beck below. The road then tested my muscles as it climbed again before edging a broad dark forestry plantation. Here I freewheeled gently, admiring the towering bulk of Thorny Pike ahead.

Without warning, a fleeting tan shape burst out of the trees to my right and I was almost knocked off my bike by a fawn bounding on to the road. It panicked and careered up the tarmac ahead of me, hemmed in by walls, before slowing down and looking back. It saw that I was still approaching and so continued to trot along the lane on its spindly legs, anxiously searching for an escape. Remarkably, I followed the young deer for half a mile, getting quite close before a farm track gave the shy animal a chance to flee.

Ten minutes later I was at the head of the dale and out of road. Ahead was only a tumble of ramshackle farm buildings and a rugged sheep track over the boggy tops to the next valley. I turned and headed back, knowing that the boys would be bouncing with excitement about the party.

'Come here and look at this!' said Barbara as I stepped through the door, her mouth half-smiling. She led me along to the kitchen. 'There.' She pointed through the window next to which the buxom Iris was gently giggling.

At first I didn't know what I was looking for, but then I spotted it. At the back of our house was the cottage owned by our occasional neighbours, Wanda and Ralph, and on the side of it was a kind of old extension which they had made into its kitchen. It had a steep stone roof and on top of the roof was our cat.

Barbara looked at me. 'Did you leave the boys' bedroom window open by any chance?'

'Possibly . . .'

Iris chuckled. 'He's been up there twenty minutes and can't seem to get down. We've tried coaxing him.'

'Can't he get back up?' I said.

'You ask him,' said Barbara. 'We're trying to get this party tea sorted.'

'What about a ladder?'

Barbara shrugged. 'Well, go on then, but you'd better hurry up because the other kids'll start arriving soon.'

I ran to the garage, fetched the wooden stepladders that Joyce had once put in a skip at Cragthwaite, then snuck through the gate and into next door's back yard, having first checked that their car wasn't about. What if they arrived while I was up on the roof? I didn't like even to contemplate the scene.

Our long-haired Siberian kitten stood on the ridge of the roof, mewing as he watched me approach. He stuck a paw out on to the slates but clearly didn't fancy the smooth, steep surface. I looked up to ascertain the course of his bid for freedom: Tom and Reuben's bedroom window was indeed open just a few inches. He must have squeezed on to the ledge and made quite a leap to reach the nearby roof.

'Silly Ulf,' I said, climbing the wobbly ladder. He watched my ascent and gave a sharp miaow, edging along the ridge towards where I was. I stretched over but could get nowhere near the frightened cat and at one point felt the stepladders wobble just a little too much. I climbed down, closed the ladder then leaned it against the wall, hoping this would bring me closer. Across the village green I saw a neighbour stop and stare. No doubt a crowd would soon be gathering.

'Stay there, Ulf,' I said as I climbed again. He paced back and forward, lifting his bushy brown tail high. The ladder did bring me closer but as I climbed I heard a protesting squeal from the Holts' new plastic guttering against which my weight was now pressing. If it broke there would be witnesses. Stupid cat!

'Nice cat,' I lied, trying pointlessly to make my knees bend the wrong way so that I could lean on to the roof tiles and reach out to the fretting feline. Resting painfully on my elbows I stretched to within about five feet but Ulf showed no interest in climbing down to my hands. Barbara and Iris peered through the kitchen window laughing merrily at my inept efforts. I could think of only one solution.

'Whose idea was it to buy a pet with vertigo?' I said, stomping into the kitchen.

Barbara was still grinning. 'But, hey, we won't need musical bumps or any other party games – all Tom's friends can just come outside and watch you. It's much more fun.'

'Careful or I'll leave him up there all night.'

'You wouldn't,' said Iris, her eyes revealing shock.

'He wouldn't,' said Barbara. 'We kid each other a lot.'

'Huh,' I said, reaching into the food cupboard before finding what I was looking for.

'What are you going to do, anyway?' said Barbara.

I showed her the can. 'Tuna.'

Outside, Ulf made a big noise again as I climbed the ladder. Four people were now watching from across the green, no doubt amused at my botched rescue mission. But this time I had a secret weapon and Ulf's keen nose registered it right away. His mewing went into overdrive as I wafted the open tin of fish; he had always been crazy about tuna, going completely berserk whenever we opened some, scratching away at the kitchen door.

'Look, tuna!' I don't know why I said it; he knew what it was as well as I did.

Once more I edged up the ladder and heard the gutter protest. I leaned agonisingly on to the roof holding out the can. Gloops of fishy brine dribbled on to the tiles.

'Come on, Ulf,' I said, trying to sound friendly through gritted teeth.

He stared at the can, his eyes huge in full hunting mode, and he edged his paws forward.

'That's it, come on.' I wafted again.

I could see his resistance was breaking: the lure was too great. But instead of padding down the roof he elected to leap. Cats are quick and I had no time to react before his barbed claws embedded in my hands.

'OOOWWW!'

I dropped the can which rolled down the roof spilling smelly tuna on to my shirt. Now safely latched into my skin Ulf wasted no time licking the roof and my clothes while I tried to stop the swaying ladder from keeling over. Barbara and Iris stood with mouths open while a little ripple of applause drifted across the green, interspersed with laughter. I unhooked the cat with difficulty, assessed the holes in my flesh then climbed down while Ulf scrabbled to reach the flakes of fish in the gutter.

The party passed off quietly, much to my relief. Tom had a splendid time with his friends, Holly gently policed Reuben, and the old-fashioned games worked a treat, although during sleeping lions one little girl did ask why I smelled of kippers.

At five o'clock the red-cheeked crowd were ushered into the dining room for their party tea and we all sang happy birthday as Barbara walked in with a magnificent candle-topped, coiled python in sponge and patterned icing, complete with marzipan forked tongue. Everyone clapped and cheered wildly, except Tom who blew out the candles and then peered at the creation.

'It's nice but I didn't mean that kind of snake cake,' he said.

Barbara's face fell. 'Oh, what did you mean, poppet?'

'One of those rolled up ones with jam in, like a log.'

We all pondered a moment then Iris piped up. 'Oh, you mean a Swiss roll?'

Tom's face lit up. 'Yes!'

There was a moment's silence as we all looked at Barbara and contemplated a factory-made 20p confection from the shop down the road. Then all the adults, including Applesett's midnight baker of serpents, broke down and guffawed while the children looked confused, waiting for a slice of snake.

The hour before parents' evening began was always tense. The reports had been sent out the previous day, appointments were made, and the classroom was scrubbed and neat, with carefully labelled wall displays including at least one piece of work by every child, however shocking. The centrepiece of the longest wall was Lisa's magnificent hawk painting, which I knew would bring admiration from all and sundry, even if nothing else did.

But at this point, with just a few moments before the evening began, my mind wasn't on Lisa but on Fraser Garth. I couldn't understand it: he was a delightful boy with no real issues in terms of learning or behaviour, and I had written him an excellent report; in fact it had been my first one, knowing that it would be easy to extol his many virtues. And yet for the past couple of days, ever since reports and parents' evening had been mentioned, Fraser had been acting very strangely.

'Are you all right, Fraser?' I'd said to him just a few hours previously, as he stood staring out of the window after all the other children had gone out to play.

'Er, aye,' he answered.

'Did you want to ask me something?'

'Erm, no.'

'Do you feel OK?'

I looked at his face for signs of paleness. He was a stocky boy with a ruddy complexion and a mass of golden hair.

'Ahm just a bit nervous, that's all.'

'That doesn't sound like you, Fraser. Is it because your parents are coming tonight?'

'Well, las' time things di'n't go so well wi' Mrs Percival.'

'Oh right, I see. Well, there's going to be no problem this evening – your mum and dad were pleased with your report, weren't they?'

'Oh aye, they were amazed.'

'So, why are you worried?'

He shrugged. 'I dunno . . . I, er, I'll go out ter play now.' He pushed open the door and disappeared leaving me somewhat confused. I decided to go and have a word with Hilda.

'Ooh, a man in me parlour,' she said as I walked into her austere classroom. 'To what do I owe the pleasure?'

'I just wanted to ask you about Fraser Garth.'

'Oh yes, nice lad but idle, like most boys of his age.'

'Do you think so? I've not noticed that – he's worked hard all year, really.'

'Well, maybe that's due to the male influence. Perhaps your growl's louder than mine, eh?' She chuckled and half-winked.

I was going to add that I hadn't really had to growl at him at all but thought better of it.

'Fraser said that parents' evening last year hadn't gone too well . . .'

Hilda looked up. 'I don't really recall it, myself. I must have spoken to five hundred parents over the years and when you get to my age they all merge into one. I always tell it like it is, though, and sometimes the truth hurts. It's like eating some of Emma's tufo.'

'Tofu. Anyway, you don't know why Fraser might be a bit nervous, then?'

'Well, I do remember his report wasn't good last time so maybe he recalls a bit of a sore backside, eh? His father's quite a brute – I bet he packs a wallop.' She laughed again and made a swishing motion with her arm.

'Do you really think that's what happened?'

'No, don't be daft – I'm only kidding. They used to back in the fifties but parents have gone soft these days. That's probably why some of them don't like the traditional way I do things.'

The bell for end of break rang and I headed back, concluding that if I was an eight-year-old boy in the dry confines of Class 2, I'd probably be lacking in drive as well.

The classroom door opened and in walked Mr and Mrs Lawson, Cathy's parents. They smiled shyly and asked if it was all right to look at her work since they were early. I told them that was the idea and pointed them towards Cathy's plastic drawer of tidy books and folders. At least there would be no problem there.

An hour later the session was in full swing with seven or eight parents in the room and the mountainous Mrs Clarkson sitting in front of my desk wearing long shorts, a vest and flip flops. She was twenty minutes late for her appointment.

'Ahm so sorry, Mr Seed. Our Ashley split 'is 'ead oppen playin' wi' dogs.'

'Oh, is he all right?'

'Aye, he's allus in t'wars tho' – needs a bloody season ticket fer casualty that bairn.'

'Right, well, Martine . . .'

She flicked back a lock of limp hair. 'I actually thought 'er report were quite good.'

This threw me considerably. 'Oh, er, right. I'm surprised.'

'Well it were tons better than what she got in Class Two.'

'I see, well, she's going steadily in some things but she does spend a lot of time calling out instead of listening.'

Mrs Clarkson gave a half laugh. 'Oh, aye, I recognise that – I were jus' same.'

'And she really needs to try harder to be neat; as you can see her books are very messy.'

'Same as me at school, again – she teks after 'er mam, does that lass.' She smiled as if expecting me to join in.

'Does she do much reading at home?'

'Gettin' Martine ter read's like gettin' honey from a pig's arse, scuse ma language. I do try but, well, we just end up 'aving a shoutin' match and then Ashley kicks off. She's no dad ter back me up, that's half the trouble.'

I looked at my watch, aware that others were waiting. 'Well, do keep trying, Mrs Clarkson. I'll have a word with Martine about it, too. Do you, er, read yourself much?'

'Nah, 'ave no time fer books.' She half laughed again and raised her stupendous bulk, causing a pencil on my desk to roll. 'Thanks any 'ow, Mr Seed.' She rumbled away and I fought to keep a straight face as Barry's parents moved forward.

Time raced by as it always did on these occasions and I enjoyed the variety of people who came into the room: the posh Quanticks, Lawrence's Labrador-centric family; Estelle's pushy but sincere mother; Anna's upright military father; Trudy's horsey mum; and Howard Sedgwick's mighty dad whose handshake mashed my fingers without him even registering. Jo Spence's parents were Dales' farmers of several generations and they looked almost like they were part of the land. They shuffled around the room, barely whispering, and sat in front of me in silence as I rattled on about Jo's progress and her astounding strength. After a while I stopped, hoping that they might respond but all they did was stand, nod, mumble something like, 'Byyy, proper job,' then thank me and leave. I smiled to myself and pondered on how many of these strange, solemn couples I had talked to over the past five years. Val had told me that many were nervous of meeting teachers, often because they couldn't help thinking back to their own schooldays when, as children of simple rural stock, they'd suffered at the hands of severe schoolmistresses.

Only two sets of parents remained: Jason's and Fraser's. I'd given

Mr Fisher a late appointment so that the rest of the evening wouldn't be ruined if he came in guns blazing, and Mrs and Mrs Garth asked to be last as they first had to prepare for bed and breakfasters in the following day.

'Evening,' said a slim, weary-looking woman I knew to be Mrs Garth. Her husband followed her into the room and nodded in my direction, a broad, unruffled man with the large muscular hands of someone who worked on the land.

'Do look at Fraser's work,' I said. 'I'm just expecting someone else first.' I guided them to the right pile and Mrs Garth dropped on to the child's chair nearby and picked up a maths book. Mr Garth correctly judged that the low plastic seats would be overly tested by his bulk and parked his rear on the table instead, while I glanced through the door for signs of Mr Fisher. Dusk was now falling but there was no one there.

I waited ten minutes then walked over to the earnest couple who were still looking through sheets of paper at Fraser's desk.

Anxious as I was, I tried to sound upbeat. 'Now then, you'll be pleased with your boy's report, no doubt.'

Mrs Garth put down the page she was holding. 'Very pleased,' she said. 'And surprised.'

'Surprised?'

Mr Garth nodded. 'Aye, well, he struggled a bit last year, like.'

'Well he hasn't struggled in Class Three; he's a lovely lad – hard-working, thoughtful and does his best. I've been very pleased with his work.'

'So are we,' said Mrs Garth. 'We can't really believe it. He's never much liked school before – his behaviour were all right, you know, but he just, well, didn't get on with reading and writing and such, but now . . . well!' Her eyes flickered.

'He's reet enthusiastic, Mr Seed,' said Fraser's father. 'I'd say he were like a changed lad, really.'

I didn't know what to say. I just sat there with a dim grin on my face. 'Er, well, that's wonderful.'

'Aye,' said Mrs Garth. 'A year ago Mrs Percival were really quite frustrated with him.'

'I wonder if that's why he looked a bit nervous today,' I said, hearing the door creak and seeing the brooding figure of Mr Fisher enter without looking at me. His eyes flicked round for Jason's drawer.

Mrs Garth drew a bit closer and lowered her voice. 'Well, you know, he's always been like that, Mr Seed, a bit of a worrier. People think because he's nice lad and helpful and lives on a farm that he doesn't have any cares but, well, he's . . . sensitive, you know.'

I nodded, half-glancing at Mr Fisher who was now skimming through Jason's exercise books with intense concentration.

'Right, well, I can honestly say I didn't realise that until today,' I said.

Mr Garth smiled. 'Probably because he's been 'appy in here with you, Mr Seed. You've done a grand job and we'd both really like to thank you.'

His wife nodded and held out a hand. I shook it and was relieved when Mr Garth then went for the gentle approach, as my fingers were still bruised from the previous assault.

'Have you looked at Fraser's work on the wall?' I said, keen for them to stay in the room as long as possible.

'No, but we will. He didn't do that buzzard painting, did he?' asked Mr Garth. 'Byyy, that's summat, is that.'

'Sadly not, but he did an excellent drawing of an eagle himself, look.' I went across to the display, trying to catch Mr Fisher's eye to see if he was waiting to speak to me. He was reading a story in Jason's English book.

Mrs Garth let out a breath of admiration when she saw her son's artwork. 'I never did anythin' like this when I were at school. I think it's marvellous.'

I showed them some models and science work before Mr Garth nodded his head towards Jason's father and lowered his voice.

'We're not, er, holdin' you up, are we?'

'No, it's fine – I'll just go over when Mr Fisher's ready.'

'Fraser's really enjoyed doing the herb garden – we saw that earlier,' said Mrs Garth, just as the door sounded again and Mr Fisher disappeared through it.

We stood and watched him hurry around the school and towards the car park.

'Well, looks like yer done fer t'night, Mr Seed,' chuckled the big farmer.

'It does,' I said, trying not to look quite as pleased as I was.

When they were gone, I switched the lights off and hurried into the main building to look for Joyce. She was in her office, jotting down a note; the door was open as ever and she was wearing her full parents' evening regalia – an expensive trouser suit, a rainbow of makeup and several pounds' worth of fashionable scent.

'Andy! How did it go, my dear?'

'Erm, well, I think.'

'You think?'

I told her about Fraser's parents first, deciding not to mention my earlier conversation with Hilda; I expected that Joyce was aware anyway. 'They were just delighted.'

'Of course they were, don't be surprised – you're a first-rate teacher. And our friend Mr Fisher?'

'This is where it gets really odd,' I said, looking through the door. 'He came in, didn't say a word, rifled through Jason's books, read a few pieces of work then just left without even speaking to me.'

To my great surprise, Joyce put her head back and broke into a wry smile. 'Good.'

I regarded her suspiciously. 'Did you have a word with him first?'

She opened her palms. 'I was in here and he just happened to pass by so I asked how things were with Jason and he said he still wasn't very happy with the way Jason was being treated by the school so I asked for specific examples and he couldn't really give any.'

'Oh, I see.'

'Then Miss Croker just happened to pass by and I called her in and asked if she had been aware of any of the staff being unfair to Jason Fisher and she said no but she had seen Jason causing trouble most weeks in the playground when she was on duty, and in assembly and in the cloakrooms.'

'What did he say to that?'

'Not a lot, so I asked if he was happy with Jason's work and he said he hadn't seen enough of it and was on the way to your classroom to do so. I added that Jason was extremely privileged to have a young, enthusiastic, talented teacher like Mr Seed this year and I know for a fact that he's been well taught and this year's school inspection concurred.'

'And what did he say to that?

'He grunted then looked at Val and said he'd better get to the classroom.'

'And that was it?'

'That was it.'

I thanked her for being so kind and a wonder. She gave me a hug and ordered me home.

I flopped into a chair when I arrived back at Craven Bottoms. At least there was peace now the boys were in bed. Barbara walked in with two steaming mugs of tea.

'Good do?' she asked.

'Very good.'

'Tell me when you've had a drink.'

'Quiet here?'

'Not really,' she said. 'Doug and Rosie are leaving.'

Chapter Twenty-Four

Marcus

The Monday of the last week of term was another day of dazzling sunshine. At lunchtime, none of the teachers could bear to be inside and so we dragged some chairs out into the sun and ate our sandwiches at the back of the school, watching the children at play on the field, with the broad green vista of Swinnerdale beyond. There were infants chasing each other and rolling on the grass, junior girls making daisy chains and boys playing cricket and football or sitting under a tree discussing tractors.

In the peace of the moment my mind switched to Rosie and Doug. How could they move away from this? I recalled the conversation that Barbara and I had had on Friday when I'd returned from parents' evening.

'Rosie came round while you were out,' Barbara had explained. 'She was quite upset, really, and needed to talk.'

'What was the trouble?'

'Well, she'd obviously had a row with Doug about something or other and it turns out that neither of them are happy here.'

'We kind of guessed that, didn't we?'

'Sadly . . . Doug hates his job at the school and Rosie just misses everything going on in York – all the social stuff and groups and—'

'Hairy people they don't have in the Dales.'

'Exactly. But they're upset because they love the house and lots of things about the village too.'

I'd slowly shaken my head. 'The work they've done on that place and the money they've spent . . .'

'I know, it breaks your heart. I'll really miss Rosie and so will the boys.'

We'd then talked about who would look after Reuben while Barbara was at work and why the country life suited some people but not others before the exhaustion of parents' evening had caused my eyelids to droop.

A low voice brought me back to the present. It was Val.

'Who's that youth on his own with the comic?' she said, squinting in the glare of the sun. I looked at the small, curly haired figure in the distance sitting cross-legged on his jumper; only one person read comics alone at lunchtime and he was in my class.

'That's Marcus Hyams,' I said.

Emma looked blank for a moment. 'Oh, the lad whose mum is a doctor? I didn't teach him.'

'His dad's a doctor too,' I said. 'They work at Hauxton and live in that big house on the Chapelgarth road.'

'Ooh, d'you think he can come and look at my bunions?' chuckled Hilda.

'What, Marcus or his dad?' said Val.

'Marcus might well know what to do with them,' I said. 'He's a really brainy kid.'

'Bit of a loner, though, by the look of it,' said Val.

'Yeah, sadly; he's usually on his own. He seems to have different hobbies from all the others – he collects action figures and his family are into their Amstrad word processor at home.'

'D'you remember when he brought some of those figures into assembly last year?' said Sue. 'He gave a talk about them.'

Hilda gently slapped her forehead. 'Oh, heavens, don't remind me – there's half an hour of me life I'll never get back. All those horrible mutant soldier things and plastic horses with armour; he just went on and on and on. If I'd had a few more Anadin in me bag I would have ended it there and then.'

Everyone laughed but I also felt a twinge of guilt and sadness: Marcus had been in my class for the whole school year and he didn't really have a friend. Could I have done more? He was a loner, for sure, and an incomer who was very different from your typical Dales lad, but there was something strangely distressing about a child sitting on his own on a day like this.

When the bell rang I wandered over to him and asked what he was reading.

'It's a sci-fi comic.'

Despite the sun, he was pale beneath his knot of curly chestnut hair. I noticed that there was a *Star Trek* strip on one of the pages.

'My boys like watching *Star Trek*, although my younger son thinks the Commander of the Enterprise is called Captain Log.'

It was true but Marcus didn't laugh.

'Spock's my favourite,' he said. I might have guessed.

At home that evening I wandered on to the village green to meet John Weatherall's seventeen-year-old son Carl for a spot of cricket practice. Ahead of us at the weekend was the annual pub challenge match between the two darts teams at The Crown, Applesett, and The Black Bull, Kettleby. I'd never played in the match before and hadn't picked up a bat or ball since college but the team was short this time and Dennis the landlord had been desperate for me to join in. I'd decided to ask the athletic Carl, our ringer, to give me a bit of reacquaintance with the basics. He was waiting by the swings, doing a little clonking keep-uppy with bat and ball.

'Now then,' he said.

'Now then, Carl.' I smiled; he was the spit of his father, down to his movements.

'What's it to be?'

'Well, I haven't played cricket for years so can we just do a bit of catching practice first so I can get used to the ball?'

'Aye, sure.'

The tall, wiry youth put down the bat and swung his arm in a big circle. He was a star footballer as well as cricketer and much admired by the girls in the village, too. He turned and tossed me the ball as we walked apart on to an area of open grass. I clasped the heavy red ball, feeling its hard leather against my hands. I was really looking forward to the match but was starting to regret practising in such a public place as two young lads came out of a house and watched us from the swings. I lobbed the ball back trying to look nonchalant.

Carl took it with one hand. 'You a batter or bowler?' he said.

'All rounder – I'm equally bad at both.' At least he half-laughed before sending a faster overarm throw towards me. I felt a painful slap as it hit my palm; I didn't drop it but I'd quite forgotten how hard and heavy cricket balls were. I made a mental note to cushion my catches more, then fired a wayward throw back to Carl. Despite its lack of direction he shuttled quickly to his left and took a smart low catch.

My partner obviously thought that I was hinting that the throws had been too easy up till now and so he leaned back and launched a high throw up into the evening sky.

'Whoaw!' I heard one of the young spectators say.

The ball sailed in a towering arc and I scampered across watching its meteoric descent with nervous attention, reaching up with my hands as I ran. The moment of impact was painful in several ways. The ball cracked against my right hand then fell to the ground while the watching boys jeered. Carl stood with his hands on hips, evidently disappointed that I couldn't take such a dolly of a catch. I, meanwhile, was staring at my fourth finger which was a very odd shape.

'I think I've dislocated it,' I said.

Carl came over. 'Aye, it's not reet that.'

Barbara was putting the boys to bed and so with great care I dialled Rosie's number to see if she could babysit so that Barbara could drive me the twenty-five miles to hospital.

'Well, I'm busy but Doug'll take you,' she said.

I tried refusing but they insisted and so I shared a long, awkward journey to Bilthorpe unsure as to whether Doug wanted to discuss their sad departure from the Dales or not. I felt stupid sitting there with a Z-shaped finger sticking up, but at least it wasn't throbbing too much.

'How's this going to affect the last week of school?' he said, nodding towards my mangled digit.

'It shouldn't be too bad – there's not a lot on during the next few days, except that I'm supposed to be refereeing a football match.'

'At this time of year?'

'It's a special Dads versus Lads game, organised by the PTA.'

'Farmers playing in wellies, is it?'

'Probably . . .' I bit the bullet. 'Anyway, Barbara and I will be sad to see you go.'

He paused. 'Well, there's only so many whist drives a man can take, and I don't think the local yokels were quite ready for our mung beans and henna, really.'

'We'll miss you, though.'

'Maybe. Anyway, you know it hurts like stink, don't you?'

'Eh? What?'

'When they pull your knuckles apart.'

Doug's crumpled 2CV rattled back into Applesett late, after a long wait at the hospital and about two seconds of agony while a prop-forward-sized nurse yanked my joint back into line. My finger was crooked but at least I could move it now. Barbara, having waited up, showed little sympathy on my return.

'Serves you right; I told you cricket is a silly game.'

'It's not a silly game, it's just that—'

'That what? The ball is too hard and your catching isn't up to it.'

'I thought wives were supposed to be loving and compassionate when their husbands are injured and end up at hospital.'

'They are but your record, quite frankly, is not the best: you either come home with a giant comedy bandage or you travel fifty miles to intensive care thinking you've got appendicitis and end up just needing a plop.'

There was a moment's silence then came what I knew was imminent from my wife: she creased over and cackled so hard that she had to hold on to the sofa. I went into the kitchen and opened a bottle of wine following a painful struggle with the cork.

The following day at school my finger looked slightly less swollen and the only activity I had difficulty with was writing on the whiteboard, with the result that everything was leaning slightly to the left.

'What's 'appened to yer writing, Mr Seed?' said Martine, as I put up the date. 'It's worse than mine.'

'Don't be rude please, Martine. I know it's nearly the end of term and you'll soon be moving on to Class Four but if I tell Miss Croker you talk to teachers like that she'll eat you on toast.'

Lawrence looked interested. 'Oh, go on, Mr Seed – tell her anyway.'

'But why *is* your writing all wonky?' asked Estelle.

'I've just hurt a finger that's all.'

'Ooh, doing what? Go on, tell us, Mr Seed,' came the call from several.

I decided that it was going to be bad enough in Applesett with all the mickey-taking I would face when Carl, via his dad, informed the darts team and thence the whole pub about my cack-handed attempt to catch a ball and the resulting injury. Instead I demanded silence from the class, to murmured 'Boos', then craftily reversed the situation by telling the children that if they were good I would give them an extra-long games session in the afternoon. It did the trick.

At morning break everyone dashed out into the sunshine except Marcus, who went to his bag, picked something up and walked across to see me.

'I thought perhaps your sons might like these,' he said, holding out a small stack of sci-fi comics. 'They've all got *Star Trek* in.'

I smiled at this unexpected act. 'Wow, that's really kind of you, Marcus. Very thoughtful – I'm sure my boys will love them.'

'They have better aliens than the TV series, too.' He maintained his sober expression.

'Erm, when would you like them back?' I pictured Tom trying to read them studiously while Reuben leaned over and scrunched the pages to a pulp.

'They're to keep.'

With relief I thanked him profusely and in a spontaneous act of friendship, thinking back to his lonely figure the previous day, held out my hand to shake.

I guessed afterwards that his six-foot-five, rugby-playing father had previously issued Marcus with stern instructions to always give a man a firm handshake. Either way, when he squeezed my fingers I shrieked, accidentally kicking the class's Skerry Hole fossil display and sending ammonites flying in all directions.

'I'll go out to play now,' he spluttered, stumbling backwards with goggling eyes.

It was a joy to be out in the afternoon for games. The sun had disappeared behind thin clouds but the day was warm and bright and the hills around Cragthwaite looked wonderful, dressed with buttercups and scattered with contented sheep. Ian, Howard and Stephen had been selected to play in the school football team the following evening against the dads and they begged if they could have some practice, even though the season was long over. Hearing me assent to this request, Estelle pushed forward.

'If they can play football then can we play netball? Jo and me are in the Girls versus Mums match tomorrow as well.'

'How can I watch two games at once?' I said, knowing that I'd dug a hole for myself here.

Estelle remained calm. 'It's all right; you can stay with the boys – the girls won't be any trouble.'

It was cheeky but she was right and we all knew it. I split the girls into two teams and asked Beverley to be umpire since her tender nose precluded her from sports for the time being. She agreed and I let them get on with it, switching my attention to the boys, who were already arguing on the field about who would be on Ian's team. Jason, unfortunately, was at the centre of it.

'Am never on Ian's team, snot fair,' he snapped.

I held up my left hand. 'Jason, it's the last week of term, nearly the end of the school year: let's not have any more disputes. You can be on Ian's team.'

For a moment he just stood there. He had been ready to strop but now there was no need and he wasn't sure how to react. He sprang over to Ian quickly as if the offer might be withdrawn, but still mumbled, 'I should be in the school team, though.'

Eventually I managed to get a game underway, although I found blowing the referee's whistle strangely difficult using my other hand. The contest followed the usual pattern with Ian dominating everything, the eager players chasing the ball like it was chained to them and the non-sporty hanging around in the far reaches of the pitch, ironically taking up the spaces where the keen ones should have been and so often receiving passes but without a clue what to do with the ball. Marcus was one of these and he soon realised that marking a corner flag was the safest option.

After ten minutes of wretched running and booting I stopped the game and called the boys over for a talk.

'Look, England has only ever won the World Cup once and it's up to you lot to do something about that but instead you're just hoofing it. Except in defence where, for some reason, you've decided the best thing is to dither. If six forwards are rushing at you and you have the ball you can't take three touches or tap it two yards to a team-mate, even if it is Ian. What should you do?'

Ian put up his hand along with the other usual candidates but I was very surprised to see Marcus, standing at the back, raise an arm also.

'Do you know, Marcus?'

'Stop fannying about,' he announced. The other boys splurted into howls of delight and I was unable to prevent myself from sniggering, too. It took two minutes for everyone to calm down, during which time Gary, Dan and Howard went over to Marcus and patted him on the back, giving their congratulations on such a hysterical remark. Marcus himself remained serious and confused.

'Where on earth did you get that from?' I asked.

'My uncle took me to the Darlington against Bury match at the weekend,' he said, eager to explain the circumstances. 'We stood in the crowd and this man was watching a defender with the ball and he called out, "Stop fannying about," so I thought that was the answer.' Once more the boys went into convulsions.

I tried to continue the game but no one could take it seriously and so we had a penalty competition instead. One curious thing I did notice was that several boys chatted to Marcus while they were waiting their turn, giving him a thumbs up and smiling at him. *Good old Uncle*, I thought.

On Thursday I didn't bother going home after school as there was so much setting up to do for the special PTA evening. A group of enthusiastic parents, mainly incomers, had approached Joyce three years earlier about raising funds for the school and she had agreed to the setting up of a Parent Teachers Association on the understanding that they organise social events as well as raffles and sales. This night was the first summer evening event following various fairs and the earlier disco. My initial job was to assemble the large wooden goals for the Dads vs Lads football match, these having been taken down in May by the groundsmen.

'How's the finger?' said Val, who was giving me a hand.

'All right as long as I don't put any pressure on it.'

'Well why are you picking up dirty great wooden posts, then?'

I looked at the two long crossbars lying in the grass. 'Well, nobody else is going to do this, are they?'

'This is a bloody PTA event isn't it? You should have got the parents to do it.'

I hadn't thought of that. She saw my face, sighed and shook her head.

With some difficulty we heaved the posts into their slots then undid the rusty bolts with pliers and fixed on the crossbar, with Val growling at me if I tried to use my right hand. In all it took forty minutes.

'I am *not* going to take all this down again afterwards,' she mumbled. 'The dads can do that, especially as there's another one to do as well.'

'No there isn't,' I said. 'I'm going to use the small five-a-side goal at the other end for the boys to defend.'

She almost smiled. 'Well, maybe yer not so flamin' daft after all.'

We dragged the metal goal up the field and Val went away to set up the netball court while I attached a net. The goal was about one eighth the size of the big one but at least it would give the boys a chance.

At seven o'clock a sizeable crowd of children, parents and other onlookers had gathered at the side of the pitch and we were ready to kick off. Eight bruising fathers stood in little groups, laughing and pointing. Some were brave enough to wear shorts, a few had managed to produce a pair of dog-eared football boots, but most were sporting tatty T-shirts, old trousers and trainers. There was one exception, however: the sports-mad Mr Fisher, Jason's father, was wearing a crisp, clean football kit with new-looking boots and smart matching socks, pulled up and tied; he even had shinpads.

The boys, mainly from Class 4 but including Ian, Stephen and Howard, bobbed up and down with excitement, looking resplendent in their all-yellow strip. The goalkeeper stood just above the tiny goal, which appeared comical in comparison to the full-sized one at the other end of the pitch. The atmosphere, with lots of quips coming in from the touchlines and the fathers all smiling and joking, was just right and I was really looking forward to refereeing the game. Ian's talented younger brothers, Scott and Robbie, stood among the spectators next to the big goal, desperate to be on the pitch but hopefully understanding that this was the last opportunity for some of the less skilful older boys to play; their time would come.

Ian, standing over the ball, turned to his team-mates and clenched his fist. Mr Reed, Anna's father and captain of the dads, looked back and called out, 'Let's show them we've still got it, chaps!' Lots of people laughed; you didn't get chaps in the Dales very often.

I gave a blast on the whistle then immediately grimaced: I'd forgotten the finger already. Ian passed the ball back and I hoped that my team would remember Marcus's exhortation not to fanny about. They soon lost it, however, and the dads started to knock the ball around, determined to show the mockers that they weren't nearly as past-it as they appeared.

The seventeen-stone Mr Garth trundled five yards to collect the ball for a throw-in.

'I'm knackered now,' he japed, before launching an enormous lob which caught out the boys completely: they weren't used to the ball travelling that far. It landed at the feet of the father of one of Emma's infants. With impressive skill he dummied to shoot, causing the boys' keeper to dive, then coolly dribbled around him and slotted the ball into the net, to much booing from the mums on the sidelines.

'Byyy, that goal's titchy,' said the scorer, who was being patted on the back by Mr Fisher. We'd played less than two minutes.

The boys looked a little crestfallen but I called over to them to keep their heads up as they kicked off again. Once more the ball was hoofed forward to my dismay and the dads passed it around surprisingly well while the poor boys, looking like fleas next to the giant farmers and builders, scurried around trying to retrieve possession.

'Nice work, team,' called Mr Reed. 'If we can keep it for the next thirty-seven minutes we've won!'

The boys harried their opponents into playing a backpass to the dads' goalie and he whacked the ball up the pitch.

'Mine!' shouted Ian, bursting after it, then taking it on his chest, turning and playing a neat one-two with Stephen. He carried it into the other half gaining speed.

'Watch him!' cried Mr Fisher but Ian sent the first defender the wrong way with a drop of the shoulder and brilliant shimmy. The next of the hulking fathers slipped trying a tackle and ended up on his backside to much hilarity from the spectators. Ian continued his burst forward and a line of huge men rumbled towards him. We could all see there was no way past this human wall but at the last second, the school's star player clipped the ball to his right where Oliver from Class 4 was in acres of space. The speedy winger dashed in towards the goal with the lumbering defence trying to turn to get back. They had no chance. Oliver whipped in a low hard cross and there, sliding in at the far post was Ian to ram home a spectacular finish.

'Yesssss!' roared the crowd. It was a genuinely stunning goal and even most of the dads clapped. I did, too, until I remembered that I was the referee.

'I-an, I-an, I-an!' chanted a little knot of children by the goalpost.

For ten minutes the game was very even, with the dads now showing the boys more respect but the jovial atmosphere remained until just before half-time. Mr Reed made a misplaced pass and Howard Sedgwick saw a chance to nip in and take the ball. Mr Fisher was nearby and jumped in, knocking Howard off his feet with a shoulder barge. I was tempted to blow the whistle but, strictly following the rules, it was a legal challenge. I was also very aware that he was still cross that Jason wasn't in the team, having heard him grumble about it earlier.

'Steady on,' said the moustachioed Mr Reed.

'Booooo,' went the crowd as a dizzy Howard climbed to his feet. I was surprised to see the petite, well-dressed Mrs Fisher joining in and laughing, too.

Mr Fisher was undeterred, however, and decided to go on a dribble. He beat two players before Ian confronted him, at which point he played a pass and carried on his run forward. The ball was given back to him and a couple of timid defenders withdrew from offering any form of challenge. Mr Fisher suddenly found himself in front of goal. He drew back his leg and smashed the ball as hard as he could towards the little goal. The cowering keeper simply ducked and covered his face, much to Ian's disgust, and the ball flew into the net.

'Yesssss!' cried Mr Fisher, jumping into the air with his hands raised.

'Booooo!' went the mums and children.

During the second half the boys, now 2–1 down, went all out for an equaliser and it looked hopeful, as some of the less fit fathers tired and stopped even pretending to run. Ian was making an heroic effort, smashing in shots and trying to beat the defence, but the dads were simply too large a barrier when they were arrayed in front of the goal.

With just two minutes left, Stephen latched on to a pass from Ian and thumped the ball as hard as he could. It smashed into Mr Spence's tree-like thigh and bounced straight to Mr Fisher, who had been orchestrating the defence, desperate to win. With the whole boys' team except one defender upfield, he saw his chance for a breakaway goal and more glory. He easily shrugged off the last opponent then darted forward into an empty pitch, knowing that the boys' goalkeeper was frightened of the power of his shots. I stood there on the half-way line watching him dash towards me, his eyes glinting.

He was so fixed on the goal ahead that I don't think he even saw me, so when I stuck out a foot as he ran past he was taken completely unaware. I flicked the ball but also caught his left foot which tangled with his right and caused him to crash, chin first, to the sun-baked turf.

'Whaaat?' he groaned, half in surprise, half in agony.

'Play on!' I called before booting the loose ball over to Oliver who miscontrolled it just inside the area. Mr Spence ambled across and tackled him cleanly. I blew the whistle.

'Penalty!'

I could hear Mr Fisher screech in protest from behind.

'Oh, good decision,' called Mr Reed. 'That was a shocking challenge.' This brought much laughter and made me feel a lot better.

Ian was given the ball and wasted no time, rifling it into the top corner to cheers and jumping celebration from the boys. I gave the whistle a last, long blast. There was much applause but I was more than aware that Mr Fisher was hobbling towards me from behind, muttering darkly. Just as he drew level, the great square figure of Mr Garth, Fraser's father, stepped in front of me; he slapped me on the shoulder.

'That were grand fun, well done, lad.'

He then swung to Mr Fisher, holding out a colossal hand. I could have sworn that I heard finger bones snapping during the handshake. 'Well played; ahm paggered but that were a real laugh, weren't it?'

As Mr Fisher croaked a faint reply I blew the whistle again, asked for help taking the goals down, then walked over to see how Val had got on, knowing that my favourite parent would be obliged to help with the dismantling and carrying.

I gulped my cup of tea and munched a piece of toast at speed. It was the morning of the last day of the school year.

'I can't believe I'm saying goodbye to those kids,' I said to Barbara who was battling to wipe Reuben's jam-coated face. 'I just wish I had something to give them.' I usually bought a small leaving present for each child but felt this time that we couldn't afford it.

'Ah, wait a moment,' said Barbara, mysteriously leaving the room. I heard a cupboard open and lots of rustling, then she reappeared with a carrier bag and held it out.

'There you are: one each.'

'Hey, where did you get these?' The bag was full of chocolate bars.

'This old boy called Stan gives them to me on my round in Ingleburn.'

'Is he trying to charm you?'

'Ha! He's about ninety-three. No, he just hands out choccies to everyone.'

I glanced at my watch. 'I'd better go now, anyway. These are perfect, well done.'

I gave her and the boys a kiss, then dashed out, delighted that I could hand out a little gift after all.

At school Joyce had mercifully ensured that there was nothing whatsoever happening on the last day and the staff were relieved to be able to clear their rooms and make sure that the children took everything with them. As a treat we let them bring games and have extra long playtimes in the warmth of the finest summer we'd known since moving to Swinnerdale.

At mid-morning Jason finished a raucous game of Mousetrap with Dan then came over to ask if could eat his chocolate in class.

'Go on, since it's the end of term. Special treat.'

'Thanks, Mr Seed!'

I spoke as he turned to go. 'Well done for asking, too. Teachers notice that kind of thing.'

He hesitated. 'What's it like in Miss Croker's?'

The question made me smile. 'I don't know – I've never been taught by her.'

'She scares me sometimes.'

'She scares me, too. But I'll tell you what: underneath she's really nice, and she's an ace teacher.'

'But what if I get into trouble with her?'

'That won't happen, will it?'

'I hope not.'

'Well, best make sure, hadn't you? You've improved this year,

Jason, so if you keep on trying hard then I think you'll get on really well in Class Four.'

He looked me in the eye. 'Really? You're not just saying that?'

'Really.'

He gave a little whoop and turned to announce to Dan the news about the chocolate, only to discover that Dan's had been eaten long ago.

At eleven o'clock there was a knock at the door and two sweaty infants heaved a big plastic bin into the room. One of them had rehearsed a speech.

'Please, Miss Perc'val says can ya 'ave a look through t'lost property.'

I had forgotten about this ritual and the class moaned when I asked them to stop playing games and look this way. I delved into the dark recesses of the malodorous container – it was like some unlucky dip. The first item was a manky blue jumper with a hole in the sleeve. It seemed vaguely familiar.

'Is this anybody's?'

'Lawrence's!' called someone from the back.

'It's not mine!' he said with disgust.

'That's been in there fer years,' said Martine.

I went radical and dropped it in a rubbish bag.

The next item was a once-white sock, which elicited laughter.

'Wait a minute!' said Howard, stepping forward for a closer look. He picked it up. 'No, Barry's had flowers on it.' Cue hoots from the boys.

'This is going to take ages at this rate,' I said. 'No more gags.'

I reached in and pulled out a crumpled red T-shirt.

'That looks like yours, Vicky,' said Estelle.

'I hope this isn't a joke,' I said.

'I haven't got one like that,' said Vicky. I looked inside the collar; there was a label saying Vicky Rushworth.

'Oh,' she said.

This procedure carried on with plimsolls, shorts, football boots, hats, coats, gloves, scarves and more being paraded to denials from all, including their embarrassed owners. Finally, I pulled out a mangled black hairbrush. There was a speckled piece of chewing gum on the handle and the bristles contained fluff, lumps of mud, hair, litter and something green which I couldn't identify. To sounds of 'Eeuurrgghh' I moved to drop it into the rubbish bag when Martine came forward.

'Ey, I bin lookin' fer that!'

The rest of the day passed off quietly until late afternoon when, restless at having to be inside on such a glorious afternoon, Class 3 were released outside for one last, special extra playtime. I sat on the bench that the PTA had so generously provided under a wide chestnut tree and yawned long and hard then closed my eyes and listened to the sounds: Ian calling for the ball, Estelle talking about her planned summer holiday, Tim scratching around in the herb garden, Jason moaning and Gary telling him to belt up. I thought of the sad, departed Ricky and of all that had happened over the year.

A swooning moment passed where I felt myself almost fall asleep but some teachers' instinct kept me aware, even though my eyes were heavy and closed. Once more I listened to the calls and noises that signalled the end of school, including some furtive whispering behind me. I opened my eyes to turn around but I was too late. I felt a slimy splat of wet and goo as something was pushed into my face. There were shouts and cheers and guffaws and the sound of feet running away. It was a paper plate of shaving foam.

I was too shocked to be cross. 'You cheeky rabble,' was all that came out as I dragged a hanky across my face and tried to see where the gunge had reached. The splat was extensive. Every child had stopped playing to stare and enjoy the prank. I wiped my tie then stood up to head inside.

'Who did it?' I said to Martine, who had come for a closer look.

'Yu'll never know, Mr Seed,' she laughed.

'Well whose idea was it?'

'Curr'n't possibly say.'

As I walked across the playground, a group of boys slipped out from behind a tree. They were patting Marcus on the back once again and laughing.

Well, at least he has some friends now, I said to myself. And, despite the mess, it was good to see Marcus coming out of his shell. I thought ahead to next year when he'd be one of the older ones and there would be other, younger children looking up to him in wonder, having heard stories about the ingenious boy who masterminded the pieing of Mr Seed.

'Daddy, can we go to the waterfall?' asked Tom, as I walked through the door of Craven Bottoms at five o'clock.

'Yeah, go paddling!' said Reuben.

'Well, it is a lovely sunny day.'

'What's happened to your clothes?' said Barbara. 'And your hair?'

After five minutes' explanation, where my wife tried and failed to keep a straight face, and a further ten getting washed and changed, I emerged into our little front garden. Reuben was standing on top of the wall, his shorts around his ankles, peeing on to the grass verge below. A car passed by on the road opposite.

It was so funny I had to call Barbara instead of telling him off.

'Whose idea was it to potty train him?' I asked.

'Wait until you see the two-er wee,' said Barbara.

'The what?'

Tom, who was listening, answered with glee. 'Me and Reuben do a wee at the same time on the toilet standing up. It's a two-er wee.'

I shook my head. 'Kids . . .'

'Hang on, when Stewart comes around tomorrow with Iris they're planning a three-er wee,' said Barbara.

'Let's get to the waterfall before I lose me wherewithal,' I said.

Buttergill Beck fell with a curtain of shimmering coolness into the dark water. It was a gentle lamb of a stream, a trickle, compared with its winter torrent. Down from the broad plunge pool, two little bare-footed boys splashed through the shallows ferrying fat pebbles and sculpted rocks to make a dam at the edge of a rippled ledge. I sat with my arm around my wife on the mossy bank watching the light play through the trees. Were we there for minutes or hours? I couldn't tell you.

'Daddy, we need help.'

'Can't Mummy help?'

'You can both help.'

The bite of the mountain water on my toes woke me up and soon we had a river dam to be proud of, deepening the flow and making our ankles cold while insects danced around us and the wagtail up ahead bobbed impatiently.

Tom stopped and clapped his hands. 'Daddy!'

'What?'

'The pirate cave. You said when the river was low we could go in it!'

Reuben's face went into a paroxysm of anticipation. 'Pirate cave, pirate cave!'

'Did you say that?' said Barbara.

'He did!' screamed Tom.

'Did,' echoed Reuben.

'I did,' I said.

'Right,' said Barbara, 'well it sounds too bloodthirsty for me so you three play in there and I'll go and get some pirate food ready at home.'

'Pieces of ate? Sorry.'

'You're very tired,' she said. 'Be careful.'

I took the boys across the narrow packhorse bridge and down the precarious slope that led to a hidden ledge below. I lowered them one at a time and warned them not to go near the edge, which dropped seven feet into a murky pool further below.

'I can see it!' said Tom.

I clambered down and there it was: the legendary little cave that we had talked about for so long but which the swift, gushing beck of winter and spring had kept concealed from us.

'Can we go in?' said Reuben, his eyes wide.

I held their hands. 'Should we dare?'

There was awe on my little sons' faces as we approached the entrance. It was just a damp, dripping hole in the rock but its darkness and mystery gave it a power that fired their imaginations such that they gripped me with genuine trepidation.

Tom's voice dropped to a whisper. 'What's inside?'

'I don't know,' I said.

'We should have brought a torch.'

Reuben reached for a cuddle. 'I'm scared.'

But then we saw the back of it and nothing was there except water and bat droppings and slime.

Tom was not to be put off. 'Daddy, you be Blackbeard and I'll be Captain Hook and Reuben can be Smee.'

'I want be Hook,' said Reuben, now wriggling down.

'Right,' said Tom. 'I'll be Blackbeard, Reuben you're Captain Hook and Daddy can be Smee.' He started to growl, while my younger son drew his arm up his sleeve and made a hook with his finger. Satisfied, he pulled a suitably sea-dogged face.

'You be Smee, Daddy,' said Tom.

I wasn't sure who Smee was but, with five weeks of holiday ahead, I didn't care.